Brl

WES GYE COLONIALISM
VELL FEUDALISM

Callum Christie

After five years in the Provincial Administration in Northern Rhodesia, Callum Christie had a very varied career.

Five years as an economist in the Ministry of Finance in Zambia were followed by a few years growing and exporting fruit and vegetables by air from Zambia to Europe.

On his return to Britain, Callum became a director of an agricultural consultancy company which specialised in agricultural marketing studies and in researching and managing start-up agricultural and fisheries projects in Africa. Finally, he established a company in Spain which produced house plants, and millions of strawberry runners for growers in Western Europe.

He has returned to his Scottish roots where he and his wife now live with one of his married sons and his family.

Published by Kirkgate Books, PO Box 3843, Glasgow G62 9DB

First published in paperback 2016

ISBN no 9781785890109

Printed and bound in the UK by Bell & Bain, Glasgow

Copyright © Malcolm Christie 2016.

The moral right of the author has been asserted.

List of cover photographs:

Front cover: the author; Queen Mother meeting Paramount Chief at his Palace; the Royal Barge, "Nalikwanda"; choral welcome at camp.

Rear cover: view across the Barotse Plain; Likishi dancer; pounding maize into flour; a traditional greeting.

Designed by Paul Futcher

GOODBYE COLONIALISM
FAREWELL FEUDALISM

Letters from a
District Officer

Callum Christie

CONTENTS

MAPS

Northern Rhodesia (Zambia)

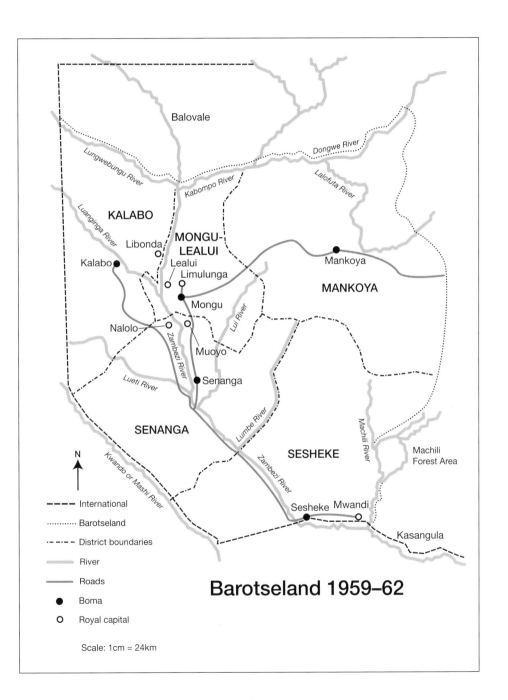

Balovale

Lungwebungu River

Dongwe River

Lalofuta River

Kabombo River

KALABO

Luanginga River

Libonda

MONGU-LEALUI

Lealui

Kalabo

Limulunga

Mankoya

MANKOYA

Mongu

Lui River

Nalolo

Zambezi River

Muoyo

Senanga

Lueti River

SENANGA

Lumbe River

SESHEKE

Kwando or Mashi River

Zambezi River

Machili River

Machili
Forest Area

N

Sesheke Mwandi

Kasangula

- – – International
.... Barotseland
- ·– ·– District boundaries
River
Roads
● Boma
○ Royal capital

Scale: 1cm = 24km

Barotseland 1959–62

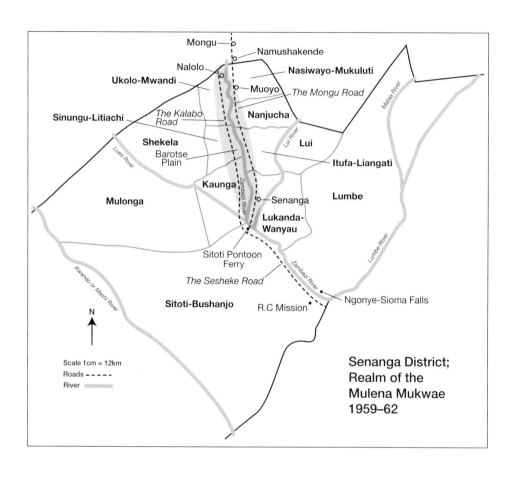

Mongu
Namushakende
Nalolo
Nasiwayo-Mukuluti
Ukolo-Mwandi
Muoyo
The Mongu Road
Sinungu-Litiachi
The Kalabo Road
Nanjucha
Shekela
Lui
Barotse Plain
Itufa-Liangati
Kaunga
Senanga
Lumbe
Mulonga
Lukanda-Wanyau
Sitoti Pontoon Ferry
The Sesheke Road
Sitoti-Bushanjo
R.C Mission
Ngonye-Sioma Falls

Mataa River
Lui River
Lueti River
Zambezi River
Lumbe River
Kwando or Mashi River
Zambezi River

N

Scale 1cm = 12km
Roads -----
River

Senanga District;
Realm of the
Mulena Mukwae
1959–62

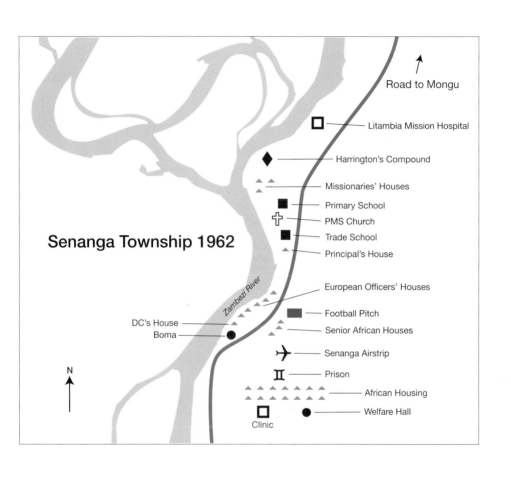

Senanga Township 1962

Road to Mongu

Litambia Mission Hospital

Harrington's Compound

Missionaries' Houses

Primary School

PMS Church

Trade School

Principal's House

European Officers' Houses

Football Pitch

Senior African Houses

DC's House

Boma

Senanga Airstrip

Prison

African Housing

Welfare Hall

Clinic

Zambezi River

N

INTRODUCTION

In September 2012 as part of a month-long visit to Zambia I revisited Senanga for three days with my eldest son, Donald, and his partner and daughter.

I did not recognise Senanga. It had grown into a small town. There was now a large prison with forbidding walls in place of the wired enclosure with traditional style huts that used to pass for a prison. Two new administrative blocks had been constructed; one for central government staff including the District Commissioner and his assistant, and the other for the Senanga District Council which did not exist until two years after I had left the District.

There was a Government Hospital staffed by a Zambian doctor and nurses, two secondary schools, of which one was part community funded, where none existed before and a regular bus service which linked Senanga to Lusaka. On the journey from Mongu, the provincial capital of what is now called Western Province, formerly Barotseland, we sped along a smooth tarred road. It took us only an hour where in the 1950s and early 60s it had taken up to three times as long. Going south from Senanga, a tarred road was under construction and was linked to a new bridge across the Zambezi. So we still had to use the same horribly bumpy track that I had followed fifty years earlier. It took about an hour to reach the spot fifteen miles south of Senanga on the Zambezi River where a motorised pontoon still carried vehicles across the river. As I write this, the switchback track and the unreliable, motorised pontoon are but a memory as travellers speed south on the new, all-weather, tarred road to Livingstone.

At intervals along the road to Senanga I saw mobile phone masts and advertisements for SIM cards for sale, sometimes on the roofs of ordinary huts in villages by the roadside. Occasionally men would be strolling along deep in conversation on their mobile phones. What a transformation in communications there had been with the mobile phone network penetrating deep into rural Zambia and, with a flood of Chinese investment (mainly Government to Government loans) creating new roads and bridges, such as the one now linking Senanga and Livingstone.

I was astounded by the warmth of the welcome I received from the present District Commissioner and his assistant, and likewise from the Police Inspector and his staff who occupied the old Boma, now a listed historic building, where I once worked. One remark of the Assistant District Commissioner struck me forcibly. "How", he asked "did you manage to tour the District in your day and visit so much of it?" It made me realise that he might have heard anecdotes of ubiquitous white district officers but had no idea of the administrative system that made it possible.

It dawned on me that one reason for my welcome was because I was seen as a rare piece of living history. I might have a story to recount that would interest a generation of Zambians who were not alive in the period of British colonial rule and had to rely on the memories of parents and grandparents for information on the closing years of British rule in their country.

That is why, approaching eighty years of age, I decided that my letters written from Senanga over fifty years ago might have an interest beyond my family circle.

I first came to Northern Rhodesia in 1959 by a combination of chance and unconscious preparation. At the completion of my Economics degree at the University of Aberdeen in the summer of 1958 I had very little idea what I was going to do at the end of four years of university paradise. Oh, to be a perpetual student! I had no sense of vocation. I thought vaguely of an academic career but the failure to obtain a First had put paid to that.

Then my friend and fellow student of Economics, Angus McDonald, applied for the Colonial Service and was accepted. It seemed a good option for me because I had been interested in politics at university and in the decolonisation of Africa including Britain's territories there.

So I applied to join the Overseas Civil Service and made Northern Rhodesia (NR) my territory of choice. As an economist I thought it was the most interesting of Britain's African possessions because it was the most industrialised and urbanised and it had large tax revenues from the copper mining companies to fund the development of its rural economy.

I was selected after interviews by both the Colonial Office and a District Officer in the NR Provincial Administration. Once I had arrived in Northern Rhodesia I found kindred spirits amongst my fellow Cadets. We were different from many of the more experienced officers who were apolitical and had little interest in the growth of African political parties. Moreover, we were from a different social background; the majority of us had been neither to public school nor to Oxbridge. So from time to time, there was tension between our generation and the older generation of District Officers, especially those who had arrived just before or just after the Second World War who were among the most senior in the hierarchy.

I suppose that this tension was centred in how we behaved towards those whom we were supposed to govern. The older officers felt that they

had to keep their distance from the governed, just as the traditional chiefs did, because they were of equal or greater importance than most chiefs. We younger officers, possibly because we knew our careers were bound to be soon cut short by the coming of African rule, were more interested in what made ordinary people tick. So the older generation played tennis amongst fellow expatriates while some of the younger ones, in addition to tennis, would play football with the locals. And whereas we were prepared to visit the offices of the local political leaders the older administrators expected the local politicians to come to them.

It was the policy of the Colonial Office to send successful candidates for the Overseas Civil Service (OCS) for a year to either Cambridge or Oxford University. The Cambridge course (the usual berth for OCS recruits going to Northern Rhodesia) was full, so I was sent to Oxford where I studied a wide range of subjects that were supposed to give a useful theoretical and practical grounding for OCS recruits before they were sent into the field. There were courses in Economics, Local Government, Imperial and African History and Anthropology. Candidates were also taught the most widely spoken language of whichever country they were selected for. I also studied elementary motor mechanics and attended a few lectures by a retired Provincial Commissioner on how to build wooden bridges and repair dirt roads.

My history tutor Colin Leys had written about the modern history of British Central Africa, particularly of Southern Rhodesia. His tutorials opened my eyes to the politics of Northern Rhodesia and its neighbours: Southern Rhodesia and Nyasaland.

I had to travel by train to London twice a week to the School of Oriental and African Studies at the University of London to be taught Bemba, the language spoken widely in the northern half of NR and in the Copperbelt where most of the large towns were situated. At SOAS I was the sole student of an experienced linguist, Dr Richardson, and his assistant for that year, Joe Chileshe, from NR. I could hardly fail to learn the language, and Joe became a friend who stayed with me and my parents during the Easter holiday and with whom I corresponded when I was living in NR.

The irony of the situation was that when I arrived in Zambia I was sent to the far south west of the territory where Bemba was never spoken. It would be nearly four years until I was posted to a Bemba-speaking part of the country. I learned rapidly that there was no unifying language in Northern Rhodesia apart from English, only a patchwork of very distinct tribal tongues.

The greater irony was that I was posted to the Barotseland Protectorate which was home to a feudal society headed by the Paramount Chief or Litunga of the Lozi-speaking peoples. In being allocated to Senanga

District, I was sent to the heart of the domain of the Princess of Southern Barotseland, the Litunga's daughter, the Mulena Mukwae. What a contrast to my expectations of being sent to the Copperbelt or some urban or semi-urban situation where I would be dealing with "modern" issues and the up-and-coming generation of African political leaders.

I quickly realised that I was privileged to be caught in a time warp between a traditional society organised on feudal lines and a colonial administration that was trying to ease it into participation in a modern democracy. It was never going to be a comfortable process.

The Political Situation in Northern Rhodesia in 1959

In Northern Rhodesia political trouble and discontent had been brewing within the African community ever since the country had become part of the Federation of Rhodesia and Nyasaland in 1953. The Federation was the brainchild of the white settlers of Northern and Southern Rhodesia. The former group, few in number but beneficiaries of the wealth generated by the copper mines in NR's Copperbelt, wanted the security of being part of the white-controlled Southern Rhodesia with its much larger white settler community. This latter settler group which depended on agriculture for its wealth wished to have access to the tax revenues that flowed from the copper mining companies in NR.

For three decades the two white settler communities had tried to persuade the British Government to agree to the amalgamation of the two Rhodesias but not until 1951 did they find a British Colonial Secretary who was sympathetic to their cause. To the great delight of the white settlers and the dismay of the leaders of the African population, in 1953 the Federation came into being. Nyasaland was thrown in to the Federation for good measure, largely because the ever-parsimonious British Government saw a means of improving that country's services and infrastructure by spreading the tax revenues from the copper mines to aid that country as well as Southern Rhodesia without any cost to the British Treasury.

The justification given by the British Government and by the leaders of the United Federal Party, (the party supported by the great majority of the white population in the Rhodesias) for establishing the Federation was that it would foster "Partnership between the races"; the extreme views of white supremacists in Southern Rhodesia (SR) would be moderated by the more liberal attitudes of the white electorates in NR and Nyasaland and by the growing black electorate in all three territories. The leaders of the African nationalist parties never believed in this rhetoric and their hostility to the Federal Government was reinforced when the leader of the main political party in SR, when addressing a white audience likened Partnership to the relationship between a rider and a horse, with the whites of course being cast in the role of the rider and the blacks in the role of the horse.

The aim of the white political leaders was to achieve for the Federation full Dominion status, equivalent to the other dominions in the British Commonwealth such as Australia and Canada.

The British Government had promised in 1953 that a Commission would be set up to examine the case for further constitutional development for the Federation which the white political leaders in the Federation were sure would lead to full independence from Britain. In the meantime, they had to be content with Federal control over most tax revenues, the military, white affairs such as segregated white education and health and major infrastructure spending such as main roads and power supplies. The largest of these investments was the Kariba Dam on the Zambezi River with its power station on the south, Southern Rhodesian, side of the dam.

The establishment of the Federation under a white electorate which took over control of most official revenues and expenditures in NR and Nyasaland from the colonial Government ran completely contrary to the policy of the British Government towards the indigenous peoples in its African Protectorates. In 1931, the then Colonial Secretary, Lord Passfield,[1] issued a White Paper which stated that "the interests of the African natives must be paramount, and that if, and when, these interests and the interests of the immigrant races should conflict, the former should prevail". The white settler leaders in NR objected strongly to this policy but it remained the guiding ethos of the colonial administration in NR and Nyasaland until Federation arrived. It did not affect SR which had been a self-governing Crown Colony since 1923 under white settler rule.

Under the sway of a white legislature, SR evolved as a country of privilege for the whites and of entrenched disadvantage for the blacks. Under the Land Apportionment Act, the vast majority of the best agricultural land was reserved for white farmers; this Act also ensured separation of the races in the urban areas where only whites could own property in certain areas. There was labour legislation which also reserved apprenticeships and employment for whites in various occupations. It was little different to South African apartheid.

Naturally the African leadership in NR looked to SR to see what the Federation and their own country might become and did not like what they saw. Federation gave these leaders a cause to fight against where previously

[1]*Better known as the social reformer, Sydney Webb.*

they were content to progress gradually to power under the guardianship of the colonial administration. Moreover, they had lost their trust in the British Government despite the majority of the Provincial Administrators being opposed to Federation because they saw it as a breach of faith to the African people.

The African leadership became ever more militant especially a young group led by Kenneth Kaunda who broke away from the African National Congress (ANC) led by the older politician, Harry Nkumbula. In 1958, the NR Government had devised a new constitution for the territory. The arithmetic of the new electoral arrangements was complicated and it was unclear if the United Federal Party (UFP), the more popular of the two white-supported parties, would gain an overall majority of elected members of the Legislative Council (Legco). An overall majority would in turn give it the right to nominate a majority of members of the Executive Council (Exco), for the first time outnumbering official members nominated by the Governor.

Kaunda felt that the risk of the UFP gaining a majority in both Legco and Exco was too great – it could well have given the UFP a mandate to claim white-controlled self-government/Crown Colony status similar to Southern Rhodesia's. Nkumbula, on the other hand, was persuaded to contest the election, at which point Kaunda led a group of his supporters out of the ANC. They formed a new party, the Zambia African National Congress (ZANC) which encouraged qualified African voters to boycott the election. ZANC supporters were accused of using strong-arm tactics in their boycott campaign. To prevent this continuing the Governor in March 1959, just a few weeks before the election, declared a State of Emergency, banned ZANC and rusticated its leaders to the rural areas.

Nkumbula's decision to contest the election knowing that the number of African seats that he could win would only be half as many as European ones proved to be justified because the seats won by the ANC prevented the UFP from winning a majority of the seats in Legco and from controlling the Exco and "Government policies".

Within Barotseland, these tales of conflict in the towns of Northern Rhodesia were just that; tales of happenings that might have come from the other side of the world. They were distant echoes of trouble that seemed to have no relevance to the traditional rulers of Barotseland and their people.

July 1959 – en route to Barotseland

ss."Winchester Castle"

19 July 1959

Dear Folks[2]

This life on the ocean wave is rather pleasant. We have had sunny weather with cool breezes which till now have kept the temperature down to about sixty-eight degrees[3] which makes sunbathing pleasant. Today (Sunday) is considerably warmer though a slight wind and clouds are keeping down the temperature to a comfortable level. James Glaze with whom I am sharing a cabin is good company.

We are sitting at a table of ten people including four South African women returning from a tour of South African war cemeteries in Europe sponsored by the SA British Servicemen's Association. Four hundred went on this tour of Europe lasting three months and about all these four can remember of their travels seems to be the hotels they stayed in and the meals they ate.

There are also two South African girls. One is very light skinned and the other has a darker complexion which led me to suppose that she was Spanish or Italian. But this being a ship on its way to South Africa another possibility has obviously occurred to the white women. She might be a Coloured (ie. mixed race) or Asian (ie. from India). The women are obviously rather shocked because in South Africa you do not share your table with people of "other" races. When the girl with the dark complexion leaves the table the four white women break into excited conversation.

"Where does she come from?" asks one. "Cape Town" replies another. They all nod their heads in mutual understanding. ▶

---

[2] I have omitted the standard introduction and signing-off from most of the letters to avoid needless repetition. A few remain and it will be seen that I sign off as "Callum". My birth certificate names me as "Malcolm" after my mother's elder brother who was killed in the First World War, aged 19. He, too, was christened "Malcolm" but was known at home as "Callum" a Gaelic form of Malcolm. This usage continued in my case with my parents invariably referring to me as Callum, and likewise my friends. But in Barotseland I was always referred by my official name of "Malcolm".

[3] Throughout the letters all temperatures are in the Fahrenheit scale: 100°F=38°C.

In Cape Town, the original European settlement in South Africa, there was obviously much miscegenation between white sailors and traders and local women before settlement took on a more permanent pattern and white women arrived. So Cape Town is home to the largest Coloured[4] community in South Africa. And though descended from white men, they along with Africans and "Asians" are all regarded as second class citizens in an apartheid system where only "pure" whites are first class and enjoy full citizenship.

I lost touch with James Glaze and recently discovered that he had become a British diplomat for much of his career, completing it as Ambassador to Ethiopia. He died in 2007.

Cape Town
31 July 1959

Dear Folks

Thanks very much for your letter which I received when the ship docked here last night. I trust you have now recovered from the exertions of the journey and are settling down to enjoy a restful holiday.

I have an important piece of news. On arrival at Cape Town I was informed by the Crown Agents that I am not going to Mazabuka. Instead I have been posted to SENANGA, BAROTSELAND PROTECTORATE, NORTHERN RHODESIA.

I am now in Cape Town General Post office on seats marked *"Europeans Only/Net Blankes"*. I feel rather ashamed to be white here.

---

[4] *The term used 50 years ago in the Rhodesias and South Africa to denote the descendants of mixed race parents.*

Yesterday's letter was written in haste because there were a couple of friends waiting for me to finish. This is now a good time to write a fuller account of my adventures (and misadventures) since leaving Southampton, though the writing may be rather illegible because of the shaking of the train.

My first letter was written just before we reached Madeira. We anchored in the bay in the early evening so we had a good view of the island while it was still daylight, but because of a breakdown in one of the engines we were late in arriving and were unable to go on shore while it was still light. As it was, we arrived at the quay about 9 p.m. in a small boat.

On dropping anchor, the ship was besieged by a host of boats from which swarmed on board men carrying merchandise, especially embroidered silks, basket work and dolls. They were zealous in bringing them to the notice of passengers and soon spirited haggling was in process. However, James and I and the two South African girls did not stay but got into one of the afore-mentioned boats carrying people ashore. The quayside was thronged with "natives" who gazed at us as though we were first arrivals from another world. It was most embarrassing walking down a lane formed by the inhabitants of the island. I can now sympathise more readily with one of the ordeals that Royalty has to face!

We were accosted by fruit and flower sellers and as we got into the town we were repeatedly invited by excited individuals to come in and look round the wares in their shops. After being importuned by the nth taxi driver we eventually succumbed on being told that we would be taken to a wine house and get free wine there. So we climbed into an open landau and set off through the town, Funchal. It is built on a hillside, most of the streets being narrow and cobbled and the pavements aglow with beautiful mosaic tiles.

The houses were painted in creams and yellows and pinks. I was entranced. We could see how the town looked because many of the streets were very well lit and in addition there was a bright moon. ▶

We reached the wine house which turned out to be a warehouse for Madeira wine and sat at a table surrounded by huge butts of wine. We were treated to samples of five different types of wine. James and I bought a bottle which we opened at table later in the voyage. We staggered back to our taxi passing other passengers from the ship on the way – there was obviously a widespread arrangement between the taxi drivers of the town and this wine firm.

We set off again in the taxi and drove through the town, climbing steadily higher along winding roads, feeling very exhilarated, singing, shouting "salud" to the locals and generally feeling very happy for the view was splendid – every so often we would get a wonderful vista of the bay beneath us, shining in the moonlight and the air was rich with scents. Then we dropped down into the town again. By the time we reached our starting point it was still only 10.30 p.m., and we felt we must do something else before we left the island (the last boat back to the ship was not till 11.30 p.m.).

So we stopped the taxi and got hold of a man who could speak English and asked him to tell the taxi driver what we wanted to do – namely, to be driven up the mountain to a typical Madeiran café where we might have coffee or a glass of wine (all the cafes in town looked horrible or were terribly crowded). So up and up the mountainside we went, by a narrow, steep and winding road until after about twenty minutes we came to a small village called Monte where, sure enough, there was a café, though a dismal looking one.

The village itself was very attractive and after buying ourselves a glass of Madeira in the café we went for a walk up a path that took us to a church in front of which there was a courtyard with a balustrade. From there we were able to look down on part of the village and far beyond and below, the bay. One of the locals who was either drunk or just naturally idiotic, kept pestering us for money for a cigarette or a drink. His only English was "Take it easy" whenever we tried to shoo him away. Eventually another young man came along and with his help, and a bribe of sixpence, the other was persuaded to leave us. By then it was time to go back to the taxi.

▶ We arrived in Cape Town in the early evening. The mountains overlooking the city were very beautiful. Five of us went into town and took a bus through the town and up the mountainside to near the foot of the cable railway. By that time, it was about 10.30 p.m. and Cape Town was twinkling below us, the stars were bright and the cliffs of Table Mountain rose white above us. It was a lovely evening. Afterwards, we went back to the ship and watched its unloading.

I am now in a Government rest house in Livingstone having arrived this morning at 7.45. All day I have been rushing around shopping, buying two months' groceries, portable radio, etc. Everyone has been very kind. This evening, the Provincial Commissioner invited me and the District Assistant who has been helping me get my goods together to a "sundowner" at his house. People here consider I am lucky to be going to Senanga – "unspoiled by civilisation". A plane calls there once a week with the mail and that is about the only contact with civilisation.

The Administrative System in Northern Rhodesia

The administration of Northern Rhodesia was concentrated on the rural areas of the territory. The main element was the Provincial Administration (PA) of which I became a member, initially as a District Officer Cadet. The PA was spread throughout the country which was divided into seven provinces and a protectorate, Barotseland. The PA in each province was headed by a Provincial Commissioner; in Barotseland he was called the Resident Commissioner.

In the towns the administrative structure was more similar to the British local government system except that the copper mining companies were responsible for housing their employees, divided into European and African areas and administered by the companies. The District Commissioner had the responsibility of ensuring that there was a sufficient degree of cooperation between these administrative authorities and various central government agencies such as the police.

Each province was divided into districts, generally six or seven in number – in Barotseland there were five. The district officer who was put in charge of a district was called the District Commissioner (DC) who was supported by up to three junior officers depending on the size and complexity of the district. The offices of the DC and his staff were known as the Boma.

The PA was the main part of the Ministry of Native Affairs; the Minister ranked number three in the central hierarchy under the Chief Secretary and, at the top of the tree, the Governor.

Within each district the PA was responsible for coordinating the work of the other government agencies which in most rural districts had no direct representative except at very junior level. In Senanga, the district to which I was posted, there was no representative of the Ministry of African Education, nor of African Agriculture, nor of Water Affairs, nor Health apart from hospital and medical assistants of which there were two. The Public Works Department had an expatriate Buildings Supervisor and a Roads Foreman who was responsible for the single main road from the southern district border to the northern, a distance of about one hundred and twenty miles. All other roads and bridges were the responsibility of the District Commissioner and his staff.

Because of the importance of cattle in the economy of Senanga District, there was an expatriate Livestock Officer. His main task was to ensure that diseases that might be fatal to cattle, such as sleeping sickness spread by tsetse flies, did not invade the district from neighbouring areas where it was endemic, including Angola which bordered our district to the west.

The Boma
Senanga
Barotseland Protectorate
5 August 1959

Dear Folks

This is just a note to let you know I have arrived here in one piece. I set off from Livingstone in a tiny Beaver aircraft (max. capacity, five passengers), the only other passenger being a girl from Australia going further upriver than myself, as a nurse in a Seventh Day Adventist mission hospital.

The air journey was delightful. The country looked beautiful in the early morning sun and we were very fortunate to see a great deal of buck, hippos, etc. below us, for we flew very low for much of the journey.

We seemed to be flying over endless forest, interspersed by a few valleys and areas of grassland. Below us was the Zambezi river meandering through the countryside. I could see no sign of civilisation except when we landed at a settlement called Sesheke, a Boma (Government Administration centre), midway between Livingstone and Senanga.

Even as we descended towards Senanga I looked in vain for signs of the township. It was only as we taxied in to land on the grass strip cut into the forest that I saw a few small houses tucked close into the trees on one side of the strip and on the other side a crowd of African onlookers and a tiny hut, the terminal building, alongside which stood four white men in a stiff row, dressed in white shirts, shorts and long stockings. They looked somehow out of place.

▶

▶ They were my new colleagues in the Boma – the District Commissioner, David Acheson, two Cadets, Iain Stuart and Jonathon Cole, and Peter Wilson, the Learner District Assistant. They are very friendly and I think I shall like working here.

Senanga is the administrative centre of an irregularly shaped district of average length one hundred miles and average breadth one hundred miles.

I am staying at the moment with Iain Stuart from Balloch on Loch Lomond – a nice chap – until my luggage arrives and I can move into a large house occupied by Jonathon Cole and Peter Wilson. I'll move into Jonathon's quarters when he moves shortly to Kalabo District just to the north of us.

The District Commissioner is young – only thirty-one years old. Stuart is about twenty-five having taken a History degree at Glasgow University followed by two years of research and teaching in Canada. He was recruited directly to the Colonial Service without doing the year's course at either Cambridge or Oxford presumably because of his age and the fact that he was married.

On Friday, I'll be going with the DC to Nalolo which is in the most northern part of our district and is the village where the Chieftainess Mulena Mukwae lives. Next to the Paramount Chief she is the most important personage in Barotseland. It will take us ten hours by boat upriver to get there.

This is written to catch tomorrow's mail plane. It is now late and I'm exhausted.

Your loving son

Callum

PS. Senanga has a tennis court – had a game this afternoon.

The Provincial Administration in Senanga District

The District Commissioner (DC) was the Magistrate for the district and his junior staff were the investigating officers and prosecutors of criminal cases of a minor nature. The decisions of the DC's court were subject to review by a High Court judge.

Most rural districts like Senanga had no police; instead the DC had 15 District Messengers who were responsible for delivering messages from the Boma to various parts of the district, for arresting suspected criminals, for supervising various public works like the repair of a rural road and for accompanying a district officer when he was on tour.

The Messengers were also responsible for looking after the district prison. Although it was surrounded by a low fence it was virtually an open prison. The working parties which sallied forth each day to carry out light jobs around the township were supervised by a District Messenger. In return the prisoners received three good meals per day and were better fed and had less work to do than the average villager. It was unknown for a prisoner to abscond.

Each year the DC and his staff would draw up the annual estimates of revenue and expenditure. The former would include revenue from the annual Poll Tax of ten shillings (about one US dollar) per able-bodied male between the age of eighteen and sixty, store and gun licences, and various other small revenue items. On the expenditure side, apart from the recurrent expenditures of running the Boma there would be the costs of repairing minor roads and bridges, clearing canals, and paying the crews of paddlers who manned the wooden pontoons which carried vehicles (usually belonging to the PA and missionaries) at infrequent intervals across the several tributaries of the Zambezi River.

There were small amounts of money available for the building of new infrastructure, such as canals and rural roads, although the largest capital budget was handled by the district Buildings Supervisor who was responsible for new staff housing in Senanga township.

Senanga was a tiny place which consisted of half a dozen houses for European civil servants and around thirty much smaller houses for African civil servants. And there was an African Welfare Hall, a Clinic and the afore-mentioned prison..

There was no trading store nor church in the tiny township. There was a grass airstrip for the Beaver flights (max. five passengers) which brought and collected the mail and a tiny brick room which housed a set of scales for weighing packages. The centre of this settlement was the Boma, the

Senanga airstrip and the Beaver which brought me there. Canadian built, the Beaver was the sturdiest of bush craft which operated throughout the world for several decades after it first went into commercial operation in 1948. It was a life-line, bringing us household necessities from Livingstone and overseas mail twice a week

administrative offices of the District Commissioner and his staff. It included a small court room.

The European community had a tennis court and later on a swimming pool too. The African community had a Welfare Association hall and later, at my instigation, a football pitch. There was also a Government Health Clinic staffed by two Medical Assistants.

About two miles from the administrative centre was the Paris Mission Society mission staffed by French and Swiss missionaries; they were Presbyterians, the French being from the Huguenot community in the south of France. The mission station consisted of a church, a trade school, a primary school and a hospital, with houses for the staff. Behind the hospital and a little way from it was a leprosarium. At that time there was quite a high incidence of leprosy in parts of Northern Rhodesia. Now it is rare, thanks to the use of new drugs to treat the disease.

Near the PMS mission was the trading store and boat building business of Arthur Harrington who had settled in Senanga many years earlier. He was over eighty, and the business was run by his son, Willie. There we bought our household requirements although the selection being limited we also had to order other goods which were flown in from Livingstone.

My first visit to Nalolo and the Mulena Mukwae

Senanga
10 August 1959

A week ago I was in Livingstone. On Tuesday I arrived here. That evening, I went with Iain Stuart, and David Acheson, the DC, to the house of Mr Harrington, an old trader who came to these parts around 1910. This old man is visited nearly every day on a rota by one or other of the members of the small European community at sundowner time to keep the old chap company (he is eighty-five). He always keeps a liberal supply of whisky and beer at hand. This gentleman, although he owns about seven stores up and down the length of Barotseland, lives in a cramped one-roomed red-brick and thatched cottage, while his son, Willie, lives with his family in a huge house next door.

The one room is dominated by an enormous bed so that we all have to huddle round a small table, its top crammed with whisky bottles, at one end of the room. The old man sits perched in a capacious arm chair next to a log fire. Iain says the old man has many colourful stories to tell.

On Friday morning, very early, (5.45 a.m.), I set off up the Zambezi river in a metal tub powered by an unreliable outboard engine, along with the DC and his wife, a Messenger and a mechanic. We were making for Nalolo, the village of the Mulena Mukwae, the royal Princess who rules over the whole of Senanga District. Over the centre of this tub there is a metal frame upon which a sheet of canvas is stretched to protect the "bwanas" (the white folk) from the rays of the sun.

Actually, it was very cold before dawn broke. We chugged upriver for fifteen and a half hours before we arrived at Nalolo, eighty miles or so due north of Senanga. The journey took five hours longer than planned because the outboard engine kept breaking down and is in any case hopelessly underpowered when the boat is carrying a full load. Barotseland is very flat and rather uninspiring, and the river winds its way through the plain. It is very shallow in many parts so that we were constantly dodging round sandbanks which added considerably to our journey. The Zambezi around these parts is

▶

quite narrow, only about a quarter of a mile wide. Since the countryside is so flat one part of the river is much like another, so although I took my camera I was hard pressed to find interesting photographs. We saw one crocodile basking on the bank on our way up and got very close to it. Then, aware of our presence it shot into the water, fast as lightning. The DC and his wife were very pleasant and friendly. Nalolo is not on the river, but joined to it by a short canal. By the time we reached there it was dark and difficult to find the junction of the canal and river.

At Nalolo we slept in the offices of the Native Treasury and next day I had an audience, along with the DC and his wife, with the Mulena Mukwae and her husband, the Ishee Kwandu (Prince of the Palace). They came out to the entrance of their compound to greet us and took us into a reception hut with reed walls and a thatched roof where we sat along one wall. We were then served tea and the Mulena's personal secretary sat on the floor and interpreted. The Mulena is an extremely charming woman and reminded me of our Queen Mother. She was unable to entertain us in her Palace because she had only recently acceded to the throne. I was told that her new Palace had not yet been completed in place of the Palace of her predecessor.

All of her subjects, including her most senior councillor, who came to see her entered the doorway on hands and knees. Barotseland for the most part is a feudal society and the divine right of kings is still a living reality here. In fact, the Mulena Mukwae is revered; it is believed that she is part of a lineage descended from God.

The Mulena Mukwae's servant had to follow this display of reverent submission to his monarch. This started even before he had entered the enclosure. Outside its entrance, he laid down the tray with its precious load of Crown Derby china with a rattle of cups while he knelt and gently clapped his cupped hands. Then he grasped the tray, rose to his feet, advanced a further few yards, laid the tray on the floor and repeated his obeisance. He rose to his feet once more, set down the tray on a table and started serving us tea. I was amazed by this whole performance.

The strange thing to me is the way in which the District Commissioner and his junior officers like me are accorded great respect. Sometimes ▶

we are addressed as "Mulena" (Chief) and we met the Mulena Mukwae on equal terms. Her Prime Minister and her leading councillors and officials all treat me respectfully. In the mornings, when I arrive at the Boma, the Messengers fall into line and salute. Villagers bow and clap their hands in salutation. I don't find all this particularly satisfying to my ego, but rather embarrassing.

Because this is a feudal society the Barotse have a great belief in established authority and since nowadays we, the colonial administration, are the ultimate authority I suppose we fit in with the feudal structure of this society, as rulers who are not to be questioned.

Most Europeans here would like to keep this state of affairs going on for ever and there is a general tendency for the Provincial Administration in which I serve to regard Barotseland as a well-nigh perfect island of content whose peace must on no account be broken.

Stay well (*mu siyale hande*)

The Paramount Chief of Barotseland and his Government

The Paramount Chief was the principal traditional authority in Barotseland and was the particular chief of the Mongu-Lealui District in which he had his two capitals. These were Lealui where he lived in the dry season situated in the middle of the Barotse Plain, and Limulunga situated on a ridge overlooking the Plain which he occupied during the flood season. He appointed chiefs to rule the other districts. His daughter, Makwibi, was the Mulena Mukwae, the Princess of south-central Barotseland.

Paramount Chief (Litunga) Sir Mwanawina III (Photo: Rev.J-L Baumgartner)

Each chief ruled with a council of advisers, usually elderly. Some of them were allocated departmental duties – Health, Education, etc. which matched those of Central Government. They seldom had any experience or qualifications in these functions although on appointment they would be offered courses on their departmental duties at the Provincial Development Training Centre at Namushakende, on the Mongu side of the border with Senanga.

The District Chief, and indeed the Paramount Chief, would always take important decisions after consulting with the council of advisers, called the Saa-Sikalo Kuta, Kuta being also the word meaning a "court" which also acted in deciding important disputes, sometimes involving members of the extended Barotse royal family. The chief adviser to the Mulena Mukwae was called the Sambi in charge of the Saa-Sikalo Kuta at Nalolo which stood on a large, man-made mound close to the Zambezi River. Like the Litunga, the Mulena Mukwae occupied a Palace at Mooyo on the ridge overlooking the Plain a few miles east of Nalolo during the period from March to July when Nalolo was cut off by the seasonal floods that inundated the Plain.

The Districts in Barotseland were divided into sub-units of traditional administration. In Senanga there were twelve. They were called lilalo (singular, silalo). Each silalo was in the charge of two indunas appointed by the Mulena Mukwae; one the senior, would be an outsider known in the Nalolo court circles; he made sure that the Mulena's interests were safeguarded. The junior induna was usually a local man who was expected to know his silalo well. Together they usually made up an effective team.

Why Barotseland was different from the rest of Northern Rhodesia

Barotseland was different from the rest of Northern Rhodesia. This difference originated in it having been given its own Protectorate status when the British South Africa Company which established the first British administration was eager to entice Lewanika, King of Barotseland, to accept the protection of the British Government (actually of the great White Queen, Victoria). The alternative was the Portuguese who were disliked by the first PMS missionaries to enter Barotseland. They recommended the British to Lewanika as did, more potently, King Khama of the Tswana people. The British had already provided protection for him and his people in a vast area, the Bechuanaland Protectorate, present-day Botswana. King Khama desired this protection because he feared invasion from the Boers who were seeking fresh areas for settlement to the west of their South African homeland. In return for mineral rights the British South Africa Company representing the British Government agreed in treaties signed in 1890 and 1900 with Lewanika to prevent settlement by Europeans in his lands except with his permission; to respect the King's ownership of the land and its resources within his territory and to respect his authority to apply traditional law in civil cases.

No such concessions were written in to treaties of protection signed by the chiefs of other tribes with the emissaries of the BSA Company in the area of what became Northern Rhodesia. So the Lozi always felt they had a privileged relationship with the British Government. This feeling was strengthened by the knighthood bestowed upon the Litunga, Mwanawina III, by Queen Elizabeth II.

The Barotse Protectorate was a protectorate within a protectorate because Northern Rhodesia was also a Protectorate. Until 1924 it was under the rule of the BSA Company and then directly under the rule of the British Government represented by the Governor. The most powerful tribal chiefs were accorded their ceremonial roles and authority in matters of tribal law although none had the rights of the Litunga (Paramount Chief) of Barotseland over land and natural resources.

In the century before the arrival of the British, wars for supremacy were fought between tribes and by rival factions within them. Arab slave traders became involved. They armed their African tribal allies with guns and together they terrorised weaker tribes in pursuit of slaves. Opposition to the British came from the Arabs and their tribal allies. Other tribes who suffered at their hands, and those who had not participated in the trade, like the Lozi, welcomed them. These chiefs accepted British protection because, although they gave up some authority over their people, they were secure against the risk of being overthrown by rivals. Only the coming of modern political leaders threatened the chiefs' close relationship with the British Administration.

Senanga Boma in 1959

A Lion Hunt

The Boma
Senanga
15 August 1959

Dear Folks

I told you of my trip upriver to meet the Mulena Mukwae. A couple of days later, I went off in a landrover with Iain Stuart to visit some villages to see how they were getting on with the building of their new court houses, to see about the thatching of a new school and to hear complaints. The part of the district we went to lies across the Zambezi from Senanga (the Zambezi splits our district lengthwise from north to south) Our journey lasting the whole day took us nearly the entire length of the west side of the district.

At the pontoon which takes vehicles across the Zambezi at Sitoti, fifteen miles south of Senanga, we were told that a pride of lions was bothering villagers nearby by carrying off a cow from time to time. We sent a note back to the Boma by runner about this. Then we called in at the house of the Seventh Day Adventist missionary and his wife for tea.

We had a Messenger with us and in the villages he translated between ourselves and the local silalo indunas (chiefs). In Barotseland, everything is done very slowly so that months may elapse between the delivery of building materials and their use. Again, unless you visit these various projects fairly regularly, the work is not done, or not done so readily. This is to be expected because the villages are all quite remote and communication is very difficult. In the floods, many villages are cut off completely from outside contacts and even now in the dry season it is only possible to reach villages on foot in many cases and at best along extremely bumpy roads fit only for landrovers.

We stayed the night in a rest house (a hostel provided in remote places for the convenience of travellers). Next morning at about 9 a.m. we arrived at the SDA mission to learn that the note we had sent back to Senanga had resulted in the Livestock Officer and the Public Works Department Manager coming out with guns in search of the lions. Lions are vermin in Barotseland and as such anyone can kill them. Crocodiles are not and only a few licences to shoot them are handed out.

Just after midnight they were in the village where a cow had been killed by lions the previous night. They had taken up their position in a tree above the cattle kraal when the lion and lioness entered the kraal. The lions were caught in the beam of their torch and one of them was shot. Both escaped into the bush.

Next morning the two men, accompanied by six villagers went into the bush looking for the wounded lion and followed the trail into very thick bush. Then they heard it growl close by and decided to retreat because they could see only about five yards ahead.

So they came back to the Mission to gather more men and guns to help beat the lions out of cover. We went with them and after an hour enough men and guns had been collected (fifteen men and four guns in all) to continue the hunt. Ian and I went with them.

We reached the spot where the lion had been heard. We split up, half the guns going across the clearing to cut off the lions' retreat while the other guns and the rest of us beat the bush with sticks and filled the air with shouts as we moved forward slowly in a semi-circle in an attempt to drive the lions into the clearing. But no lion appeared. Then we beat through more really thick bush, much of it very prickly. Eventually, just as we were on the point of giving up, the wounded lion was spotted and shot. The lioness was also seen but she sped off before anyone could shoot.

There was great excitement amongst the beaters. The lion lay stretched out under the low branches of a thicket. Several of the men prodded the prone body with their long sticks to make sure it was indeed dead. Being reassured it was, they hauled it into the clearing and two or three of the bolder spirits knelt over it and shouted taunts into its ear.

The lion was slung over a pole cut from a branch and carried in triumph through the village where it had carried out its raids and thence to the mission where it was laid out in the middle of the school compound. A crowd from another village nearby came to view the beast and all the school children were marshalled by their ▶

teachers to march in single file past the lion, like crowds passing through a cathedral to gaze on the bier of a departed monarch.

So within a week of arrival I have been involved in a lion hunt. During the hunt I was too busy keeping out of the way of briar bushes to really feel afraid. In any case, I felt that if the lion did spring upon us it would be most unlikely to pick on me. Nevertheless, I stuck as close as I could to one of the men with a gun.

Lions in this area are rather rare. They usually keep well away from human settlements. All the Europeans here think I am fantastically lucky to have seen one so soon. The Veterinary Officer[5] who shot it had never seen one before and he has lived in Northern Rhodesia all his life.

Now Iain Stuart is out on tour and the DC is on a Boundary Commission on our international border with Portuguese West Africa[6] for two weeks. All my kit arrived yesterday and I have moved into my house which I share with Peter Wilson the Learner District Assistant.

Senanga
24 August 1959

I am gradually settling down to the office routine. As yet I do little except look on and try to understand what I'm supposed to do. Into the office come a steady stream of people wanting jobs with the NR Government, gun and ammunition licences, "situpas" (identity cards), or making complaints about something or other – matrimonial disputes, food shortages, contractors wanting leave to start building a school or dispensary, etc.

As yet I can do little in this line because of my complete ignorance of local conditions - for example, in the case of an Induna complaining of a lack of maize in his area. To judge whether it is a reasonable complaint one has to know when the harvest was

[5]His proper title was Livestock Officer to denote that he did not have a degree in Veterinary Science but instead a qualification in livestock management.
[6]Now called Angola.

24

▶ taken in, whether or not it was a good one in his sub-district and if not, why not, the reputation of the Induna and so on.

With other complaints, one has to know the regulations on the subject. Quite a lot of the work, too, involves some knowledge of accounting procedures. Whenever money is involved as payments, advances or receipts, various forms have to be filled. Here, again, I am just feeling my way. In the next few days we shall be going through the books of the native sub-treasuries (one in each silalo) in the district.

So at the moment I am reading up various books of regulations – Financial Orders, General Orders, etc. I'm also reading various tour reports written about different parts of the district for the past thirty years. Most of the past week has been spent in the office. However, I was out on three short trips driving a five-ton lorry (both the Boma drivers were out on tour with the landrovers). On one of them I went with the Learner District Assistant to value a barge for the Resident Commissioner at a spot 26 miles away on the other side of the Zambezi.

Coming back on the pontoon, we saw a couple of chaps in a speedboat whom the pontoon foreman said were crocodile hunters. Just that morning we had received a telegram from the DC of Sesheke further down the Zambezi that these chaps were coming into our district and that it was not known whether or not they had a permit to shoot crocs. After taking the lorry across, we went back to the opposite bank on the pontoon and walked to the hunters' camp. We asked them to show us their permit (issued on the authority of the Litunga with the fee going to his Treasury) and they did so. The Zambezi is let out in four stretches for six months of the year to professional hunters, each stretch being fifty to eighty miles long and if the hunters are really expert they may leave with several hundred croc skins. Last year, one of the hunters had been trapping crocs alive to take to zoos in the US. I must say these hunters looked as hard as nails – they would have to be! They hunt at night with a strong torch whose beam picks out the eyes of the croc for the hunter to shoot at. After we had interviewed these men we had to be canoed across the Zambezi, the pontoon having closed for the night. It was very beautiful ▶

slipping over the perfectly calm waters of the great river in the gloaming, though my heart was in my mouth every time the canoe rocked with the exertions of the paddler. It is most unhealthy for the occupants if a canoe capsizes – and I don't mean they will catch their death of cold – hardly time for that in these crocodile infested waters.

I have been out duck shooting this week with the other officers at the boma. For me the trips are very enjoyable for they are made in the last hour of daylight and first of dusk when the air is cool, the flies have gone, the mosquitoes have not yet appeared and the colours on the river in the setting sun are marvellous – a pink sheen on the river, purples and reds and browns in the woods and various shades of greens and yellows on the plain. Moreover, the bird life of this place is fantastic – herons, cranes, fish eagles, spurwing and other geese, all huge birds, ducks, and many small birds of brilliant hue.

The past week has been nice and cool, cold to those who have been here for a while. I have been out visiting quite a lot of the other European homes here. They are all extremely hospitable and friendly. I don't talk politics here except with Iain Stuart. It would create too much misunderstanding. Besides, it is rather presumptuous of me to air my views until I have had first-hand experience of the situation. So I keep my mouth shut – a new experience!

Senanga
30 August 1959

I have now almost completed my first month in the Provincial Administration in NR. The days have certainly flown past, especially since I have been of some use in the office. During the second half of this week we were very busy checking the books of the native Sub-Treasuries that operate in Senanga District. The chaps in charge of the Sub-Treasuries are, of course, Africans whose job is to gather in the taxes and act as court clerks in the Native Court of each silalo. They are paid seven to ten pounds per ▶

month, which strikes me as being far too low even in relation to other wages in Barotseland. A cook gets three to five pounds per month, a District Messenger seven pounds to over fifteen pounds (for the Head Messenger) while the chief African clerk at the Boma gets about twenty pounds per month. I am paid eighty pounds per month. Compared to his salary the Court Clerk is handling large sums of money in taxes and court fines.

The result of paying the Court Clerks such low wages is that embezzlement by them seems to be rife and half of them have been removed for this offence in the last two years. Naturally, the Government loses a lot of money in the process. The trouble is that the Barotse Native Government which pays the Court Clerks is perpetually short of money despite the fact that Barotseland is fairly heavily subsidised by the NR Government. Taxation consists of an annual tax of ten shillings Government Tax, and ten shillings Native Government Levy on every male African between the age of eighteen and sixty. I have been informed that of the NRG Tax, only one shilling, finds its way into central government's coffers, the other nine shillings being remitted back to the Barotse Native Treasury.

This region is potentially rich agriculturally, as it should be considering that one of Africa's largest rivers waters it. Every tour report that I read talks of the potential for greater crop yields, the suitability of the region for rice growing, etc. But little or no advance seems to have been made in this direction. The trouble seems to be the reluctance of the Paramount Chief to see the country develop and change but by far the major reason is the lack of cash to pay for public utilities, in this case, roads, without which agricultural development is pointless. It is no use peasants growing foodstuffs for export if communications are too bad to allow them to be despatched reasonably quickly and cheaply to the main centres of consumption. The problem is so great that the Provincial Administration here seems to have given up hope of Barotseland's development, in the absence of the miraculous discovery of oil, gold or diamonds, and so for the most part is content with routine administration work.

▶ A week on Tuesday I shall be going on my first tour, to the Shekela silalo. I shall meet Iain Stuart in Shekela as he will be passing through on his way back from his present tour. He will show me the ropes, accompanying me for the first two or three days of my tour. Then I'll be left on my own.

The tour will last 10-15 days. Touring is popular with District Officers both because it tends to be more interesting than office work and because touring officers get an allowance of twelve shillings and sixpence[7] for every night spent on tour. This allowance covers living expenses so that for the period one spends on tour one's salary remains untouched.

I am told, by the way, that as a bachelor, I should manage to save about three hundred pounds per annum. At that rate, I'll soon be a millionaire!

There is a District Officer here at the moment, sent to help out while the DC was on a Boundary Commission on the Portuguese frontier. Now that the DC has returned, this chap will be leaving. He is a real pukka English type, his father being a high-up gynaecologist in London. He is one of those types who seems to know all the Top People.

Rereading my comment that "this region is potentially rich agriculturally" I think now that I was mistaken. Yes, there was plenty of water in the Zambezi River; the trouble was that it flooded the entire Barotse Plain on either side of it each year in a manner that to this day has never been controlled. How then do you grow crops around the year on this Plain?

In the open woodlands and grasslands beyond the Plain the soils are mainly Kalahari sands, soft and infertile. Most of the villages are grouped along river tributaries of the Zambezi and dambos, depressions amidst the sandy plains which have moist soils around them for most of the year. In a good season a surplus of maize and other foodstuffs can be grown but getting them to market is very arduous compared with other areas of Zambia. This is because the soft sandy soils of Barotseland (now called Western Province) make it impossible to use a bicycle to carry a sack of grain or groundnuts, unlike other areas where the soils are formed from much firmer, often lateritic soils.

[7] *About £0.60 in present day money although much more in real terms.*

I have to take four main sets of exams. In January 1960 I hope to sit General and Financial Orders, Stores Regulations and Colonial Regulations. In April, I intend to take Lower Lozi and perhaps Lower Bemba. In October 1960, I'll aim to sit Higher Lozi and in the following August, Law. I have got quite a deal of homework to do in my first two years.

My first monthly pay check arrived this week, about seventy-eight pounds!! Am I worth all that?

Did you know that I have been writing all these letters from over four thousand feet? Rather a good excuse if my writing proves illegible. It is also a good excuse if I get beaten at tennis.

Now to answer some of the questions Mum asked in her last letter, though I fancy I may have answered them already.

What are my living quarters like? Well, if you have received the slides you will see what the house looks like from the outside. I share the main front veranda and the main hall which is a large sitting room entering into the dining room. Peter Wilson who shares the house has his own set of rooms and on my side I have a self-contained set of rooms consisting of two bedrooms, a bathroom and a room I use for studying.

Have I got a servant of my own? Yes, by name Jameson.

My trusty cook and housekeeper, Jameson, in front of my first house

▶ Will I have to buy a lot of extras? All depends how well I live. But within the next week I shall probably buy some lengths of cloth from one of the local stores for curtains and cushion covers to be made up by a local tailor. I have already bought pots and pans and I still have to buy some odds and ends such as milk jug, etc.

Nearly all luxuries and semi-luxury goods whether in the durable or foodstuffs category have to be bought in Livingstone or Mongu and these tend to be very expensive. But it is quite possible to live very well off the local produce. Local fish (bream) caught the day you eat them cost sixpence or nine pence[8] each and are delicious.

Senanga
14 September 1959

Although the last two days have been cooler, as a whole the weather during the past week has been really hotting up with maximum afternoon shade temperatures ranging from 92 to 97°F.[9] Rather warm. I have given up wearing long trousers to the office and have fallen into line with the other officers and now wear shorts. My theory was that I should wear warm clothes for as long as possible so that when the really hot weather came I would have something cooler to change into.

During the past week I had my first taste of touring proper. I went out to one of the silalos in the north-west of the District, called Shekela, where I met Iain Stuart returning from a tour of one of the other silalos. It took nearly seven hours in the landrover to cover the eighty miles from Senanga to Shekela so rough are the roads in Barotseland.

The last five or six miles were along a track, purely imaginary in places, through the bush. I can assure you it is rather a fine sight to see the bushes and saplings folding beneath you as the gallant landrover ploughs its way forward. I drove most of the way in second gear of which I am perhaps inordinately fond so that I had to stop on two occasions because of insistent knocking noises from the boiling water in the radiator.

▶

[8] *In present money, 3 pence or US 5 cents.*
[9] *37.5°C - 40.6°C.*

I was glad that I did not enjoy the experience of one of our drivers the week before. While driving one of the landrovers on his way to pick up the DC who was on tour, he was chased by a lion, he swears for nine miles (seems to me to be a bit excessive) but strange things happen in this country. This happened in one of the most isolated and sparsely populated areas of the district and in such parts (apart from the game Parks) there is more game than in any other part of Northern Rhodesia – elephants, giraffes, lions, etc. In one area, huge herds of buffalo roam, three hundred strong, eating the ground bare as they go. So wherever we camp while on tour, a large fire is built outside the door of our compound beside which the Messengers sleep with loaded guns. This latter is an extreme precaution because wild animals keep well away from fire as a rule.

I might as well describe the layout of a District Officer's camp. In the centre is a wall, six to eight feet tall made of reeds and straw built to enclose a circle thirty feet or so in diameter. At its entrance, between sunrise and sunset, when the DO is present, the Union Jack is flown (an exercise known as "showing the Flag"!).

In the middle of this circle is the DO's hut of one or two rooms where he eats and sleeps. In the circle, too, are subsidiary enclosures where the DO's lavatory seat and canvas bath are placed.

Iain Stuart taking a village census

▶ I arrived at Shekela in the early evening and next morning Iain took me round three villages on a sample tour.

That night, the villagers came to the fire outside the gate of our compound to stage a dance for us. I was fascinated by it all especially when some of the men danced solo. In those dances they imitate wild animals and their animism is terrific.

Early next morning, at 6.30 a.m., I set off on my own with an entourage of two Indunas, Messengers and carriers and visited four villages. It involved a long hike of eighteen to twenty miles over mostly sandy soil which makes walking very tiring. After midday, too, it gets very hot as the accumulated heat of the day seems then to be unleashed. Usually you try to complete your inspection of villages by midday, having walked, say, ten miles, rest in the afternoon and write up your report in the late afternoon and evening. But this day I did not get back to camp until 3.30 p.m. with the entourage sadly wilted.

My cook opened a new tin of salt the other day to fill up the empty salt cellar. I wondered why the "salt" had little effect on the flavour of my dish. Investigation found that he had opened a tin of the Andrew's liver variety! Nothing like a good dose of an emetic now and again.

I shall write more about Shekela anon for I am going back there to continue my tour on Thursday after the Minister for Native Affairs (MNA) and the Resident Commissioner have come and, I hope, gone.

PS Heard on BBC on Sat that Dons beat Dunfermline 3-1. Jolly good.

Got letter from Joe Chileshe and heard him on wireless again.

Lunch for the Minister

Senanga

20 September 1959

As you know, the Resident Commissioner (RC) and the Minister for Native Affairs and his wife were here last week. They came to us for lunch and we served them with cream of mushroom soup, fried steaks of bream (the best fish locally for eating), cold beef and salad, and a trifle made of jelly with fruit mixed through it, with a layer of custard above and a layer of clotted cream to top it. Really quite swell and the DC's wife told me that the MNA's wife had remarked to her on the excellence of the meal we had provided.

The Minister was DC here from 1940-42 and he and his wife used to live in this house, so it was quite a sentimental occasion for them. She was very charming and easy to talk to. The Minister is a big man, at least 6 feet tall, inclining to stoutness. His name is Billing, and from it I had pictured a man just like that.

He was very affable with a bit too dominating a manner for my liking. An Oxford man, rowed for his college, bit of a snob. Wish I had taken up rowing – definitely the OK thing to do! The RC, Gervas Clay,[10] is also a rowing man as seem to be most of the other bigwigs in the PA. He is a dried up looking man with a dried up looking moustache and a dry sense of humour. He insisted in making much banter of the Scots and Scotland which it was difficult to counter, in jesting style, without being rude. I think it is a bit off for a man much senior to another, to use a type of jest which deserves an insubordinate answer unless the two are well acquainted.

I made a ghastly faux pas by calling my cook who was waiting at table by the MNA's name on a couple of occasions. "Billing" I called out instead of "Jameson". I naturally did not realise this at the time but my confreres Iain Stuart and Peter Wilson told me about it to my consternation. I expect to receive my dismissal papers any day now!

▶

[10] *"Old" Gervas Clay whom I thought looked ancient was 52 at that time and lived for a further 50 years, dying aged 102 after eating an entire box of Belgian chocolates – according to his family.*

At the DC's cocktail party that night, all the Europeans in Senanga (with about two exceptions) were there, and that meant the missionaries were there, too. Now this was almost a unique occasion, because the European community is divided in two, between the missionaries and laymen, and seldom do they mix, except on business.

The Rhodesians that I have met here are uniformly suspicious and even resentful of the missionaries. Our DC is typical. He is a Rhodesian, very friendly and informal. He regards the missionaries as responsible for all the trouble in Northern Rhodesia. He sees them as unrealistic idealists who put ideas into the African's head which he is not able to understand because they are contrary to all his previously held beliefs and traditions. The only missionaries that he approves of are the Capuchin Fathers; in this area, Irish. They are looked upon as men of the world, realists who have always a whisky to offer you whenever you visit their mission and have no illusions about the native.

Most Europeans would not go so far as the old trader, Harrington, who said when I visited him one night "mad dogs and missionaries ought to be shot". As for the Church of Scotland missionaries, "they are Communists". The RC thinks the Church of Scotland sends out poor types most of whom can't stick it, he says, for more than two or three years while the General Assembly of the Church of Scotland, although it said a lot, did little to help the African in practical ways. They had had to close down a mission station and a hospital, he said, for lack of funds in the last year or two.

The Minister of Native Affairs had heard of "a man called Macleod who does a lot of talking, doesn't he?" Iain and I just had to grin and bear it.

Certainly, as I think I have said before, these Rhodesians do try to be just to the Africans. They admit that the colour bar is wrong. The tests for full rights as a citizen are to be applied without discrimination to black and white alike. Yet the DC said in conversation to me one night that he would not consider inviting any of the African clerks, not even the Head Clerk, who work at the Boma, into his house for a meal or a drink. The reason he gives is that they are not sufficiently civilized – for example, he believes

> that their honesty is only maintained because of fear of the consequences, not because they have accepted the European code of ethics.

This is a long way from the presence of missionaries at a social gathering of the rest of the European population. I might say, too, that part of the reason for the non-mixing is that the mission station is built some two miles from the Boma.

As it turned out, the cocktail party went very well and everyone mixed, thanks to the bonhomie of the Minister. The missionaries here belong to the Paris Mission Society[11] their parent body being the Reformed Church in France. They come from France, Belgium and Switzerland.

The army is here just now on a recruiting campaign. Barotseland is one of the few areas where relatively "uncontaminated" Africans are to be found for recruitment to the Army and Police.

"The man called Macleod" was in fact the newly appointed Colonial Secretary who made decisions affecting Northern Rhodesia and Britain's other colonial territories. Ultimately he was the boss of all colonial civil servants, from the highest to the lowest. He soon made it known that he was above all concerned to safeguard African interests in the Federation. This was possibly not appreciated by some of the old guard civil servants like Billing.

[11]*See page 16.*

Letters from Shekela Silalo – Land of Sand

Yela Camp, Shekela Silalo, Senanga

25 September 1959

Dear Folks

This is Friday evening, but this letter has to be written now if it is to catch the first plane out of Senanga next week (Tuesday afternoon). I shall send a mail runner off to the Boma early tomorrow morning and if he goes hard he will reach Senanga on Tuesday morning at the latest.

I am miles out in the bush at the moment camped about a quarter of a mile from a village with my following of fourteen carriers, two district messengers, one cook, two camp labourers and the Barotse Native Government representatives – two Indunas, two Kapasus and the Court Clerk.

I started off from Senanga the day before yesterday, with the DC. We spent one night at a camp on the edge of the Zambezi Plain. The place was infested with insect life because just below where we were camped was the swampy plain. Mosquitoes abounded and much larger insects as well. We had dinner out in the open air and large moving objects constantly landed on our lamp or on the table, attracted by our Tilley lamps[12] placed there.

Despite the distractions, however, we dined well on thick vegetable soup, roast duck (shot by the DC that afternoon) with green peas and roast potatoes and cabbage, strawberries out of a tin and custard.

Next morning, we again got up early – at 5 a.m. We drove further up the Plain edge and then cut inland over the escarpment that forms the Western boundary of the Zambezi plain and descended into Shekela. We arrived about 11 a.m. at Shekela Kuta and, while the DC tinkered with the landrover and then looked over the Tax Receipt books of the Court Clerk, I went with the senior Induna to inspect the school buildings and garden. ▶

---

[12]*A type of pressurised paraffin (kerosene) lamp that emitted a brilliant white light. Its main drawbacks were the fragility of its mantle and the heat it gave off.*

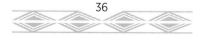

On my previous visit I had gone into the school and met the two teachers that work here and made a cursory tour of inspection. This time I had a proper look round though one of the teachers was ill with pneumonia and the other was away collecting material for basket making as there is a female basket making instructor for the younger children.

The children are being provided with new dormitories because eighty percent live too far away from their villages to go home after school. In the garden, maize had been planted and there were also mango trees. I feel that in a school of this type where children are only taken up to Primary 2 and hardly any go on to Middle or Upper Primary education because the nearest schools in these categories are at least 20 miles away, the garden is the most important part of the school.

The senior Induna has agreed to help with the growing of rice in marshy land that lies next to the school garden. This marshy land is like the land on the Zambezi Plain, very wet but rich. The senior Induna is one of two rice growers in the district and for this place is very progressive. He was accused of witchcraft because his crops were so good when he came to this silalo three years ago.

As we left the school the Induna said sadly "Sir, this is the most backward part of Barotseland!"

In the evening, I saw the head teacher and told him of the Induna's offer. He, too, is a "progressive". His son is one of two children to have gone to the next silalo where the nearest Middle primary school is, for "higher" education. As he said, "The people here don't appreciate education."

Yet having looked through some dozen or so villages on the two days of my previous visit and today, one can understand why the people here do not value education very highly. They have food in reasonable plenty and very few other needs. Apart from food, their main requirement is money to pay for taxes, blankets and some cheap clothes.

The money is procured by the men who go to the mines in South Africa. The mines run a highly organised company to recruit men here. It is called WENELA – the Witwatersrand Native Labour

▶ Association. In the last village I visited today, out of twelve men, five were working in South Africa and one in Southern Rhodesia. I see from previous years' tour reports that on average a quarter of the men are in South Africa at any one time. They go for eleven months at a time, then come back to be replaced by another batch.

Food is plentiful because, except in cassava growing areas, the crops have been good. Cassava,[13] a crop that takes three years to mature needs dry soil and in the heavy floods of '57 and '58 much of the cassava crop was completely ruined and the new crops have not matured yet.

Most people also grow maize, millet, etc., though the heavy floods of '57 and '58 destroyed much grain. There was widespread hunger and Government had to import grain for sale. Even in hungry years, the people seldom die from lack of food because of the availability of forest fruits, fish and game,

Today I must have walked at least sixteen miles. We started at 7 a.m., having first hired carriers. Plenty of applicants, so I left one of the District Messengers to sort it out and thanked them all for coming along; some must have walked eight to ten miles.

View across a dambo in Shekela   ▶

[13] *Cassava, also known as manioc, is a tuberous root. It was introduced to Africa from Brazil by the Portuguese and is now a widely grown perennial crop providing plenty of carbohydrates but little protein. Its leaves which are rich in protein are used as a relish. It is popular because it grows well in poor soils.*

The countryside we walked through consisted of wide depressions or dambos that are quickly covered with water when the floods begin to rise in February. Along the sides of the depressions the trees grow thicker and the grass is long and tussocky. In the depressions on drier ground there is low stumpy grass and scrub and the occasional tree.

The villages are built on ridges or old termite mounds often formed by anthills and at least for the duration of my visit are clean. I make a point of looking inside one hut in each village. In one that I looked into today there were pictures from "Readers Digest" pinned to the wall. The owner was illiterate.

The huts should be a minimum of twelve feet square.[14] Many are smaller and with round huts it is difficult to know if they have the regulation floor area! At the villages, the District Messenger who accompanies us gets the people to bring food for buying to feed the carriers, which I pay for and deduct from their wages. I find it most amusing to see the D/M bargaining. He is a real old-timer, as hard as nails. The other D/M goes with the carriers straight to the next camp and sets things in order. My cook goes with them so that a cup of tea is ready when I get into camp.

For dinner tonight I had soup, a huge tomato omelette (eggs are less than a penny each here), paw-paw and custard to finish. Nae bad, lad. To think I get paid for camping and used to do it for fun back home and not nearly so luxuriously.

I got a letter this week saying that on the basis of a report on my work in London, I would be exempted the written part of the Lower Bemba provided I passed the oral part in April. So I think I'll have a stab at it, if only because I may get a trip to Lusaka out of it.

[14] *As laid down in a recent Hygiene Ordinance of the Barotse Government. It was based on the belief that the larger the hut, the better the health of the family living in it. The inside walls of the hut were supposed to be smeared with mud to reduce the prevalence of insects. In Barotseland, in contrast to areas where there were clay soils which enabled people to make sun-dried, or less commonly, burnt bricks in house construction, the universal construction materials were poles cut from the surrounding woodland and grass or reeds from the surrounding grassland and reed beds. The walls of poles, in-filled with grass were then smeared inside and out with mud sometimes mixed with cattle dung to present a smooth appearance. It made the walls more weatherproof against rain and they could be decorated as shown in the photograph.*

A decorated house in Shekela

Have just heard the Goons with half an ear, most of my attention on this letter.

To settle a query of Mum's, mosquitoes breed profusely in Barotseland especially in the Plain. I trust that the Paludrine that I take daily will keep the malaria away.

My most precious possession was my transistor radio which was light, robust and efficient. My favourite station was the BBC World Service from London. What a miracle it was to hear these modulated British accents recounting the latest news from around the world, as well my favourites like the Goons and best of all Sports Report with its memorably rousing theme tune. Every weekend, I would strain to catch how my home team, Aberdeen (the Dons), had fared.

The Camp beside Mulikela's Village
Shekela Silalo, Senanga.
1 October, 1959

As you may surmise from the address (not to be used on letters dispatched to me!), I am still on tour and enjoying it though it is strenuous work – eleven to eighteen miles per day plus censusing and inspection of villages. It is quite a good day's work under any conditions, I would say, and certainly so in the present climate. We are now in the middle of the hot season during which the Malozi say "the sun burns you up by early in the morning". So far I have stood up to the heat OK. I should think that the low humidity has a lot to do with it.

Thinking back to my last letter, I have a feeling that although I spoke in general terms about being "on tour", I gave no detailed description. This then is how a typical day's touring unfolds.

The alarm goes at 5.30 a.m. though I have usually wakened already from cold. It is around 50°F[15] degrees, a forty to fifty degree[16] drop from the day maximum temperature. I think the low humidity explains the terrific variation in temperature between night and day.

6a.m. – breakfast: - paw-paw, scrambled egg and a cup of tea. Then after brushing my teeth and filling a vacuum flask with tea, I call for one of the District Messengers – a signal to the camp that I am ready to start.

From their huts, the District Messengers, Indunas and Kapasus suddenly appear and the carriers get off their haunches around the camp fire. The Senior D/M brings with him two carriers who will carry my folding table, a couple of folding chairs and my touring box. It is a small tin trunk with census books, other miscellaneous forms and papers, snake bite outfit (I still have to see a snake, thank goodness!), packet of raisins and vacuum flask.

6.30 a.m., we set off from camp leaving the rest of the carriers to pack up the camp under the supervision of my cook, the junior D/M and a kapasu. It is still chilly and the walk is pleasant. The ▶

---

[15] 11°C.
[16] 25° - 31°C.

villages are about three to six miles apart so we walk along narrow paths for one or two or more hours before we reach a village. When a village is near we come across a group of the women of the village who, kneeling, clap a welcome, then stand and break into song, walking at our side, clapping in rhythm.

Around the village, the "gardens", i.e. small fields, are to be seen. Some are already planted with maize and they are the first part of the village I inspect. Where plenty of maize has been planted, the headman is praised. Where none, or little, he is asked for an explanation. It varies from a complaint that there is no wet soil to the soil being too sticky. Usually the underlying explanation is the same, the headman has not sufficient drive.

Then we go into the middle of the village where there is usually a small thatched shelter built in which I sit while taking the census. The carriers have already set up the table so I usually dump my hat and camera, which I am carrying everywhere on this tour, and then proceed to go round the village with my entourage, accompanied by the headman. I examine the huts, measuring the occasional one to see that it comes up to standard and look inside one or two to see that the huts are smeared with a mud plaster both inside and out. Huts and gardens are things to which I pay most attention. Where a village's huts are particularly poor, the induna tells the headman that he is going to fine them, and sometimes, where the village is very small, most people having deserted the headman for another, the headman is told to shift with his remaining adherents to someone else's village. The grain bins are looked into to see what the food situation is and a cursory inspection is made of rubbish pits and latrines.

I go to the open-sided hut where I am going to hear the census, take out my books while the villagers kneel in a half circle in front. Sometimes, before I start reading out the names from the census book, I deliver a general word of praise or admonition, translated by the Induna or the Court Clerk. Often the Induna does this off his own bat, knowing my general feelings about the village and adding comments of his own.

> I then read out each man's name, asking him the name of his wife(s) and the number of children, boys and girls, he has. These men are ones paying taxes. Then come the names of those who are exempted from tax-paying by reason of old age, or physical disability, then the names of the unmarried women. ▷

More than fifty years later I recall one headman in this silalo. There were two reasons for this. The first was that he reminded me of one of my cousins despite the difference in age and skin colour. It was the expressiveness of his face, half smiling, alert and intelligent. The other reason was that he had twelve wives. Polygamy was quite common in the District but this was more than I ever came across in three years of village inspections. In completing the village register I had to write down the name of each wife and as he told me each name I asked him as part of the census, how many children she had. The answer to the first was "None" and after the second wife, "None" and so it went on. There was a degree of anticipation building up amongst me and my companions. Had he scored a blank on all of the twelve?

At the twelfth, who was younger than the rest, after reciting her name, he announced triumphantly to my question of how many children: "One". At which I laid down my pen and joined in the applause which the headman acknowledged with a slight bow.

> Young men who want to pay taxes are then considered and if the Indunas think they are old enough I write down their names. Often there are men present who want to shift to or from the village and the Indunas consider their petition. If they grant the petition, I make the necessary adjustment to the tax register book.
>
> Then details of cattle possessed, ploughs, children attending school, tribe, crops cultivated and crafts pursued are taken and general requests considered. Eg. A hunter wanted to shoot lions raiding the kraal; permission to cut trees to make cassava gardens in the woods, etc. Then off to the next village. Generally, three villages are visited each day, the time spent in each varying according to size; usually half to one hour.
>
> My footwear could be more comfortable. My newly purchased boots give me blisters and chapped ankles. ▷

Village in Shekela Silalo with a central termite mound, paw-paw trees in background

General information about this area. Its name, Shekela, is derived from a word in an old dialect, "musheke" so that Shekela means "Land of Sand". This is quite apposite because except near the permanently wet bottoms of the numerous depressions ("dambos"), the soil is very sandy which increases the difficulty of walking. In the woods, the fallen leaves and the tufty grass make for a firmer footing though the path is churned into soft sand by the scores of feet that have gone before.

There are many cattle but in general they belong to people living on the Barotse Plain to the east who send them to Shekela for herding when the Plain is flooded each year.

There are two main types of people living here. First, the Ba-Simaa who have been settled in these parts for two hundred years or so. They are agriculturalists, herdsmen and craftsmen in wood and fibres.

Second, the Mambunda, sometimes called "Mawiko – people of the west", because they have moved here in the present century from Angola to the west of Barotseland, or from North-Western Province of Northern Rhodesia. They are people of the woods,

▶ hunters whose main crop is cassava, the only foodstuff that grows well in the sandy soil of the woods where they live. Their huts are much less well constructed than those of the Ba-Simaa. They are woodworkers and blacksmiths, making spears, axes, etc. They worship inanimate objects which represent their ancestors – such as a piece of stick stuck into the ground.

The women's songs change with the times. Nowadays, they sing about the District Officer's "jeepie" (landrover) that bumps its way along roads, and through the forest. Another song that is heard in nearly every village is "When I saw the shirt, I thought it was my darling".[17]

Shambwe's Village
Liamanyinga Pan
Shekela Silalo
Monday 5 October 1959

Dear Folks,

This is my last full day on tour. This afternoon, a landrover should arrive so that I shall be able to leave for Senanga first thing tomorrow morning.

I am feeling particularly elated for when I reached camp a mail-runner was waiting with my mail which consisted of four letters from you and the first of the Manchester Weekly Guardians ordered by Willie Farquhar.

Mum sounds as though she is rather sorry for me being on my lonesome out on tour. I can assure you that so far I have not felt a bit lonely. Why this is I can't really explain. Partly it is because I am being kept busy walking between and visiting villages, resting from that, learning Lozi, writing up a diary of the tour that has to be made into a tour report at the end and with all that I have scarcely time to listen to the wireless or get any light reading done. ▶

[17] "My darling" was the young woman's husband or boyfriend returning from the mines in South Africa whom she had spotted a long way off walking across the plain towards his village.

I feel at home, now, with the people around me which also staves off loneliness. The fact that I can now pick up a little of what people are saying is I think the chief reason for this. Besides, the Court Clerk of the local native court who is also the tax gatherer, and the chief Induna can both speak English and are both very friendly and helpful.

On Saturday we entered a part of the silalo where a New Apostolic Church is situated. The women of the villages in this part greet you with hymns instead of the traditional secular songs found elsewhere. Again, today, Sunday, the day when we rest, we were met by hymn- singing villagers, one of the hymns being a Christmas one whose tune I knew well (the chorus goes "Hail thou ever blessed morn, Hail Redemption's happy dawn" etc.). It was very exhilarating for the men joined in the singing as well, a thing that does not happen in the pagan villages where the singing seems to be left exclusively to the women.

At the village where my camp is situated is the church building and the houses of the two evangelists and the lay helper – very good buildings, though the ordinary villagers' huts are very small. I met one of the evangelists and asked him to use his influence to get the people of the village to build better huts for themselves.

Senanga
Tuesday, 6 October 1959.

I am now back in a proper house from which the mosquitoes are largely excluded, thanks to mosquito wire mesh that covers the porches and windows.

I received a letter from Dad today in which he asks whether the camps are permanent or not. They are semi-permanent being built in exactly the same way as native huts – a framework of poles filled in with reeds and smeared with mud inside and out. These buildings have to be renewed every so often and a camp may change its location because of a shift of one or two villages which would leave the old camp isolated. The camps are built by the villagers – sort of tribute work.

> I hear that I'll soon be off on tour again - a long one probably lasting a month. The sooner I get off the better, because the rains will be here soon.
>
> Am told it was 101°F[18] in the shade last Friday.

I interspersed my regular weekly letter to my parents with less frequent ones to friends in Britain and elsewhere. They were written from a slightly different perspective, possibly franker and less reassuring than the letters to my parents. The main recipients were my closest friends, Christian Fraser and Willie Farquhar – both friends from university.

Letter to Christian Fraser

Senanga
11 October 1959

Dear Christian

I hope none of my friends will ever again refer to this continent as "Darkest Africa". There is no escape from the sun during the present season, and from 9 a.m. I am in a lather of sweat. This is a bit of an exaggeration; from 12 p.m. until 5 p.m. would be more exact. For it is in the afternoon that the whole heat of the day seems to accumulate and burst forth, penetrating every corner. This afternoon I am going to try sitting in a bath of cold water! In fact, the water is running now so you will enjoy the unique experience of reading a letter that has been written in the bath.

Work these days begins at 7 a.m. and goes on until 1.30 p.m. Quite a stretch but it makes sense not to have to work in the afternoons.

On tour of a sub-district, it is different. Just this week I returned from one that lasted a fortnight. I would set off from camp at 6.30 a.m. and sometimes not get back till 3 p.m.

It is quite extraordinary the way this district falls into the traditional picture of the colonial world in Africa - the District Officer travelling on foot with a retinue of native chiefs, district messengers and carriers. The DO is treated with enormous respect everywhere he goes, at least in its outward forms. I came to Africa ▶

[18] 43°C.

▶ prepared to find everything different from any of the pictures I had formed from reading about it. Yet here is Joyce Cary's pre-war colonial setup in nearly every detail.

There is first, a small European community composed of decent friendly people full of prejudices and an inability to understand what people in the outside world are thinking about the colonial situation. Even the most knowledgeable of the Europeans have these prejudices because of their lack of social contact with Africans.

Second, the African is wonderfully deferential except a few who have been to the line of rail. Witchcraft-ridden to some extent – how far no European knows. Two years ago in this and other parts of Barotseland there were a great number of witchcraft trials following a murder by a witchdoctor in the sub-district that I have just finished touring. In the investigations that followed, hundreds of people were brought to trial on charges of sorcery and many hundreds of witchcraft materials were confiscated. The two chiefs who accompanied me on this tour said witchcraft still goes on but more secretly than before.

Talking to the people, however, one would never guess this, except, perhaps, amongst the most backward of the tribes in the district called the Mambunda. Some of these people still wear skins instead of European clothes. They live on the edge of the woods and spend most of their energies in hunting and blacksmithing, making spears, axes and the like. They are notoriously blind to the advantages of education so that few of their children go to school. They live in small rickety huts and frequently are in search of new parts of the forest to clear and grow their cassava.

The investigations showed that even amongst those tribes that look upon the Mambunda as "ignorant savages" witchcraft was practised. How deeply ingrained it is and to what extent education, most of it provided by the missions, and Christianity can exorcise it is a matter of dispute. Rhodesians say it will take one hundred to two hundred years and this is the chief reason they give for arguing that the vote should not be given to even outwardly civilized, educated Africans. Even the educated ▶

> African is regarded by them as being inherently lazy and corrupt and Ghana is cited as a terrible example of what happens when self-government is given to the "nigs".
>
> I stayed up on Thursday to hear the first of the election results; pretty well as I had expected though the Conservatives' victory was much bigger than I expected. They left me gloomy especially to hear the cries of glee from the Rhodesians here. But they may crow too soon. From what I gathered from my Conservative friends at Oxford, the Tory Party may be rediscovering its conscience over Africa.

Reading the final paragraph with the benefit of hindsight some fifty years later, I'm quite impressed by my perspicacity at how misplaced the optimism of the white political leaders and their followers was after the Tory victory in the election of October 1959. Within a few months Harold Macmillan would tell the South African parliament that there was an unstoppable "wind of change" blowing through Africa which white political leaders would have to come to terms with.

Who was Christian Fraser? She was a friend throughout most of my university days but only one of a wide group drawn from various social networks – my fellow students of economics, the Student Christian Movement of which she was a member, the hockey club and the student newspaper of which I became editor in my second year. A student's life can be a very gregarious one and mine certainly was.

I didn't really become attracted to her until after I had completed my degree at Aberdeen and moved to Oxford for a year of study sponsored by the Colonial Office. During my Easter vacation from there I met some friends for coffee in the Aberdeen Students' Union. While chatting with them Christian swept past in an elegant mid-calf trench coat on her way to meet a friend. She looked somehow different to the young woman I had known as a student; she looked more poised, more self-confident and more attractive.

I had no chance to speak to her because a short time later she swept out again hardly glancing at me. I asked around – where was Christian based; no one seemed to know. All I knew was that she had completed a postgraduate degree in Social Work at Edinburgh University and had taken up a social work job in England. Not long after returning to Oxford I was reminded that the College May Ball was only three weeks away and my immediate thought was to contact Christian to invite her to the Ball. I managed to find her address from our mutual university friend, Willie Farquhar, and then sent her a telegram two weeks beforehand with the invitation to the Ball. Luckily she was able to come. We spent an enjoyable weekend together, at the Ball, punting on the river, strolling along the river towpath to the Trout Inn near Oxford and savouring the warm sunny weather of early summer.

That weekend was my passport to writing to her throughout my three years in Northern Rhodesia.

> Senanga
> 12 October, 1959
>
> There are two hippos wallowing in the river below the house and they have been molesting the paddle (canoe) ferry these last few days. Yesterday morning, they forced a man to dive from his canoe and swim for shore to get out of their clutches. In the afternoon I went down to where the canoes cross, carrying people and goods across the Zambezi. Incredibly beautiful watching the canoes slipping over the calm water, lit up by the dazzling afternoon sun. Also exciting because the hippos were just a little way down stream and drifting towards the crossing, raising their heads every so often and emitting a bored bellow and a great spout of water. A small bird with magnificent colouring also circled near me and close by was a jacaranda tree aglow with its beautiful blue flowers.

Hippos are one of the most dangerous animals in Africa. Although they are not carnivorous they are bad tempered and will attack intruders to their territory. With one bite they can sever a man in two.

"A small bird with magnificent colouring" illustrates my ignorance of the beautiful and abundant bird life around me. The small bird with the magnificent colouring was the carmine bee-eater which nests in the sandy banks of the Zambezi in September and October.

Carmine bee-eaters

It has been jolly hot this week. On a couple of occasions the temperature reached 102°F[19] degrees . Today has again been very hot. The rains will come any time now and then it will be sticky and hot.

Tomorrow, at 6 a.m., I hope, I set off on tour. I should have gone off on Friday, but a hitch occurred because one landrover got involved in a minor smash while the other was in the workshops in Mongu having an overhaul. However, I am now taking so many people on tour with me that I have decided to go in the lorry! I shall be accompanied by an Agricultural Assistant, a Medical Assistant and a Surveyor, all Africans, besides a driver to take the lorry back to Senanga. So quite a sizable entourage and I shall probably need about twenty carriers.

The surveyor is coming because I want a decent map made of the silalo (sub-district) which I am touring. No good map showing the location of all the villages exists so that I have little idea what route I shall be following or how long it will take. My tour will be the first to be made on foot of the area for over twenty-five years and it is probable that no District Officer has tramped the whole of this region. This is because until this year the extensive tours have been made by landrover.

The Zambezi River as the light fades

[19]*44°C.*

> ▶ It is wonderfully beautiful here just now. The river is very low but the foliage is at its most variegated. There are quite a lot of jacarandas around here, with their lovely blue-purple flowers. I have been out visiting three times this week and on two of these occasions we all sat outside on the stoep (veranda), the moon full and the Zambezi a glimmer below us. Hard to excel and no mosquitoes to irritate us.

It was a retreat from modern touring when the Resident Commissioner, Gervas Clay, reintroduced foot tours as the principal mode of village to village inspections. He was a very conservative official who obviously believed the old methods were best. I and several of my fellow Cadets in Barotseland thought it was a total waste of time to take weeks instead of days to tour a silalo.

Now I am older and perhaps wiser. Looking back, I can appreciate that it was an entirely different experience for the villagers to be visited on foot by the District Officer and Indunas and their retinues. Imagine the slow approach of the important visitors who can be seen for miles away advancing over the open sun-scorched plain. They are met by the women of the village who sing at the tops of their voices for the few hundred yards into the village.

The visitors talk with their menfolk, inspect grain bins and houses and gardens and write in their books all the information about each family and its possessions of livestock and ploughs. It's a leisurely affair. Surely each family is important in the eyes of the District Officer, and the representatives of Barotse royalty, the two Indunas. It is a big occasion which will be talked about for months to come.

Compare that with the whizz-bang visit by the same important people who arrive in a landrover showering the villagers in a cloud of dust. A quick visit and then off to the next village. Little time for the women of the village to sing. Not much time to observe the visitors closely and note their mannerisms and peculiarities. Not nearly such a memorable occasion.

The other case for making me and my fellow district officers walk from village to village was that it made us appreciate how hard life is for villagers. It certainly did in my case and has lived with me to this day. I learned that life in the villages is hard and it takes a hero to emerge and pioneer a new crop, open a trading store or start a small enterprise such as rearing hens and selling eggs to nearby townships. It always angered me to read in a newspaper of certain African leaders berating "lazy villagers", forgetting their own roots in doing so.

I go to Church

This morning I went to church for the first time, I am ashamed to say, since coming to Senanga. I could plead some excuses – that the service is wholly in Lozi, that the church is a two mile walk from the house and that no Europeans from outside the mission go. The main reason, however, was just sheer laziness. I always forgot to ask about the time of the service until yesterday when I asked the Head Clerk, Mr Nyumbu, who is an elder of the church (Paris Mission Society). There is also a branch of the New Apostolic Church here. Three European[20] evangelists belonging to this church breezed into the office last week on a tour of branches of their church in Barotseland. Apparently, the headquarters of the Church is in Johannesburg.

To get back to my going to church. I was jerked out of my inertia by a short argument between myself, Iain, and Mr Nyumbu. It concerned the claim made by an African woman for compensation following the death of her son at a mine in South Africa. This was the second time she had come to ask for it. On the first, Iain had taken the particulars of her claim both on behalf of herself and of the younger brother of the dead man – an idiot of about ten years of age. Iain filled in the requisite form but did not write a very enthusiastic covering letter to the Compensation Bureau in South Africa because he felt the woman had little right to money, for though single when her son had left for the mines, she had married before his death and at that time could no longer be said to be dependent on the dead man's earnings. The claim was rejected, both on behalf of herself and of the dead man's brother.

On Friday, the woman came in again and I was advised by the District Messenger to call in the Head Clerk because he knew the particulars of the case. The facts of the idiot brother then came out – most important, that the woman's new husband had no obligations to her son by her previous husband. Now this made the boy even more dependent on the earnings of the deceased and made the compensation claim on his behalf a valid one. ▶

[20] "Europeans" did not necessarily mean people from Europe, only that they were white. In fact, I recall that they were from the USA!

▶ I saw Iain about it, and he apparently had not been made fully aware about all the facts pertaining to the claim of the boy. He was a bit annoyed about this and said a few words about the untrustworthiness of the testimony of Africans. This made Mr Nyumbu annoyed and he said "Sir, you do not understand the African. You think they all come telling lies". And for that moment his eyes glittered with resentment and bitterness. And then he became the polite clerk again.

Iain was rather upset at this and as he told me after dinner when we discussed this together, he had been the only one on the station to make any attempt at understanding. He has now and again invited a clerk to tea, chaired meetings at the Welfare Hall and looked over the houses in the compound to rectify any deficiencies in them. Neither the DC nor the Cadet who was here during the past year till I arrived had done anything in this line.

To cap the story, I decided I had better do something to achieve "understanding", hence church. Also I feel the lack of "community worship". In so far as my Christian faith is concerned, I am a gregarious creature – I like to feel that others are praising the same Lord as myself and at the same time.

So, with some apprehension, I went along. The church is a red brick building, quite pleasant to look at, simple in design and white washed inside. It is quite a typical Presbyterian kirk, the main difference being the thatched roof. As I drew near I heard the sound of a hymn being sung. I was sure I had still a few minutes to spare and asked an African who was near whether the service had begun. When I got inside I found that it hadn't; they were just practising under the lead of a precentor who sang the note and the first line of the hymn.

The service although entirely in Lozi seemed to me to be pretty much like an ordinary Presbyterian service. One hymn at least was familiar "Praise God from whom all blessings flow". The main difference was that there was no Old Testament reading and that the sermon was punctuated with one or two hymns. Also, during general prayer, thanks were given for protection first by Queen Victoria and now by Queen Elizabeth! The service was taken by our friend the African clerk. He is a very helpful chap and seems to be ▶

▶ highly respected in the African community. On several occasions I have been asked to consult him on community matters.

After the service, I had lunch with one of the missionaries and his wife. They are Belgians. The French lady doctor Dr Casalis in charge of the hospital was there, too. It was very enjoyable though I do wish I could speak more French.

Sunday morning at the PMS church, Senanga

Letters from Bushanjo Silalo – Land of Wild Game and Foul Wells

Mutomena's Village
Sitoti-Bushanjo Silalo
Senanga
24 October 1959

I take up my pen now because clouds, heavy and black, have rolled up, thunder is rumbling nearby and I am expecting to see for the first time since my arrival, RAIN.

From the address you may deduce that I am out on tour once more. I started on Monday intending to leave at 6 a.m. I had such a job rounding up my entourage that it was nearly 7 a.m. before we got going – in a five-ton lorry. After twelve miles we reached the Zambezi which we crossed on a motorised pontoon. Then we continued along the other side of the Zambezi going south, down river. Two hours bumping and frequent gear changes took us to a place called Sioma where a mission station is established, run by an RC order – Capuchin Fathers.

I called in because they have several primary schools in this silalo and they might have wanted some supplies taken out to them.

On tour with the 5 ton Bedford lorry

A mile further along the main road we turned off to the west along a well-defined rough road into the bush. This road runs for about sixty miles till it reaches the Portuguese border.[21] It is maintained by WNLA which uses it for transporting lorry loads of Africans to and from a depot one hundred miles south of Sioma, called Katima Mulilo, which is one of the large African settlements mentioned by Livingstone in his Journals.

I have been reading during the last three days "Livingstone's Travels" which is an edited collection of Livingstone's Journals by James Macnair. What a remarkable man Livingstone was. He seems to have been the first European to have travelled through Barotseland. He had a terrific insight into the mind of the African and a wonderful sense of humour that helped him to brush aside disappointments.

The seeds of pawpaw which today grow in nearly every village in these parts were brought by Livingstone in pots all the way from the west coast for they were hitherto unknown here.

So far, I have found that nearly all the villages of this area have to rely on well water and invariably this has the colour of coffee or tea because of being contaminated by cattle dung and urine that seeps into the wells.[22]

This is the chief cattle area of Barotseland and huge herds are attached to each village. These villages seldom own the beasts for, as in Shekela, people on the thickly populated flanks of the Barotse Plain send their cattle here to be herded in the wide open spaces when the Barotse Plain is seasonally flooded. This region is especially favoured because the grass grows luxuriantly. It is called the Silowana Grasslands.

Next day I again made use of the lorry to take me the eighteen miles to the site of the next camp.

On the third day I walked twelve miles to the next camp, visiting two villages en route.

[21]Now the border between Zambia and Angola.
[22]A year and a great deal of correspondence later, I persuaded the Health Department to sink proper wells lined with concrete casing, throughout this silalo to remedy the contamination of the drinking water.

In the afternoon we walked a further eight miles to visit the villages we had censused. In one the huts were well-built and large, in the other two, just the opposite. In such villages the people always justify themselves by saying that they want to move to a new site because there they will have either better gardens, or better water supply or a better site for building.

By the time I got back to camp I was utterly exhausted physically, though mentally and spiritually not so, for I find the villagers very refreshing. They are on the whole gay and hospitable in spite of the squalor.

The following morning, I walked sixteen miles visiting four villages en route, three of them well-nigh empty, the majority of the able-bodied having gone to help build my camp. This I reached to be greeted by a great crowd of women cavorting, singing and hallooing with high spirits.

In the afternoon I spent over three hours taking the census of about ten villages, listening to complaints and it was after 6 p.m. before I was finished. A good day's work, tiring and often tedious; yet I feel enormously privileged to be working with these people, however frustrating it is and however slight the effect of all my urging to build better houses and wells.

Why I should feel this sense of privilege, even exhilaration, is difficult to explain. Partly, I suppose, because I am physically as fit as ever I have been, partly because of the character of the people as I have mentioned.

That afternoon a man asked to be exempt taxes. As he did not appear to be over middle age I asked the reason for his request. He said he had a sore back and lifted his shirt to prove it. There was a great lump at the top and a pus-filled huge open sore at the base. "Spinal TB", the Dispensary Assistant said. It must have been giving the man considerable pain yet he did not droop but even smiled.

Yesterday, and again today, I have been using this camp as a base to visit the villages censused on Thursday but not visited. The huts ▶

▶ in this village are very large and well built. Why they should be so much better than those in the surrounding villages I do not know.[23]

The nearest river is about twenty miles away yet the people here are so fond of fish that they go there to catch them and even go to the Zambezi some forty to fifty miles away. They return with huge sledge loads of fish which they split and put in the sun to dry. While they are still moist they are covered with huge swarms of flies. Ugh!

Half way through writing this letter I had tea with the Agricultural Assistant and the Medical Assistant. We talked about changes in this silalo, progress in developing it and Barotseland as a whole. They say changes are taking place as more and more men see more of the world and visit the townships and the line of rail. When they return they tend to build bigger houses and generally be more civilised.

They asked me if DOs toured silalos in Britain. So I delivered a probably incomprehensible lesson on local government and its difficulties and advantages.

On tour with carriers. Senior District Messenger Kachana nearest camera. Note the white sandy soil. Kachana always carried a shotgun which frequently provided fresh meat for the pot

[23] As I wrote in an earlier letter, the explanation for the varied quality of house-building between one village and another probably lay in the character and leadership of the village headman.

Am now at the end of my second week on tour which may last for another one or three weeks depending on how urgently my presence is required at the boma.

This silalo is divided by its physical geography in two –the other part which lies on the banks of the Zambezi and this part that I am touring that lies in the bush, separated from the riverine lands by a broad belt of forest. The part by the river was censused earlier but no report was written so it is undecided as yet whether I will tour it.

By mail runner today I heard that Iain Stuart has been transferred to Choma on the line of rail. He was due for a shift because Cadets are usually transferred after a year.

The past week has been fairly routine. One day, however, was very hard – a twenty-five mile trek visiting eight villages en route. By the time I got to camp I was utterly exhausted as were the rest of my entourage but at the entrance the junior D/M was waiting with a handful of mail including two letters from you and one from Willie Farquhar. A real godsend.

The day after, we walked nineteen miles (there is a surveyor with me with an assistant who pushes a bicycle wheel with cyclometer attached) but at a much faster pace than the previous day and the increased energy expended was more than compensated by the shorter time spent walking under the merciless sun.

On our epic march the villages stood about two to three miles apart and between each the women always accompanied us to the next singing and clapping their hands to the rhythm made by the castanets. This of course helped to shorten the journey.

The week has also been marked by showers of rain and one or two electric storms, the sky lit by great flashes of lightning.

On Saturday (yesterday) the Agricultural Assistant, the Hospital Assistant and the Surveyor came to tea. I learn quite a lot from these tea parties of mine. The Hosp Asst is an intelligent chap with ▶

a good sense of humour and a sceptical attitude to life. One of the topics of conversation was housing conditions in the African compound. The houses are two-roomed, some of them are falling down and as one said, you trip over the pots on the way to bed because there is no pantry in the house, no bathroom, no flush lavatories and no running water – water has to be brought up from the river.

The Hosp Asst worked previously on the line of rail and enjoyed a much better house. He said adjustment was difficult on coming to Senanga – "I nearly resigned". He says that the house is well-nigh impossible to keep clean because it is so small.

Since 1955, too, it has been proposed to have a communal water tap installed in the compound[24] but it has yet to materialize. I cannot express the shame I felt in comparing my standard of living with theirs, whatever the economic justification for such a state of affairs. If the DC were more interested much more could be done. Iain Stuart told me something of the compound housing conditions a short time before I came on tour and how he found it impossible to interest the DC in the matter.

One question they asked, and it was asked the previous Sunday by the Induna and Court Clerk and by the Induna and Court Clerk in Shekela was "Do you have as many religions in England as here?" The cynical are amused, and the ordinary African plainly puzzled by the various rival Christian missions. "Which one" they ask, "has the truth and how are we to choose between them?"

I try and explain that these are not different religions but different denominations of the same religion, different glimpses of a truth that is impossible for man to grasp in its entirety and that after all, they all regard Jesus as the Son of God. They remain, however, politely disbelieving.

Well, there is little else to write about except that in one village I came across a hut with glass windows! Quite an outstanding event!

---

[24] *The absence of a tap bringing water to the compound meant that the women and children had to bring water in buckets from the river a few hundred yards away. Two years later, under a different DC, new houses were built for the African civil servants and piped water was supplied.*

My astonishment at seeing a house with glass windows was because it was so rare on account of the cost of glass and the almost superhuman difficulty of carrying panes of glass for scores of miles over very bumpy roads and then footpaths without breaking them.

Senanga

Sunday 8 November 1959

Back home again, and quite glad, too, because my last week on tour had its fair share of discomfort.

In the first place, I got a poisoned foot. This happened a week ago when somehow or other I grazed the top of my foot – I think it somehow was either pinched by my boot or else I had a bite from an insect and walking aggravated it. It began to swell a little and I got the Hosp. Asst. to bandage it. Next morning (Monday) it was still a bit swollen so I had it bandaged and because I could not put my boot on I wore four stockings on it. I managed quite well thereby and walked the twelve miles to the next camp with little difficulty, though I must have presented rather a comical sight to the villagers, semi-bootless.

Next day, as it was still swollen, I repeated the practice of the day before, but this time had to walk 14 miles and by the end walking had become rather painful and my foot more swollen than ever. Next morning it was even worse so I wrote to Senanga asking for a vehicle to pick me up because I did not know how long I was going to be out of action. Besides, it had been arranged that I would meet a vehicle on Saturday (yesterday) so this meant it coming out a day earlier and going right to the furthest point of the silalo from Senanga. Then I intended using it to complete the tour – there were only eight villages left, or walking in to meet it if my foot healed before the vehicle's arrival (it would be two days at least before it did).

So Wednesday and Thursday I spent lying in bed getting penicillin injections and compresses on my foot and generally having a nice lazy time and getting a lot of reading done. The foot made good progress now that I was resting it as I should have done in the first place. But it had not completely cleared up by Friday when about midday the Boma lorry was heard. That ▶

afternoon I used it to visit another four villages and slept at the next camp en route to Senanga. Then next morning (yesterday) we visited and censused the remaining four villages and by 6.30 p.m. we were back in Senanga.

Today my foot is ninety-five percent better, and the bandage I put on tonight should clear it up completely.

The main reason I am glad to be back is that once again I shall be drinking reasonably clean water. During the past week I have had some bouts of diarrhoea which can be painful and embarrassing. One day I was inspecting a village when I had to dash for the woods and just yesterday, taking a census of an assembled throng from four villages I had to flee. Must be quite a laugh for the rest of them – the white man has many advantages and great wealth but much use they are if he doesn't have their iron belly! Pills that I had with me helped but sometimes they were used when the assault had become so fierce that it was impossible to check.

The final piece of misfortune came on Friday afternoon after setting off in the lorry. We came upon a herd of tsessebe who looked upon this strange object with curiosity and just refused to run away. So with inward reluctance I gave way to the importuning of my companions, took the Boma rifle (a Lee Enfield .303 probably dating from the First World War), inserted a bullet, and for the first time in my life, pulled the trigger. As I had long suspected such an act was more dangerous to me than to the beasts I was aiming at. The bullet ploughed into the earth about twenty yards in front of the tsessebe, to the mirth of my companions. Worse still, the kick of the gun gave me a terrible crick in the neck. What a life!

I hardly got any sleep that night especially as Jameson nearly broke my spine rubbing in embrocation given me by the long suffering Hosp Asst. I had told him to rub hard and he obeyed my instructions with spirited devotion.

The blossoms on the flame trees outside the house are now fully out. I must take some photographs but they will not, I suppose, convey the extraordinarily beautiful framing they give to this house.

▶ This morning as I lay in bed enjoying a nice long lie I heard the beating of a drum and lusty singing and saw a procession making its way towards the Boma. Not till lunch time did I find out what it was all about – Remembrance Sunday. In the absence of poppy sellers out in Sitoti-Bushanjo, how was I to remember?

Senanga
16 November 1959

Dear Folks

For the past week the sun has been obscured by clouds for most of the time and it is now very comfortable and pleasant – the perfect temperature, not too hot nor too cold. Working in the office is now much easier just because of this fall in temperature.

Another good result of the rains is that it has settled the dust so that at the end of the day you are no longer dirty and grubby. The roads are far better because the landrover's wheels can get a better grip on the damp sandy surface.

The river is rising slowly, an indication of the rain that must be falling around the headwaters. The rain when it comes falls with great intensity, so far only in short, sharp showers. The lightning is quite spectacular – great brilliant forks of lightning across the sky.

I was at old man Harrington's on Saturday. He was in a great story-telling mood. He is eighty-five and has been in Northern Rhodesia since about 1905. He speaks about the early Administrators of Northern Rhodesia some of whom I have read about as being quite outstanding men. He tells of how he walked into the office of Wallace ("an old woman") whom I know to have been Administrator in the Western half of Northern Rhodesia when it was under the control of the British South Africa Co. and demanded a permit to buy ammunition. To get rid of Harrington without argument, Wallace asked how much ammo he wanted. "Ten thousand rounds", said Harrington and Wallace signed on the spot for this amount – anything for peace. One can understand his point of view when one remembers that Harrington and his mates ▶

used to go into the cinema in Livingstone on a Saturday night to watch the film show, aim their rifles and loose them off at the baddies on the screen if they got bored.

Now he has mellowed. He is tolerant as European Rhodesians go in race matters, not only because his half-caste son runs his business now, but also because he keeps well up to date with current affairs. He gets a wide selection of Rhodesian newspapers sent to him and listens to his wireless a lot.

Funnily enough, in the train at Cape Town I met a chap from the UK who was returning from leave to work in Northern Rhodesia. When I told him I was going to Senanga he said, "Oh, you'll meet the Mayor, Mr Harrington, then". I told old Harrington that he was known as far afield as Cape Town. He replied "No doubt – by the police!"

The Boma
Senanga
23 November 1959

On Thursday night we had a dreadful storm and at about 8pm one of the Boma clerks and the Dresser at the dispensary came to ask me if I would drive the clerk's child to hospital as she had a temperature of 104°F and her feet were swollen. As luck would have it, the only Boma landrover on the station was broken and I had to plunge through the howling wind and rain and fearsome lightning to look for a landrover at one of the other houses. We managed to find one belonging to the Roads Foreman and returned to the compound to pick up the girl. Then a three-mile drive to the hospital which was much further than it sounds for it must have taken at least twenty minutes to get there due to the combination of bumpy road, landrover with half its springs broken and need to save the child from being bumped around too much.

Yesterday morning at 4 a.m. I was awakened by Jameson, who had been aroused by a District Messenger and the poor old dispensary chappie and one of our drivers – permission sought to take a landrover and carry a chap who, it was thought, had his skull fractured by his wife an hour or two previously.

When the office opened, I questioned the wife who admitted to the deed and then when the radio opened up told the Mongu police about the matter. Then I drove to the hospital prepared if need be to take a dying deposition from the husband. Luckily, his strength had picked up and though I have not heard since, I doubt if his skull is fractured. The trouble is that he nearly pegged out from loss of blood – the Dresser at the Dispensary had not bound his wound tightly enough. Anyway, the doctor allowed me to see him and take his statement. The chap's head was swathed in bandages; otherwise he did not look too bad though I suppose it is rather difficult for an African to look pale.

Mum asked if I had met a witchdoctor – what a question – such people do not advertise themselves (to us at any rate). But superstition dies hard. For example, on two or three occasions people have come to ask permission for the drums to be beaten in the compound in order to drive the evil spirits away from a sick person. On one occasion, it was the second-in- charge of the district messengers who made the request.

Last Saturday evening, I visited old Harrington. I was the only one there and I got him on to speaking about his early days out here. He used to work in an architect's office in London but he got tired of a life bounded by the 8.37 a.m. and the 6.05 p.m. commuter trains. So one day he told his boss he was going to Africa. His boss offered to make him a partner but H was adamant and signed up with the British South Africa Co. to work as an architect in Northern Rhodesia.

He arrived in Rhodesia in 1897 on about the third train to run from Cape Town to Bulawayo. He worked in what is now the Eastern province of Northern Rhodesia and then was sent to build houses and offices in Mongu, the administrative capital of Barotseland.

Then in 1905, he was given a posting to the line of rail, but he did not want to go back to town life, so he set up as a trader in Senanga, ninety miles downriver from Mongu. And here he is to this day.

Africans to him are either "boys" or "niggers", and educated ones are merely "savages with suits"! He is so outrageous in these

▶ opinions that I just don't protest – on these matters there can be no agreement with this old man of eighty-five. Outwardly, at any rate, he won't change his opinions though I should think the Duke of Edinburgh's visit to Ghana and such like events shake him inwardly quite considerably.

Senanga
29 November 1959

I shall be going on tour tomorrow morning (Monday) so I am writing earlier than usual this week.

The tour will be a short one. I am being sent out to inspect a main road that is being realigned to take it permanently above the flood level, a causeway across a pan (dambo) that is being reconstructed, one or two bridges and some canals in the north-west of the District that are being dug for the first time or reopened after having been neglected for over thirty years.

The Barotse Plain is drained by a complex system of canals and in the old days was kept open by slave labour. In 1906, the Paramount Chief abolished slavery but in 1925 another proclamation against compulsory unpaid tribute labour was made by him so it is only comparatively recently that slavery was completely abolished.[25]

The most immediate effect of its abolition was that the tasks that previously were done by compulsion were not done at all. The people, though free, have not been taught to use their freedom constructively. Canals became blocked with weeds and fish traps, land became permanently waterlogged, less land was cultivated and food production fell.

Mr Harrington has told me that prior to 1925 people came to him to sell maize at extremely low prices and every year he exported ▶

---

[25] *Actually, unpaid labour was still used to build the camps that I and other district officers used when touring the silalos. I am not sure why they were not constructed using paid labour. There was no overt opposition to this from the villagers probably because they were so used to doing what they were ordered to do by established authority. It would have taken one or two days of effort by the people of a large village or two or three small ones to build one of these camps of poles, thatch and mud.*

about three hundred bags. Now, far from being a surplus area, maize is imported into Senanga District.

This year a powerful effort is being made to reopen old canals and dig new ones. This is being made possible by a large increase in development funds partly from a new reserve fund of the Barotse Native Government, partly, I believe, by an increase in Colonial Welfare and Development funds. In our District £600 is being given by NRG and at least as much by BNG.

In Kalabo District just to the north, however, £20,000 has been spent in the last year or two on canals. Kalabo has suffered badly from heavy flooding so it has priority. It has also got a very go-ahead DC which counts for a lot when it comes to getting a share of limited funds.

I shall also be going to Shekela which I toured in September to see how experimental rice growing is getting on and to visit two or three villages that I did not manage to visit when on tour.

The head of the PMS Mission in Senanga and his wife and child came to tea on Friday. His name is Mr Zwahlen and he comes from Neuchatel in Switzerland. He has been in Barotseland since 1936 and I suppose knows as well as any European the people of this Province.

According to him the effects of slavery are to be seen in the excessive politeness (of the old timers at least) and the excessive softness of the people. They always look to government to help them. They don't try to help themselves first.

In part, he is quite right. Yesterday, for example, I was talking to the Chairman of the African Welfare Society in Senanga I asked him if they had a table tennis table. He told me one had been made at the Mission Trades School for them and that it was still lying there awaiting transport. I asked him if it would not be easier to get some men to carry it to the Welfare Hall (only one mile away). He looked at me as though I was a trifle mad.

On the other hand, in another District[26] in Barotseland, where Cooperative societies have been set up, the villagers have built their own roads so as to make it easier to bring their bags of maize

[26]Mankoya, now known as Kaoma.

to market. The members of the Producers Coop are paid a fixed price for their maize and the profits from the sales of the maize are shared amongst the producers.

Self-reliance is, I suppose, a difficult thing to learn but it will come as the cooperative movement spreads and local self-government becomes more democratic.

Mr Zwahlen is not very happy about the changes that are taking place in Barotseland and Northern Rhodesia generally. "The African picks up all the worst features of European civilisation – the desire for material goods for example – and none of the best. He sees and covets the rewards of our civilisation but fails to realise the background of endeavour that has made it possible."

"People are far less respectful than they were when I came to the country", he avers, "and young fellows with merely primary education fancy themselves as the goods. They listen to the wireless but misunderstand what they hear".

Most grievous of all to this missionary is the way in which all Europeans are lumped together, missionaries and all, and judged as one without any distinctions. As proof of this, Mr Zwahlen mentioned a well-known PMS missionary who has worked in the Territory for several decades. She was attacked and robbed outside her home in Livingstone.

Another thing he mentioned that I remember; old ways of thought die hard even amongst church members. In the two years he has spent in Senanga only one wedding has been celebrated in church because the people don't like taking the Christian vows – to love, honour and obey **till death us do part** – far too long a commitment they feel for any sensible man to take!

In fact, Zwahlen seems to me to have the air of a defeated man – a terrible thing to say I admit. The combination of western materialism and age old superstitions and habits of thought have prevented the Gospel from making the progress he had no doubt hoped for when he first came to this country as an enthusiastic young man.

Last night a District Messenger came to say there had been a fight in the compound between a man and his wife. The man had come off worse – been bonked on the head with a stick. He had been taken to the Dispensary to have his head bandaged and was now on the rampage threatening to kill his wife. So the D/M put the woman in prison for her safety and came to report.

I thought he had acted wisely and told him I would come and see the woman and her husband this morning.

This I did. The bloke, one of the station hands, had a splendid tonsure, the bare bit being covered by pink Elastoplast. It was quite a sight and humiliating for him. He was still angry, His face twitched as he recounted the incident of the night before. So I told him not to be such a silly dope – that if he wanted to get his own back it was far better to take the matter to the Native Court; if he tried hitting her, he not she, would be put in jail.

He agreed he would not beat his wife so I said she could be let out of prison. There was a Senior D/M present so I asked him if he thought it would be safe to let the woman out. He said he would take the man to the Head Messenger to get the latter to talk to him just to make sure. Husband and wife bashing seems to be in vogue here just now!

Near the start of a tour- I'm still looking quite neatly turned out apart from the crumpled stockings. By the end of a day of hard walking or bumping along bush roads I was much more unkempt. I am standing on the low escarpment overlooking the Barotse Plain. This was a delayed action shot with the camera balanced on the front of the landrover

I become a Civil Engineer

Senanga
7 December 1959

Last week I fairly gallivanted around the District inspecting canals, bridges, culverts and roads – just the job for a man with a B.Sc. in Civil Engineering like me. I now realize the epithet that sums me up – PRACTICAL![27]

I left Senanga on the Monday and drove to a village some forty or fifty miles away on the other side of the Zambezi Plain. There I descended from my landrover to inspect a new court building. No building – just a heap of bricks. Why? No cement and they had not got round to writing to us about it. So I told the bricklayer to go ahead and dig the foundations.

How big? Make it twenty feet by forty, I said and a room for the Court Clerk. A masterly decision, crowning years of research into the optimum size for this kind of public building.

A bridge under construction (photo Rev JL Baumgartner)

I drove with one of the local Indunas to inspect a bridge and causeway being built over a low-lying annually flooded piece of ground. I cast an experienced eye over the towers being

▷

[27]*I was being ironic; my degree was in Economics, a subject long in theory and short in practical matters.*

constructed for the bridge, examined the timbers for woodworm and took a note of requirements for materials from the foreman. Then I drove ten miles along a side track to inspect a new canal that is being dug.

When I started I felt full of beans. Development is a great thing I was thinking. By the time I had driven five miles along this twisting, bumpy, swampy, tree-strewn track I was fuming; "What's the good of development – they (the Africans) don't want it or make use of the public works etc. once they've been provided". Thence to camp.

Next day I drove about twenty-five miles to another village where another court house is being built. The walls were there but no roof – the corrugated iron had been sent to a place at the other end of the District by mistake. I checked the tax collection books of the court clerk and then proceeded another thirty miles to Shekela.

At Shekela I visited the school gardens to see how their rice was getting on. This was by way of an experiment initiated by me. It was not doing too well, unfortunately, because of the drought we have been having.

The day after, Wednesday, I drove another twenty miles which brought me to the northern border of our District. Here I had to inspect a canal which the DC of the district to the north (Kalabo) said was filled with fish traps, weeds, etc. in our District. So I disembarked at a village close to the canal, unpacked my camp kit and set off for the canal. There followed an exhausting day's activities. The heat was terrific and I was on the go until 5 p.m. First I examined some canals adjacent to the canal of foremost interest. Then I walked for a mile or two into the next District to see what state the canal in question was in the complainant's domain. It was terrible, I noted with partisan glee – blocked with weeds, lilies, etc. and even a monstrous fish trap. I measured the water flow rate (by seeing how long it took a piece of grass to pass between two points a few feet apart!), then proceeded down the canal till I reached our own District. Here the canal ran through bogs so rather than get all my clothes all mucked up I took them off and dived into the canal to the consternation of all. Then I swam and waded along the canal until the D/M who was with me pointed to a lagoon that lay ahead. "Likwena", he said. "Crocodiles" – so out we scrambled, bog or no bog and rejoined the other messenger who was on the path some distance away holding my clothes.

I dressed and we skirted the lagoon at a distance. On the other side we found a canoe which we commandeered, paddling along the canal for a mile or two until it became too shallow. Then we walked along the bank of the canal (no bog by this time) until we reached its junction with a tributary of the Zambezi. From there, a long trudge back to camp.[28]

Next day I drove to the store of an old trader situated fifteen miles inside the next District to repay four gallons of petrol Iain Stuart had borrowed a month or two back. This old man had a stroke a couple of years ago and is now a parcel of skin and bones. His son, a Eurafrican, runs the store and seemed a very pleasant type.

The old man received me in his bedroom and during our chat sat on the edge of his bed in his pyjamas. He lamented that he had not long to live, that he was only seventy-one while old man Harrington was eighty-five and that he had recently received pills which, had they been available two years ago, would have prevented his stroke. Very cheerful conversation. However, he perked up a bit and bade me farewell very courteously when I took my leave.

I went to a PMS mission station nearby to pay back another four gallons of petrol borrowed by the thirsty Stuart, was given a cup of tea and set off to drive down a new road cut through the forest on the top of the ridge that borders the plain in these parts. Coming in the opposite direction I had followed the old road along the foot of the ridge where the trees were fewer and the soil firmer. But this road floods in March and April and moreover has to pass through numerous villages. The new road runs straight as a die through the forest. Along most of it only the trees have been cleared – grass and light scrub remain. Looking along the road was for all the world like seeing a green carpet unrolled as far as the eye could see.

▶

---

[28] *The point of all this effort was to estimate the extent of the work and the cost of the labour required to clear the canal.*

> The soil (sand) was so soft that I had to plough along for most of the way in low ratio, at about fifteen miles per hour. Now that the trees have been cleared, the men will dig parallel tracks, the width of a wheel base apart, fill them with dry grass and cover with soil again. This improves the surface by making it firmer but it requires constant maintenance. In the absence of gravel deposits there is little else one can do.
>
> Eventually I struck the old road again when the ridge petered out not very far from the causeway that I visited on Monday. Here I had to leave the landrover to go and inspect another canal. The going was very rough in places and I had to be carried across various boggy places and streams on the backs of my District Messengers (I had two with me). I don't really like this devoted service, preferring to fend for myself but these D/Ms, especially the old school one called Kachana, seem to be genuinely hurt if you deny them an opportunity to display their readiness to protect your life and limbs with their own. In this case, it was only a matter of saving me the bother of taking off my boots and stockings.

The other merit of this primitive system of road construction and maintenance was that it was very labour-intensive and provided scarce paid employment to the local men.

Letters from a Land of Flooded Valleys and Rivers

Senanga
Sunday 13 December 1959

Dear Folks

An early letter this week because I shall be going on tour tomorrow.

During the past week I actually made a start on it by visiting some villages that stand fairly close to the Boma. One can see the effects of civilisation on these villages – the traditional crafts – basket making, mat making, etc. – are little practised but quite a few men are working as carpenters making chairs, tables, and other furniture for people in the township. Compared to the rest of the district, the people in this area are highly educated so that a number are employed in good jobs – the army and police (they live outside the District) and clerical posts in the Administration, while others work as labourers in the PA and the Public Works Dept.

Some of the villages I visited which are on the Plain have twin villages in the forest, along the ridge that borders the Plain. When the flood comes in February they will shift to these villages and return to the plain when the flood recedes in May-June.[29] This "omboka" system as it is called is practised by nearly all who live on the Barotse Plain, from the Paramount Chief downwards. A few villages remain on the Plain all the year round where they are fortunate enough to have their houses on the highest of the mounds that dot the plain.

The people go to all this trouble to build two villages for themselves mainly in order to be near the river for the fishing. The other reason is that they have gardens on the plain where they grow maize which should ripen a few weeks before the flood comes. Disaster occurs when the flood arrives too soon for the harvest to be gathered in.

---

[29] *Actually, most villages moved from the Plain to their villages on the escarpment edge in March and moved back in July-August.*

The unhappy Councillor and his Son

Beside Luchanana's Village
PO Senanga
Sunday 20 December 1959

This is proving to be a most enjoyable tour – a holiday really – I am beginning to understand how DO's manage to do without their local leave (official) because this is it (unofficial). In fact, I had to wrestle with my conscience before I decided to rest in camp here today. But in the end, my well-known devotion to the Sabbath won. Compared to my last tour, my hours of work have been short although on average they have been the same as those I put in at the office. But instead of sitting at a desk I have been canoeing (i.e. being canoed), walking, arguing, explaining, exhorting, listening and censusing.

An interesting event was the completely unexpected visit of one of the PMS missionaries to my camp last night. He had been on tour further up this valley and returning to Senanga he had stopped near here to camp for the night when he heard that a DO was also camping in the vicinity. So he paid me a visit. I had only met him twice before, and that briefly.[30]

It turned out that we were both Associates of the Iona Community.[31] When he discovered this he shook my hand fervently, just as Stanley did when he met Livingstone on the shore of Lake Tanganyika.

We talked for a couple of hours. He was greatly agitated at the decision of the local people to ask the Roman Catholics to take over a new school about to be built near this camp. This part of the District has been a PMS stamping ground for many years and hitherto there has been a tacit agreement between the missions to keep out of each other's area. But now the RCs have halved their boarding fees. In the past, RCs, PMS and the Local Education Authority all charged twelve pounds per annum boarding fees – now the RCs are only charging six pounds. The result is that where ▶

---

[30] *His name was Jean-Louis Baumgartner. He and his wife, Renéé, have remained our friends until the present day.*

[31] *This is an ecumenical Christian community centred on the restored Abbey on the Island of Iona off the west coast of Scotland.*

new schools are being set up the people are asking the RCs to run them even in PMS areas. I think this is a little off – an attempt to bribe souls as well as threatening an unedifying fight to the death between the RCs and other missions.

He told me that he is one of the few missionaries in his society still engaged in basic evangelical work. Most of his colleagues, in Basutoland, French Cameroons, etc., are merely administrators, managers of schools, etc., having handed over basic evangelical work to African pastors.

From that we went on to talk about witchcraft. He told me that even his best evangelists believe in the supernatural powers of witchdoctors; that if they put a spell on a man, he cannot recover; that they can cause lightning to strike down a man. Further, he himself knows of Africans, turned away from the local hospital as incurable cases, being cured after a witchdoctor's healing session.

No doubt in some cases, the mental effect is so great as to mend the physical ailment. This explains the cases of people who believe themselves bewitched; they develop a physical disease because they are mentally certain of the power of the witchdoctor and eventually may die unless they can get a more powerful medicine to counteract the one used against them. Thus last week, the Livestock Officer in Senanga lost his cook who complained he was suffering from "muba" a favourite bad medicine used by "bad" witchdoctors. He took off his shirt to let the LO see the muscles of his body twitching. The LO sent him to the hospital but during the night he ran away and has not been seen since.

About the tour itself. This silalo lies astride a couple of river valleys up one of which I have been travelling during the past week. The villages lie on both sides of the river, which explains the canoeing that I have been indulging in. The valley is two to three miles wide. There is no pronounced flow of water in this part of the valley for the outfall of the river into the Zambezi is impeded by a bar of rock. Thus water lies over a wide area and to get from one side to the other one has to canoe a tortuous course through the rough reeds and lilies. I found it very pleasant slipping through the reeds often finding a passage through packed reeds where none existed to the stranger's eye. I must say I enjoyed every minute of these canoe journeys. The paddler uses a long pole with one end shaped as a blade so that he can paddle or punt as the depth and clearness of the water best suit.

Indunas Nalonge (left) and Sambiana (right) with the Court Clerk between them being canoed across the Lui River, and a villager on either end with a pole for punting and paddling

There are two main tribes living in these parts. One lives in very small huts on the forest edge and depends mainly on cassava and millet. They are suffering badly from lack of food because the bad floods of the previous three years rotted their cassava and it takes three years for a new crop to mature properly.

The other tribe lives in the plain on mounds or on the land between the forest and the plain, or have two villages, one in the plain and one higher up on the plain edge to which they shift when the heavy rains come. They are well off this year because they grow maize on perennially moist soils unaffected by this year's drought (which has killed what little grain the forest dwellers have planted). Already the maize cobs are becoming ripe and I have eaten quite a few "green mealies" this week – boiled and then spread with Stork margarine.

▶ This silalo has been quite well served by schools because there is a Middle Primary School in this valley. The Upper Primary School is at Senanga only fifteen miles from the central part of the valley.[32] This one area supplies the province and Northern Rhodesia with teachers, clerks, policemen and soldiers some of whom have built splendid huts in their home villages to go back to when they return on leave or to work on the land when they retire.

One hears much about the strong sense of family responsibility in the primitive community but having visited innumerable villages where the old people are left to live in small reed and grass huts about five to six feet in diameter, I doubt it. One could understand this happening where a man's children had left the village to seek work. But it also happens when they are living in the village. The younger generation may have excellent huts for themselves but their poor old folk are just allowed to languish in these horrible little hovels.

I met the Katengo councillor for this region on Wednesday. He presented me with six mealie cobs and I returned the compliment by inviting him to lunch. The Katengo Council is a popularly elected body of some fifteen members representing the whole of Barotseland (three from each District) and its function is to bring up and discuss popular grievances with the Paramount Chief. The Katengo Councillor is paid three pounds per month and six to ten pounds for each of the two sittings of the Council that take place every year, a total yearly income of 48 pounds!

This particular Katengo councillor is an ex-school teacher in a Roman Catholic school who lost his job after working in it for twenty-two years because he decided to take a second wife. For ten months, he told me, the mission tried to persuade him to divorce her but he preferred to lose his job and pension (due in three years' time) rather than go against the sentiment of the people in his village. He shook his head sadly. "I made a mistake, sir, but an African wants to have many children and I had only two by my first wife". ▶

---

[32] *The building of lower and middle primary schools and the only upper primary situated at the PMS mission at Senanga, was the responsibility of the three missionary groups which provided primary schooling in our district. These groups were the Paris Missionary Society, the Capuchin Fathers (Roman Catholic) and the Seventh Day Adventists. The teachers' salaries were paid by the Government. In the first four years of primary school, teaching was done in the vernacular; in Barotseland this was Lozi. Thereafter it was in English.*

His elder son has a BSc from Fort Hare University in South Africa and is teaching in the Secondary School in Mongu and his younger boy is in his fourth year at Senior Secondary School in Lusaka. As he got down to eating he became quite confiding."

"You know, sir, I was in my hut this morning when you came into the village. I did not come out to meet you because I had not washed my face. And I was ashamed for my people when I heard you scolding them for their bad huts.

"Oh yes, sir, this life is difficult compared to life as a teacher. Now I have to sell some of my oxen to pay for my younger son's school fees. And last year, when I returned from the Katengo Council meeting I found someone had come into my garden in my absence and stolen all my maize.

"My son enjoyed Fort Hare but it was very hard for him in his holidays to come back to the village. He was not happy here".

On Friday, I invited the two silalo Indunas to lunch. One of them is an ex-prison warder who worked for eighteen years in Bulawayo before being recalled by the Paramount Chief to be an Induna.

The senior Induna's son was attending the Royal Dick Veterinary College in Edinburgh. Two and a half years later when I was home on leave his son, George Akafekwa, spent a week with me and my parents. I took him to climb Lochnagar, near Balmoral, the Queen's residence in the Scottish Highlands. It was a clear day and from the mountain's summit we could see for many miles across the countryside to the east coast of Scotland. "Isn't this beautiful, George," I exclaimed.

"I suppose so", he replied somewhat mournfully, "But I would rather be looking at the Barotse Plain!"

Years later, George became Zambia's Director of Veterinary Services.

Summer on Lochnagar, George is definitely feeling cold!

A funny sort of Christmas

Senanga

27 December 59

Dear Folks

Christmas has come and gone and tomorrow morning I shall be back to work as usual.

On the afternoon of the twenty-fourth, a service in English was held at the mission. The DC and Laurie Jarratt, the new District Assistant, read the lessons, the service, English Evensong, being taken by the missionary I met out in the bush a few days previously. Most of the European inhabitants were there, as well as some of the boys from the mission Trade School. Afterwards we were given tea at one of the missionaries' houses.

At this jolly tea party, one of the items of gossip was the disappearance some weeks ago from the Barotse Native Government capital of Lealui of Prince Akashambatwa,[33] one of the sons of the

---

[33] *I had already heard about the Prince's alleged murder because the rumours of it had spread by bush telegraph throughout Senanga District. Everywhere I went it was one of the most popular songs the women sang, about the murder of the handsome Prince. It reminded me of a Scots border ballad in all its gory details.*

late Paramount Chief and the discovery since then of some parts of a human body. It is being alleged that the present Paramount Chief, anxious to secure the succession for one of his own family (the chieftainship is not hereditary but elective) did away with this fellow who was looked upon as a likely successor to him.

The chief celebration at Christmas was Christmas Eve dinner at the DC's house. Before that, we had all been down at old Mr Harrington's for a warmer-up drink. Then after about half an hour there we all left for the DC's, taking the "Old Man" with us. It was the first time he had gone beyond his own yard for a year. He is, as you can imagine, very shaky on his pins, though considering his age he is quite a good advertisement for Standfast whisky. He drinks a bottle a day and in the morning he mixes it with milk!

Just when I was giving up hope, at 11.45 p.m. we went in for dinner; two courses – roast turkey, ham and cranberry sauce with mixed veg followed by plum pudding which was brought in a halo of blue brandy flame.

After dinner was over, the crackers were pulled and we all put on cute multi-coloured hats and went outside to reseat ourselves on slightly damp chairs. Sporadic games kept the party going till about 2 p.m., at which time we dribbled home and slept in late next morning.

I was exhausted, actually, because the night before I only managed to get two or three hours sleep for the rain was continuous and torrential and fairly battered the corrugated iron roof making a metallic drumming noise. In addition, I gradually became aware of a persistent dripping noise close at hand. Eventually I got up and traced the noise to the bathroom next door and there, in the dark, stepped into a large puddle; the roof was leaking.

I slept in on Christmas Day... Then, across to the Jarratt's for Christmas dinner; goose and guinea fowl – extremely delicious – and substantial helpings of Christmas pudding and not too bad wine. Also there was Jonathon Cole who was a Cadet here until a fortnight after I arrived and was then shifted to the Development Centre at Namushakende some sixty miles north of here.

Next day, I again slept late and made lunch for Jonathon Cole who spent the morning bidding farewell to his old friends in Senanga. He has just been to a fortnight's course in Lusaka. Says that the senior officers there are expecting big trouble in Northern Rhodesia next year. Every three months, eighty new policemen are being trained and sub-police stations are opening up all over the country.

But of all this hubbub, we in Barotseland remain ignorant. There is little sign of any particular interest in the 1960 talks about a new Constitution hereabouts.

The other chief item of news is the rising river. During the past week in which we have had a great deal of rain, three to four inches in one night alone, the river has been rising rapidly. I expect it will overflow the far bank in front of the house fairly soon and the plain will gradually disappear beneath the flood.

Happy New Year

Love

Callum

1960: A MOMENTOUS YEAR FOR NORTHERN RHODESIA

1960 was the year when the Queen Mother came to visit the Litunga (Paramount Chief) and was treated to a right Royal welcome. Her visit symbolised the close relationship between two royal houses – the British and the Lozi one. This relationship was immensely important to the Lozi rulers because for them it was a guarantee of the inviolability of the treaties of protection signed between them and the British Government. These pre-dated and were separate from the treaties of protection signed with the other chiefs in Northern Rhodesia.

In August, the Barotse National Council passed a motion which sought the agreement of the British government to allow Barotseland to secede from Northern Rhodesia if the latter became independent. Of this there was little mention in my letters probably because I was blissfully unaware of it while touring around the distant parts of the District. The Barotse ruling elite feared the rise of the new African political class as much as the white Rhodesian politicians and as the year went by they drew closer to the latter.

Outside Barotseland the most important event was the visit of the Monckton Commission which had been appointed to review the constitution of the Federation of Rhodesia and Nyasaland. This review of the Federal constitution had been guaranteed by the British Government when the Federation was founded in 1953. The Federal Government was dominated by white politicians who expected that this review would result in a recommendation to grant full independence to the Federation. Their expectations were boosted by the re-election of a Conservative Government at the General Election in October 1959. The Conservative Party was regarded as the party which supported British "kith and kin" in Africa. Moreover, the majority of the members of the Commission were conservatives and their Chairman was a former Conservative Cabinet Minister.

The African political leaders in NR regarded the Commission's visit and terms of reference (which excluded consideration of the right to secede from the Federation for either Northern Rhodesia or Nyasaland) with deep suspicion. They feared that its conclusions would merely rubber-stamp an agreement between the British and Federal Governments to allow the latter to become totally self-governing and so end the Colonial Office's responsibility to safeguard the rights of the African people. They therefore decided to boycott the Commission.

But events were about to show that the British Prime Minister and Colonial Secretary were preparing to introduce a new direction for British policy in Africa that swung the balance away from support from white settlers. The first hint of this came in three key speeches which the Prime Minister, Harold Macmillan, gave in Nigeria, Southern Rhodesia and South Africa in January 1960. In the last of these, delivered to the South African Parliament he said "The most striking of all the impressions I have formed since I left London a month ago is of the strength of this African national consciousness .... The wind of change is blowing through the continent .... Our national policies must take account of it."

He still spoke of his hopes for partnership between the races but it should have been clear to everyone that times were a-changing.

Outside the borders of Northern Rhodesia, the winds predicted by Macmillan blew fiercely. In the Belgian Congo the Belgian Government capitulated and handed over power to totally inexperienced politicians after hastily arranged elections. Chaos followed quickly and thousands of Belgian expatriates fled the country.

The Monckton Commission issued its report in October 1960 and to most people's surprise stated that the Federation could not continue in its present form. Africans in both Northern Rhodesia and Nyasaland would have to be allocated a majority of seats in their countries in the next Federal elections. Even in Southern Rhodesia they would have to have increased representation in the Assembly.

A constitutional conference to discuss the future of the Federation took place in December but broke up in short time because the white settler representatives were not prepared to agree to the shift in the balance of power recommended by the Monckton Commission.

Later in the same month a Northern Rhodesia Constitutional conference got under way but was boycotted by the white-supported United Federal Party as soon as new electoral arrangements that favoured the African parties were put forward.

In March, the Sharpeville riots in South Africa left over sixty Africans dead. Several thousand Africans had staged a demonstration against the Pass Laws which required all adult Africans to carry a pass giving them permission to leave their home reserves and move to urban areas in search of work. International condemnation was widespread and from that time South Africa became increasingly isolated. Two years later it was expelled from the British Commonwealth.

As I recount in my letters, even in isolated and tranquil Barotseland, faint tremors from these political earthquakes would be felt throughout the year.

A Scottish Hogmanay, Senanga Style

Senanga
5 January 1960

Dear Folks

It is difficult to know how to begin one's first letter of a new decade. In fact, this is my second attempt. The first began with a page and a half of philosophy and thanks for all you have done for me in the past. But, really, we are a family that does not need to be explicit about the things we feel most deeply so I'll plunge straight into the normal recital.

Hogmanay was very enjoyable, possibly because it suits the pagan atmosphere of this place. A party was held in my house which was swell for the occasion. The painters had just finished repainting the main rooms a very light cream and the picture sent out by you had come back from Lusaka, framed, and hung resplendent, a tribute to your taste.[34]

There were also Christmas decorations, an artificial Christmas tree and coloured balloons to make the place look festive.

We capped it all by using candles for illumination and a very lovely scene it was. All the guests (fourteen in all) were delighted and praised the house, your picture and the decorations. We had a very good time for the party went with a swing with ordinary dances, novelty dances and various games, so much so that not even the Senanga dipsomaniac, the Roads Foreman, had time to get tiddly.

Just before midnight I packed them all out of the house into a covered porch outside the kitchen (it was raining cats and dogs at the time), giving them each a mango and the darkest man a piece of charcoal so that they would not enter empty handed. I left them to shiver till the last stroke of midnight had sounded. Then a knock came at the door and the tall dark man (the dipsomaniac) entered clutching his little bit of charcoal. The rest entered one by one. I shook hands with each man and gave each of the ladies a kiss. All were rather impressed by the solemnity of the occasion. I think it ▶

[34] *A painting of Kings College, University of Aberdeen.*

was the first time that most of them had gone through this ceremony and all felt, after they had got over the initial bewilderment of being suddenly chucked out by their host, that the New Year deserved to be marked in some such way.

Then we all joined hands to sing Auld Lang Syne in which I was expected as the only Scot present to lead the singing to actions.

When they had all gone I slunk off to bed and turned on the wireless just in time to hear the tail end of a Hogmanay party from Scotland on the BBC.

At the moment we are busy in the office preparing the annual report, and the statistics of every manner of thing. I am also trying to do some swotting for an exam in General Orders and Colonial Regulations. These are the various rules that govern my official life. As yet, I have done very little work, but no doubt, with a little luck, I shall manage to pass though it is staggering the number of eventualities that are legislated for. There are about four hundred General Orders which deal with regulations for officers in NR and about one hundred Colonial Regulations dealing with the Overseas Civil Service.

Love – and stay well

Counsel for the Prosecution

Senanga
12 January 1960

The past week has been quite hectic culminating this morning in my exam on Colonial Regulations and General Orders which I polished off no bother, I hope!

Firstly; there has been the need to help the DC prepare his annual report for the District – i.e., doing the hack work of facts and figures. Then I have been plunged straight into preparing the estimates for the coming year, in conjunction with the DC and the District Assistant (Laurie Jarrett). Thus I am preparing estimates for salaries, uniforms and roads, the DC is doing vehicles etc. and the DA is doing station upkeep, travelling on duty allowances etc.

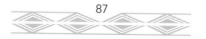

▶ To crown it all, I have been sifting the evidence (a slick way of saying that I have been putting weary questions to a set of liars each one more adept than the next) in a case of attempted theft of a drum of petrol. This last business opened on Wednesday of last week and involved me in going back to the office each afternoon for fresh interrogation sessions. The facts of the case are as follows.

The African clerk at the Government Roads Branch depot in Senanga owed money to an African trader on the western boundary of Senanga district. Not having money to pay back this trader, he offered in a letter, which has come into our possession, to give petrol instead.

He got the petrol by false entries in his ledger. The trader sent in his lorry complete with driver and lorry boy with a load of maize and instructions to collect the petrol from the clerk. They went to his house on the morning of Boxing Day but he told them to come back in the evening. They did so and the three of them went to the Roads Dept. petrol store. They allege that they got hold of the night watchman who opened the doors of the store for them and helped to push out the drum of petrol onto the road. It is at this point that the stories of the principals diverge.

The Clerk: I got him to confess his guilt and he tells me that all four of them were in it – he went home after seeing that the other three had pushed the drum of petrol well into the bush. He left them while they were still pushing it as he'd had quite a hectic time that day celebrating.

The Lorry Driver and Lorry Boy: Their testimony is consistent – it has been impossible to make one contradict the other; a bit too good to be true, I think. They say that after the drum of petrol was rolled out of the store they said to the clerk and the night watchman that they would come with the lorry the next day and collect it – i.e. in broad daylight. The other two protested at the delay and seeing that the decision was final they started to roll the drum into the bush. The lorry driver and his assistant then concluded that the drum could not have been honestly bought as they had been led to believe and walked off saying that they would have nothing to do with it. ▶

> **The Night watchman:** says that he knows nothing about the actual taking of the petrol – he was in his house nearby when that happened because it was raining hard. When the rain stopped, he left his house to make sure the store was OK but found the door ajar and the marks of a drum having been rolled away. He decided to try to trace it and got the assistance of a twelve-year-old schoolboy living nearby. Together they followed the tracks and found the drum at a point in the bush between the petrol store and where the lorry driver and his assistant were sleeping with their lorry. The watchman had started to push the drum back to the store when the lorry driver appeared. Next morning the watchman reported the driver to the European in charge of roads in this district for attempting to steal the drum of petrol.

> Each of the two sides pleading innocence have their witnesses, some of whom I have managed to discredit but some I have not yet had time to interview. I think that I shall prosecute tomorrow and probably get all four charged and convicted. But where a man pleads Not Guilty the Magistrate is put in a ticklish position because he does not like to be jury as well as judge, especially as he is also the DC, so he may well acquit all but the clerk.

Petrol was a very valuable commodity in a remote district like Senanga, particularly for a trader who was based one hundred miles from the centre of the District on its western boundary. To buy petrol or diesel for his lorry he would have had to send it to the provincial capital, Mongu, eighty miles to the north of Senanga. There was a commercial petrol station there where fuel for his vehicles could be purchased.

A forty-four gallon drum of fuel was worth the equivalent of three months' salary for the Roads Department clerk. His monthly salary, certainly no more than twenty pounds, would have left him with very little left over and if he was not prudent in handling it he would have been regularly in debt. He could augment his official salary by cooking the books, which would not have been too difficult because his boss, the dipsomaniac road foreman, was careless and given to driving his vehicle when drunk. It was a temptation for the clerk to steal the drum of fuel to pay off his debt. He would have got away with it if the three others had not got cold feet and alerted the foreman, or perhaps had not been bribed by the clerk to keep their mouths shut.

This type of crime by low-paid clerks who handled quite large sums of money in proportion to their salaries, such as the Court Clerks of the silalo Native Courts, was very common. Had these men been better paid their temptation to defraud the Government would have been less acute.

Senanga
19 January 1960

Dear Folks

I have been busy again this week finishing estimates of recurrent expenditure and completing the various returns for the previous year. This last day or two, for example, I have been trying to untangle the mess into which the leasing[35] of land to traders, missions etc. has got, in order to put in a reasonably accurate return of leases to the Resident Commissioner's Office.

Last Friday we tried the clerk who attempted to steal the petrol. He made it easy by pleading guilty. The other three were let off because there was not sufficient independent evidence to make certain that the High Court would not reject our findings.

The weather has been very hot these last few days; max temp 97°F but seeming hotter than similar temperatures experienced in October because of the humidity. There are clouds about but not rain-bearing ones. Today was terrible – quite early in the morning I was clammy with sweat. At 2 p.m. a storm broke out bringing an invigorating cold wind, hailstones, and lashing rain. Unfortunately, it did not last long so it has become hot and clammy again. It is still so despite the fact that it is now nearly 10pm. Last night the minimum temp was 81°F.

This period of drought is very bad for the crops which had shot up during the month of rain that came before. They are now beginning to shrivel in the sun.

The river is continuing to rise fairly rapidly because of the effect of rains that fell three or four weeks ago two to three hundred miles upstream. It is this water that moves down the Zambezi at about ▶

[35] Trading stores, whether white-owned or African, and mission station land had to be leased from the Paramount Chief in whom the ownership of all land in Barotseland was vested – one of the traditional rights that he retained in the original Concessions which he signed with the British South African Company in 1890 and 1900.

five knots per hour. Sometimes the flood comes with great suddenness and because of its disconnection with the local rainfall conditions, with little warning.

It comes downriver like a tidal wave if there have been particularly heavy rains in the headwaters and it is possible to go to bed one night seeing the river on its normal course between its banks and the plain all visible and next morning wake to find the true course no longer discernible and the plain like an inland sea.

This morning I went with Laurie Jarrett to inspect the Boma paddle barges. The Boma owns two or three small canoes, two eight-man paddle barges and two sixteen-man paddle barges. They are used for carrying food supplies, building materials and touring.[36] From March to July, when the plain is covered with water, much of the touring will be done by barge and it is during this period that silalos that border the plain are visited and toured because then the people tend to be more concentrated having shifted from their scattered villages on the plain to more closely grouped settlements on the forest edge of the plain.

In the afternoon I went duck shooting with Laurie while his wife, Sheila, waited in the Boma steel long boat for us to return. We motored up river intending to land on the plain to seek out the duck which settle on flooded depressions there. As we were chugging along a couple of ducks flew across our bows. I put the shotgun to my shoulder, took a rough aim and fired – and was catapulted backwards off my seat to land flat on my back on the bottom of the boat. The ducks sped on.

We left the boat and went to look for the duck. Almost immediately we saw some. They saw us, too, and rose in the air. We loosed a volley of lead at them but they flew off without a feather out of place. Every other duck within the vicinity was awakened from their reveries by the din and all rose and flew far away for we failed to see any more on our wanderings. Shooting duck in these parts requires undertaking certain discomforts such as wading through waist-deep water that has filled depressions in the plain and in the drier areas being cut to pieces by sharp pronged reeds.

[36] *The barges were the best way to send supplies across the Barotse Plain and the flooded valleys of the Zambezi's tributaries which were well-nigh inaccessible to vehicles during the Flood Season.*

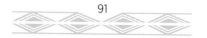

Nothing much of note has happened here this week. I have been kept fairly busy and this week will be extremely so because I have been given most of the work to do in connection with the quarterly balance audit of the Native Treasury's books.[37]

Last night there was a party for the Livestock Officer and his wife, who are leaving Senanga. They are going to join his brother on a farm near Mazabuka on the line of rail previously worked by their father. They are a very friendly and helpful couple. They treat and pay their servants well by the wage standards that exist here and in their day to day business dealings with Africans treat them with politeness. Yet I doubt if they would ever consider the possibility in their lifetime of having an African friend to stay with them for a week's holiday as we had Joe Chileshe. They are of the Gradualism School to which all Rhodesians seem to belong though there is a great variety of grades within it; think a hundred years until Africans are "civilised" enough to share in the government of the country with Europeans and in the full range of professional jobs that Europeans do. The alternatives to rapid African political advancement seem to me just as dangerous. Living in the midst of a colonial situation convinces me that it is essentially immoral (because of the built-in racism in society). To preserve law and order we are having to curtail individual liberties.

The hope is that in so doing we give ourselves time to educate the people so that they are able to make a parliamentary democracy work. What does not seem to be realized is that a democracy is more than a series of forms – regular elections, secret ballots, etc. ▶

[37] *So much for Indirect Rule whereby the Colonial Office ruled their African Protectorates through the traditional rulers. If this was the case anywhere in Northern Rhodesia one would have expected it to have been in Barotseland where the Litunga had more powers reserved to him than any of the other Paramount Chiefs. Actually, it was an indirect rule supervised by the district officers in the Provincial Administration. We audited the books of the central Native Treasury of our District as well as the accounts of the court clerks who gathered taxes and court fines in the individual silalos. We also inspected the records of these courts to ensure that there were no miscarriages of justice. Auditing the books of court clerks and of the central treasury was extremely boring but the court records were frequently entertaining containing as they did fruity details of cases of adultery which together with land disputes constituted the majority of cases heard by the Indunas in the silalo courts.*

▶ It is also an attitude of mind towards the settling of political problems. How Emergency Orders are expected to instil this spirit, I would not know.

A case of witchcraft was brought to the Boma today. A witchdoctor had danced in a village and pointed out someone as a witch. This is the third case to arise in the last fortnight. A letter also arrived today to say that an old man had disappeared from his village. It could involve witchcraft so I sent off a District Messenger to investigate.

Though this place is obviously ridden with superstition, it is nothing to what it was forty or fifty years ago when witches were put to trial by ordeal (sounds like medieval days in Europe) by being ducked in the river (if guilty, you sink), or being forced to immerse one's hands in boiling water (guilty if blisters come up), or by application of poison (guilty if you die). The African clerk, Mr Nyumbu, who teaches me Lozi told me that it was largely by the efforts of the PMS that these overt acts of cruelty were ended.

I still believe that it was better to agree to rapid political advancement for the African majority. The alternative was bloody civil war such as had occurred in Kenya and which I foresaw coming to pass in the Rhodesias and South Africa. Thank God Northern Rhodesia did not go down the same route as Southern Rhodesia because in the end the British Government had the guts to stand up to the white settlers in NR. It was still a Protectorate directly ruled by the UK Government unlike Southern Rhodesia which was a Crown Colony ruled, except in foreign affairs, by the local power elite – the white settlers.

Colonialism was acceptable for a period so long as it was used to train Africans to acquire the skills necessary to run a modern state. That is how the African leaders saw it, too, until they became frustrated at the slowness of this process.

"Emergency Orders" were the powers which were used by the Governor of Northern Rhodesia to declare ZANC, (referred in the Introduction) illegal, to rusticate its leaders to rural areas and to imprison its President, Kenneth Kaunda.

This letter also shows only too well my ignorance of the African belief in witchdoctors and witchcraft. What I failed to realise was that there was a profound difference between witchdoctors and witch finders. The former attempted to heal patients who were suffering from physical as well as mental illness. They did so by a combination of traditional medicines using plants found in the bush, psychological healing techniques and group therapy, bordering on a frenzied collective effort to rid the patient of his or her illness. There were also bad witchdoctors who dealt in poisonous medicines to harm or kill the enemies of their clients.

On the other hand, there were witch finders who sought to identify the persons who were thought to be visiting sickness and death on others in their community. These witch finders used much the same techniques as were employed in medieval Europe to identify witches and in both continents they usually victimised old women. A case of which I had personal knowledge happened three years later when I was District Commissioner in Luwingu in the north of the country. A witch finder entered the District and went around the villages terrorising old and vulnerable people. His technique for identifying a witch was to make her eat maize porridge which he had prepared and into which he mixed powdered glass. This lacerated her internal organs. If she failed to survive her meal of porridge she was clearly a witch because everyone knew that there was no harm in eating this staple dish.

The witch finders were feared and revered by many of the people and it was very difficult to have them arrested because of the problems in proving their guilt and because the mass of the people believed that they were serving society by ridding it of people they feared most – witches.

Senanga
2 February 1960

Your query about the red headgear on the heads of the village women – these are red felt berets – the favourite hat wear of village women – kept carefully in a corner of the hut but brought out on big occasions. I think that some of my shots of these women coming to greet me and my party give some impression of the movement, liveliness and gaiety of such situations.

One matter I had to deal with today might interest you. It concerned a case of cursing. Cursing is a serious offence in the eyes of Africans and an injured person if he proves his case is awarded compensation. If the cursing was particularly defamatory, the guilty party is treated as having committed a criminal as well as a civil offence and fined one to two pounds, or one month's ▶

imprisonment. Moreover, in this case the complainant is a member of royalty. Royalty in Barotseland is anyone descended from a Paramount Chief in direct line and since there have been several Paramount Chiefs, the royal class is quite a large one. Because royalty is concerned, the case has to be held at the District Kuta in Nalolo. It is the central court of the District at which the leading councillors of the Mulena Mukwae act as judges.

Local women walking by my side on approaching their village

Since the accused and the complainant are wives of two employees at WNLA and the witnesses to the cursing are all WNLA employees, I have had to write to the WNLA representative here and ask him to allow some of his employees leave to appear as witnesses in this case. Nalolo is eighty miles away so he will lose their services for a week or so. He will have some nice things to say on the subject of African ideas of law. Just as well Europeans cannot be had up in the African courts for cursing!

In the last week or so, the tide seems to have turned against the attempt by the white settler in Africa to perpetuate his domination. The progress of the Kenyan Conference,[38] Macmillan's speech in the South African parliament[39] and the statement of Major Patrick Wall[40] that if it were confirmed by the Monckton Commission that African opinion in the northern territories was determinedly opposed to Federation, the ties of the Federation would have to be loosened and a weaker association of the three states set up with NR and Nyasaland remaining under the Colonial Office and SR getting complete independence. A statement from a quarter such as this must come as a severe blow to Welensky.[41]

I am gradually becoming more of a security risk for ducks when I venture out with my shotgun. Last Wednesday I brought a duck out of the sky to its evident astonishment. When hit, it sort of stood on its tail, fluttered its wings and then zoomed downwards in a steep bank straight at my feet. I jumped sideways with a startled yelp, rather shaken by my prowess.

On Saturday, I went out shooting with Laurie Jarrett and Mike Bircham (WNLA). We travelled upriver and got off at what we deemed a suitable spot. We waited for some time but nary a bird. Then over the horizon I saw a flock of duck appear and as luck would have it they seemed to be flying straight for me. So I snuggled down behind a clump of long grass, cocked my gun and put it to my shoulder. Sure enough on they came and as they flew over me I raised my gun, took aim and fired – and a duck dropped like a stone to the ground.

▶

---

[38] *The conference in London that was to lead to majority African rule in Kenya and to Independence within a couple of years.*

[39] *The "Wind of Change" speech.*

[40] *A Conservative MP in the House of Commons, noted for his support of the Federation.*

[41] *Welensky was the Prime Minister of the Federation of Rhodesia and Nyasaland and leader of the ruling party, the main white settler one, the United Federal Party.*

▶ Curiosity of the week: I had to take particulars from a man being tried this week on a charge of witchcraft. I asked him his occupation. His answer: "Naka"[42] (witch) doctor!

He got six months, though considering that he had shortly before emerged from Mongu prison on a similar charge, I doubt if prison acts as much of a corrective. He had strange clouded blue eyes which probably explains how he came to take up his present profession.

Lunch with the Mulena Mukwae

Senanga
23 February 1960

You will be surprised but no doubt gladdened by the news that I have passed my exam in General Orders. Today's post included a letter from the Resident Commissioner himself congratulating me on being such a brilliant fellow. I enclose his little testimonial; sweet of him and all that, but fancy telling me to work hard for my other exams – you would think he was my Dad!

I got home on Wednesday from an enjoyable two-day visit to Nalolo. I went with the DC. We set off at about 5 p.m. from Senanga and drove along the Mongu road for about sixty miles. It took only two hours because it is in good condition, the rains having flattened and hardened the sandy surface. This road lies along a forested ridge bordering the Zambezi Plain. Then, about 20 miles south of Mongu we turned down off the main road and made for a promontory off the ridge on which is situated a permanent camp – a thatched roofed house of burnt brick for the use of officers on tour. This camp is situated close to the "camp" that the Mulena Mukwae and her Court move to when forced to flee from their mound in the plain by the rising flood waters of the Zambezi.

▶

---

[42] *The Naka was probably a witch finder, not a witchdoctor, someone who was using charms or some form of trial by ordeal to identify a witch.*

Next morning, we travelled about a couple of miles by landrover and another half mile on foot in order to reach a small canal where a barge was waiting to carry us to Nalolo. It belonged to the Ishee Kwandu, the Mulena Mukwae's husband, and like all royal barges had a canopy in the middle of the boat under which dignitaries (the likes of me) can shelter from the sun. The barge, some thirty feet long and six feet wide, was manned by ten paddlers, five in front of us and five behind.

The DC, David Acheson, waiting for the Ishee Kwandu's paddle barge to be ready

Our progress to Nalolo could hardly be described as express. It took us three and a half hours to cover the seven miles to Nalolo. Partly this was due to reeds blocking the canal for the first quarter of the journey, but mostly it was the Zambezi current which we had to battle against. As we approached the Zambezi the current in the canal flowed ever more strongly against us; finally, we reached the mighty river. There we hugged the bank and made a laboured journey upstream, the paddlers thrusting their long paddles into the water with great energy and encouraging each other with shouts in order to keep us moving. It was a stirring sight to see the poles sweep up and down in unison against the blue sky and the fast flowing water.

▶ Eventually we reached Nalolo which is built on a mound on the plain, close to the banks of the Zambezi. The great mound, if not built entirely by human agency is probably partly so. The capital of Barotseland, Lealui, is built on a similar artificial mound and in the days of the early missionaries was large enough to hold twelve thousand people. These mounds on the plain are very highly prized because they enable people to stay close to their rich plain gardens from which they hope to harvest heavy crops before the flood comes. In the old days they also had a military value.

When I visited Nalolo in August, it was necessary to walk about half a mile from the canal to the mound of Nalolo. Now the water reaches right up to the edge of the mound. We stepped out of our barge to be welcomed by the leading induna of the Mulena Mukwae's court. We made our way up to the room in the office block of the court where we were to stay. There we were informed that the Mulena Mukwae would be pleased if we came to lunch. So we went with the Mulena Mukwae's secretary to the entrance to the courtyard of the palace where she and the Ishee Kwandu were waiting.

There followed some chit-chat around a coffee table with a coronation mug (E2R) on it and I wondered how on earth we were going to get all our plates on such a small surface. But following some whispers and thumpings from behind the scenes, the Mulena Mukwae rose and conducted us through a pair of curtains to the next room where a table, bigger than the last, still rather small, was laid for lunch.

I must tell you that we were served lunch off beautiful crockery of dignified contemporary design. I longed to turn over a plate and see the make and apparently the DC was of the same mind.

When the lackeys had cleared away the tea cups we sat on chatting, or at least they chatted in Lozi and I held my peace. I could understand most of what the DC and Ishee Kwandu were saying because the former speaks Lozi capably but not rapidly while the Ishee Kwandu was a Government clerk from 1928 till 1951 and is used to speaking in the simplest terms possible to slow-witted Englishmen.

▶

However, I could make little of what the Mulena Mukwae said, which did not matter very much as she left most of the talking to her husband contenting herself for the most part to wonderful beaming smiles whenever anything remotely funny was said. Actually she is a most delightful woman, very stout (she waddles rather than walks) and when she smiles her whole face, eyes and double chin take part; very striking and beautiful.

The Mulena Mukwae Makwibi (photo Rev. JL Baumgartner)

About the middle of the afternoon, the DC decided it was time to announce the real purpose of his visit – to get the Mulena Mukwae and her Court to agree to her being presented to the Monckton Commission when part of it arrives in Mongu. This struck our hosts dumb for a minute. Then the Chief Minister was called in. He clapped his way into our presence to show respect to the Mulena and then squatted on the floor. The Mulena Mukwae squinted across to the Ishee Kwandu and whispered "Go on, say something". So he spoke up and the MM gained confidence to say her little bit. It was eventually agreed that next morning the DC would address the whole Saa-Sikalo Kuta (the Royal Council) and explain about the Monckton Commission.

Shortly afterwards we left the Princess after having been with her for three hours.

Just after we left a messenger came from the MM with a present of a couple of large fish and twenty-five eggs.

Next day, I had to do some work with the Treasury Clerk while the DC addressed the Council.

While this was going on a great event took place in the heavens which stopped all proceedings down below; two jet planes were describing vapour trails in the blue sky to the wonder of all. Goodness knows what they were doing over the middle of Barotseland – showing the flag perhaps.

At midday we had finished our work and went to the MM to say goodbye. We stayed at the Palace for an hour or so, drank tea and ate biscuits, shook hands and departed.

The Ishee Kwandu, the Prince Consort of the Mulena Mukwae, in front of the Palace

Into our barge once again, we fairly sped along especially when we got into the Zambezi where the full-throated current carried us along. Then into the canal and here, too, we went fast having the current flowing with us until we reached a small lake. We crossed this and entered the canal on the other side where the current flowed against us and reeds pressed in on us. So progress was slow which was a pity because as we brushed the grass in our passing, mosquitoes and flies were aroused from their slumber and swarmed into the barge.

Eventually we reached our landing point only to find that the landrover which had been sent on to Mongu to have the ravages from my encounter with a tree made good had not returned. We had to tramp some three miles to get back to the rest camp through sand which has been described as the worst in Barotseland.

Luckily, the landrover turned up about two hours later and at 7 p.m. as dusk was falling we were able to set off home. On the way we saw a couple of polecats by the side of the road and a little later a mongoose jumped into the road and hared off down the road with us in close pursuit. We were at thirty mph and yet the animal continued to larrup along in front of us for about a mile before suddenly bounding into the bush.

Regarding the Royal baby,[43] old man Harrington had somehow made up his mind that it was due in January and when it didn't appear, he was convinced that it was all a fake, a plot of Machiavellian cunning devised by the English aristocracy to deceive poor innocents like himself. What exactly these plotters were to gain by their machinations was not quite clear but somehow it would conspire to dish the White man of his rights in Africa. He opines "The Royal Family aren't what they used to be what with Prince Phillip dancing with niggers in Ghana. Victoria wouldn't have had that"!

Last week when I visited him he was quivering with rage having just read of an attempt to sabotage a train in Rhodesia by throwing petrol bombs at the driver and fireman in their cab. Dastardly, but Mr Harrington's remedy was to line up all the inhabitants of a village near the line and shoot them all every time such an outrage happened. "We are too soft; the Germans did it, and the Portuguese, and that's what we should do". His other plan is to station a guard on every coach armed with a sten gun to shoot at anyone who seems to be attempting sabotage.

I have to try and divert him from such subjects for fear he becomes apoplectic and on to more innocuous subjects, such as Princess Margaret's engagement to a photographer. How clever of you to give me a camera before sending me out into the world; it is obviously the thing to make things click!

There is not much that is new this week but on Friday one part of the Monckton Commission arrives. I think that most of the witnesses (village headmen and teachers) will be against Federation mainly because they fear an end to the treaties between the British Crown and the Paramount Chief. This was the reason given to me by the Katengo Councillor for this part of the District. At a meeting of the people at a nearby Native Court he had been told to oppose Federation when he goes to Lealui, the capital of the Barotse Native Government, to give evidence to the Monckton Commission.

▶

[43] *Prince Andrew, born on 18th February, 1960.*

▶ This is directly opposed to the Paramount Chief's advice on Federation though there is no intention hereabouts of boycotting the Commission.

It must be said that Barotseland does not seem to have been adversely affected by Federation. Nor has it done much good. Thus we are still very short of dispensaries and hospitals and this is about the only sphere which is Federal in these parts. Had this been another Nyasaland, of course, hospitals and dispensaries would be springing up all over the place to convince people of the economic benefits of Federation.

Nowhere in my letters do I do more than report without comment on the attitude of the Barotse establishment to the Federation. It is almost as though I accepted it as a fact of life that they would prefer a white-ruled Federation to a black-ruled Northern Rhodesia. The Paramount Chief and the rest of the Lozi establishment realised that within the Federation their existing powers and authority would be respected, whereas in a Northern Rhodesia ruled by a new class of politicians who did not come from their establishment or anyone else's, their authority might be greatly diminished.

Health was a Federal responsibility. As far as the ordinary person in Barotseland was concerned the activities that affected him remained in territorial (Northern Rhodesian) hands such as the Provincial Administration and African Agriculture and Education.

Letter to Christian Fraser

Dear Christian

I can't remember when last I wrote but I think it was just before my "Sanders of the River" tour. This was a tour of a sub-district lying astride a tributary of the Zambezi. I spent about half my time walking up one edge of the river valley and the other half in making excursions by canoe to the other side. It was marvellous gliding through narrow lanes of water banked by reeds and dotted with beautiful water lilies.

Most of these dugouts are extremely narrow, some only nine inches wide, and so very easy to capsize. On most of these expeditions I sat for fear of rockin' the boat. The Africans from chiefs to children are marvellously expert handlers of canoes. They wield long-poled paddles which they use for punting when the depth of the water allows it, much the same as punting on the Isis in Oxford. Apart from me, the other passengers in the canoe stood upright all the while, so good was their sense of balance.

The villages and their people on each side of the valley presented a vivid contrast to each other. On the one side was a tribe which cultivates large areas of maize in valley gardens and is served with a large Primary School. There one finds some villages with extremely well-built huts, some very big. One that I measured was forty yards by twenty yards. The owner had four wives, four entrance doors and four double beds! Some huts had framed windows with mosquito netting or glass in them.

They are the hard-working Lozi.

On the other side was a forest tribe, a tribe of hunters and shifting cultivators growing cassava and millet, living from hand to mouth and constantly on the verge of starvation.

Their huts are tiny. They are half resentful, half amused, that I and my retinue of superior Africans from the plain should object to the way they run their lives. They don't want progress because they don't accept our materialist ethics. Yet though they may be

▶

The local hairdressing salon; a Mambunda lady having the full treatment. (photo Rev JL Baumgartner)

hollow-cheeked the men file their front teeth to enhance their appearance and the women tease out their hair into long scalp-clutching curls which they and their admirers obviously think very fetching. Moreover, the women sing, wiggle their hips and love to be photographed. They are the Mambunda of whom I've written before. There is another side, their susceptibility to disease and their fear of witchcraft. Belief in witchcraft is still widespread as the missionaries will tell you. Even African evangelists believe in the supernatural powers of witchdoctors. In some cases, this belief has a good end. Witchdoctors undoubtedly have cures to certain illnesses from their deep knowledge of plants, trees and herbs. In other cases, they may effect a cure by means of auto-suggestion or whatever the psychological process is called. But mostly, I believe, the influence of witchdoctors, especially witch finders, is a baleful one, the least of which is to prevent people going to the mission hospital in good time.

Worse still is the possibility of terrorization when witchdoctors, those that are really witch finders, not doctors, "divine" witches when misfortune strikes at an individual or a community. We have had to deal with two or three cases of this in the last month or two. There is also the general fear of being bewitched by someone who has stronger medicine than oneself. Thus the brain of a crocodile is said to be very strong medicine. In a recent case before the DC here, the accused was charged under the Witchcraft Ordinance for having in his possession a device for the practice of witchcraft. But Mr Nyumbu, the Head Clerk, with twenty years in Government service who is teaching me Lozi felt the accused should have been charged with attempted murder.

The Monckton Commission comes, and goes

Senanga
8 March 1960

Dear Folks

The Monckton Commission has come and gone and normality once more descends. The day before saw frantic activity around the Boma – weeds removed, a surrounding wall of stones whitewashed and various blots removed from the landscape. On the great day, a considerable furniture removal took place as various offices were denuded of their tables and chairs which were than lugged over to the court room where the Commission was to conduct its hearing.

Not until that morning did we learn of the composition of the party that was going to visit us:

Lord and Lady Monckton, Sir Charles Arden Clarke, Sir Lionel Heald, Sir Charles Tennant, Mrs Elspeth Huxley, Aidan Crawley, Wellington Chirwa and one or two less well known luminaries.

At 2.15 p.m. the sound of aeroplane engines was heard so I strolled down to the airfield with the Jarretts, just in time to see the two planes carrying the Commissioners swoop down and land.

The planes taxied to a halt just in front of the assembled throng of Africans come to witness the arrival of the "Lords from England". The DC rushed over with a set of steps to the first plane to come to a halt, to enable the incomers to descend to terra firma. The first man out of the plane, whom everyone took to be Lord Monckton, introduced himself to the DC and then introduced the other members of the Commission to him.

The DC had made no cut and dried arrangements for making introductions to the leading Senanga citizens but as Laurie and I were standing in front of the crowd which stood by the side of the road leading to the Boma the DC introduced us to the various Commissioners. After shaking hands all round we walked with them to the Boma. There a great crowd of witnesses who had come in from the nearby villages were gathered in the shade ▶

of some trees outside the Boma. As the "Lords" approached they all sank to their knees and clapped their hands in the traditional Lozi greeting.

Until half an hour before the arrival of the Commission, only 8 persons had come to the office to say that they wanted to give evidence, but just before the arrival of the Commission, forty or fifty turned up with the intention of giving evidence. The DC persuaded them to appoint a spokesman which they were ready enough to do because they were unanimous in their opinion of Federation.

The Commission went into the Courtroom and started interviewing the first 8 witnesses, 6 of whom elected to go in together. Apparently they were not at all sure why they had come nor what they wanted to say. Indeed, one of the Commissioners came outside and asked the DC what on earth had caused them to come and give evidence.

Then, after the eight had been interviewed, the Commissioners came out and sat down at a table that we had set up under the trees where the multitude of witnesses had gathered.

The acting chairman of the Commissioners (we had discovered by this time that Lord Monckton and his wife had not arrived and that Aidan Crawley was sick in bed in Mongu), Arden-Clarke, asked the assembly why they had come.

"Because the DC told us", was the answer, meaning that they had received a circular from this office stating that the Commission was coming, that its purpose was such and such and that anyone could come forward to give evidence. So the chairman painstakingly explained why he and his fellow Commissioners had come to Senanga.

There followed evidence, very brief, that all those present did not like Federation because it threatened their special Protectorate status. So Arden-Clarke assured them that whatever happened, the Barotse treaties with the British Crown would stand good as long as the Barotse wanted them.

▶ Naturally, few Africans in these parts know much about Federation and their opposition is based on a desire to hold onto the status quo, whatever its imperfections, rather than venture on uncharted seas where they might find themselves much worse off than at present. Indeed, as I may have mentioned already, in much of the local talk about Federation, it is obvious that many Africans don't realize that Federation is already in being but they are shrewd enough, perhaps, to see that in a completely independent Federation their treaties would not do them any good.

The Commissioners came to the DC's house after they had heard all the witnesses. In his front garden, overlooking the Zambezi, and the Zambezi plain stretching without a break to the horizon, they had tea. They were very impressed with the view and I think they all relished their deliberations with the unsophisticated villagers of Senanga. The ruling by which all Civil Servants were excluded from giving evidence in a District such as this cut out at a single stroke ninety percent of those Africans who are reasonably well informed on political matters.

The only people besides the Commissioners at this tea party were the DC and his wife, myself, the missionary in charge of the Mission at Senanga and the doctor from the mission hospital. The reason for this was the difficulty in getting sufficient deck chairs etc. to seat everyone, for the tea was served out of doors. No African was present except two members of the Commission. This is typical of the Senanga social set-up.

A day or two ago, when out in the Boma motor-powered long boat, I passed a couple of hippos huffing and puffing in great style. The DC has reluctantly decided that one will have to be shot as they are proving obstreperous of late. A day ago they upset a canoe and, naturally, there would be quite an outcry if a life was lost in such a moment. All the same, hippos are gradually being eliminated and this is thought by some to have caused the silting up of canals and rivers which these huge monsters had previously helped to keep clear with their movements.

Earlier in the evening I visited Mr Harrington. He has an interesting view of the recent disaster at Agadir. ▶

"It all comes from digging things out of the earth and putting nothing back; that is why you get the earth cracking".[44]

Ah, well, it all goes to show that there is as much innocence amongst the very old as amongst the very young.

The river has been rising much faster of late. Until a fortnight ago it was rising at the rate of one and a quarter inches per day. Then the rate rose to two and a quarter inches. A week ago it rose to three and a half inches, on Monday it rose four and a half, Tuesday, six inches and today (Wednesday) seven and a half inches.

You can well imagine that at this rate a very considerable rise in the water level is taking place. The curious thing is that for the last fortnight or so we have had little rain in Senanga. The rise in the river is obviously caused by rains that fell in the headwaters of the Zambezi some hundreds of miles away, three weeks or more ago. Much of the plain is now under water, though it does not appear to be because the long grasses of the plain continue to show above the water. Thus you often see the rather weird apparition of men canoeing over apparently dry land far from the river.

Senanga
15 March 1960

I suppose I should thank you for your regular and ever welcome letters but I guess you know that life would be rather desolate for me without them.

There is not much to report this week. The chief item of news is that I am once again sharing the house. An addition to the PA staff arrived yesterday, Adrian Thomas by name. He is slightly younger than myself since he was engaged two and a half years ago as an LDA. Now he has just returned from vacation leave in England and is starting his second tour, this time as a DA – District Assistant. This a rank lower than District Officer, reserved for those, usually non-graduates, who have not done the Oxford or Cambridge course which I did.

[44] A disastrous earthquake took place at Agadir in Morocco on 29th February 1960. 12,000 people died.

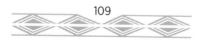

▶ The villagers living on the plain drove their cattle across the Zambezi last week in order to graze them on the higher ground on the edge of the plain beside Senanga. It was quite a sight seeing great blocks of horns sticking out of the middle of the Zambezi while the herds of long-horned cattle were floated across the river. The technique of taking the cattle across the river involved the minimum of effort because they were driven into the water at a bend on the river and the current hitting this bend carried the cattle out into the middle of the river. From there on men in small canoes on every side of the herd nudged them gradually towards the opposite bank where they landed several hundred yards downstream from their starting point *(see photo on page 237)*.

Very soon the Mulena Mukwae will be shifting from her capital in the middle of the plain to one on the forest ridge. I believe this is quite a colourful ceremony and with the DC intending going with his family to see it, I might be able to go as well.

With the flooding of the plain and the coming of cattle to the high ground hereabouts, we are now infested with flies which come seeking dry land under their own steam and on the backs of men and cattle. Luckily, very few get into the house as it is well protected by mosquito netting. However, when walking outside you have to try to get used to them walking across your face and clinging by the score to your back.

The evenings are cooler now and it is very enjoyable to step outside the house just before going to bed in order to give the dog a little exercise and savour the slightly warm breeze against the cheek, breathe the scents that are borne on it, hear the faint tap of drums from a village down on the plain or further along the forest ridge, follow a firefly's progress among the branches of a tree and gaze at the star-filled sky.

In Northern Rhodesia every African male over the age of eighteen has to have an Identity Certificate and has to carry it with him. If he does not have it when he is working or visiting a town outside his home district he can be arrested, though I don't think he is prosecuted if he can produce it later on. I don't know what the difference is between the system here and the South African one. Presumably it is that once a man has his IC he can move wherever he likes within Northern Rhodesia while in South Africa he needs a pass every time he moves from town to reservation and vice versa.

I suppose the chief justification for having Identity Certificates is that they provide the only paper evidence that most Africans have of their identity. Europeans have bank books and other documents which they can produce if they want to prove their identity but the largely property-less Africans have no such trappings of existence.

The other main reason for the IC system is that it helps to prevent youths from flocking from their villages to the line of rail until they are old enough to look after themselves and have imbibed good old tribal traditions.

I for one have heard of no bitterness on the part of the African community towards this IC system though no doubt it exists amongst the growing professional class for whom an IC is now superfluous for the reasons that make it superfluous for most Europeans.

I am writing today because tomorrow I go on tour for four days. It will be by landrover to visit several Kutas and check the tax collection books of the Kuta clerks, inspect a road and two or three culverts and arrange with the Indunas of one of the Kutas the dates on which I shall tour their silalo.

The route I shall follow is more or less the same as the one I took when I went out on my canal, road and bridge inspection tour. You will not be surprised to hear that two of the new culverts that I inspected then have been washed away by the floods – ah me, the dangers and trials of this mortal life!

Actually, I have come to the conclusion in the last week that the Provincial Administration is out of date. In the interwar period, when Britain ran her colonies on a far thinner shoe string than at present, the highly gifted amateur in a number of trades was the answer to providing a basic administration with the minimum of personnel. These were the days when there were few or no Education Officers, Road Engineers, Building Foremen, Cooperative and Development Officers, etc.

Now, even on a small station like Senanga, there are technical officers to cope with the specialised problems of house building, road building and livestock. Despite that, the PA staff has increased greatly. Before the war this was a two-man station and sometimes only one. In 1951 it became a four man one and has been that ever since.

The purpose of this increase in staff is to give closer administration but the powers that be also are alive to the fact that it is not enough to go round villages counting heads. Thus we are now entrusted with a large budget each year with which to dig canals, construct roads and bridges and build various permanent and semi-permanent buildings. It strikes me that we are now achieving the least results with the most amount of money.

I believe the money would be more efficiently spent if one of the PA staff was replaced by a Roads Engineer, another by a builder and yet another by a trained Development Officer. That would ▶

leave one PA officer, namely the DC, who would act as coordinator of the technical officers in his district and continue as JP and general administrator, tax collector, etc.

This sort of process has already happened in the urban areas where the DC and his staff sit rather awkwardly alongside elected urban councils in the European areas and township management boards in the African areas.

Senanga
6 April 1960

This is a very hasty scribble because in one and a quarter hour's time I leave for Mongu for the Lozi exam. Now I have the collywobbles though I think I shall scrape through.

Last Friday I returned from a gruelling four day landrover trip up and down the edge of the Barotse plain on the other side of the river. I was driving every day from 7 a.m. till 3 or 4 p.m. and along roads which bear little resemblance to most of the roads you have seen.

Early morning view of the flooded Barotse Plain

> On my final night in camp I was feeling like death warmed up and then, hey presto, your letters arrived along with the Manchester Guardian Weekly. After reading all that I felt considerably easier in body and mind and slept well.
>
> Now I have recovered from the bumping, the heat and the dust. My oral Lozi much improved as a result of only speaking that on the trip – (English) swearing also much more fluent!

Senanga
12 April 1960

I'm afraid I have an item of bad news for you. I have failed my Lozi oral. I thought I had done reasonably well but I must have been wrong. I was quite surprised as were the other people (such as Laurie Jarrett) who have heard me burble away in Lozi in the office – they thought I would have no trouble in passing. No excuses, it just means I must try to speak Lozi more often.

I don't know about the result of my written exam as yet. Here again I thought I had done reasonably well but with the melancholy outcome of the oral I can no longer feel sure of having passed the written.

Every newcomer to the Provincial Administration had to pass exams in one of the main vernacular languages, in my case Lozi the main language of Barotseland. The exam had to be passed at Lower level within one's first tour of three years and by the end of a second tour the exam had to be passed at Higher level. Both exams came in two parts, Written and Oral.

It was possible to take the exam as many times as was necessary, as they were held twice a year in each province. I passed my Lower Written at my first try and my Oral at my second. Then I went on to take and pass my Higher Written and Oral Lozi exams a year later.

If you failed to complete the Lower standard of language exam within your first tour you would not be confirmed as a district officer and your career in the Provincial Administration would probably be at an end.

Back to Shekela

Shekela Silalo
17 April 1960

I am at present out in the back of beyond touring Shekela Silalo which is the one I toured first of all after coming to Senanga. I am enjoying myself enormously despite blisters because it is a splendid change from office work. All one has to do is trudge along, think up a few things to put in the report at the end of it all, count heads, check that taxes have been paid, listen to complaints and inspect huts. Mentally very relaxing if physically tiring.

Unfortunately, word has come from the Boma that I must cut short my tour because the DC is going on a three week holiday on medical advice. He had to take to his bed with a fever and a very high temperature twice during the week before I left to go on tour. Laurie Jarrett has to go to Lusaka for an interview and Adrian Thomas, the newly arrived District Assistant, has been called up to do two weeks Territorial Army training.

There has been little change in the silalo since my last tour, though there are some new huts being built partly as a result of my last tour, partly as a result of fines administered by the Indunas in the Kuta here. Also, rice is growing in the school garden and some villages have tried growing it. Thus is progress measured. Perhaps someday this area will be flowing with milk and honey, but it will take a long time.

It might be possible to grow oranges and coffee on a large scale here but these could not begin to bear fruit for many years yet. I intend taking out some orange trees to the Induna who is a keen farmer and, later, a new variety of cassava. Others in the silalo might then gradually copy him. I think this is the only way to make progress amongst a people who on the whole seem disinclined to disturb their present mode of existence.

This is the season when the crops are gathered in – maize, sorghum, and millet. Cassava, groundnuts, sugar beans and sweet potatoes will be harvested a little later. So this is the time when people have full bellies. This year, the crops have been generally good though some areas have done poorly by planting for early

▶

rains which did not materialise. Unfortunately, these same areas are the ones that most require a good harvest because they planted early in the hope of getting an early maize crop to appease their hunger.

It was interesting on today's walk to see how observant the African is. A lion's spoor was pointed out – faint paw prints, invisible to me until I stopped and stooped to observe. Then, later, the path that a snake had taken in the sand was pointed out.

Yesterday, we saw a snake hanging in a tree beside the path. From what I have read of snakes, I think it was of the harmless kind but we gave it a wide berth. Africans regard every snake as poisonous.

I am writing this letter sitting in a mosquito tent, which is not a place for mosquitoes to live in – just the opposite, being a construction of mosquito netting supported on poles, about ten feet long, wide and high. It is supposed to provide a sanctuary where one may work unmolested by mosquitoes and other winged monsters. However, it is rather defective because the door doesn't shut properly and some Charlie has put his feet or head or something through the walls at several points thereby creating gaping holes, excellent ingress opportunities for flying insects with homicidal or suicidal tendencies.

Actually, there is only one mosquito that I have seen though it has been actively nibbling me and I haven't yet nabbed him. However, there are hordes of flying ants and beetles and a couple of monsters about a couple inches long which have just at this moment given up the fight against the burning hot glass of my Tilley lamp and are lying dormant on the ground.

An envelope lying on the table at my elbow is shuffling across the table in a mysterious fashion no doubt propelled by one of my aviator friends trapped beneath it.

Senanga

26 April 1960

Dear Folks

I am now back at the Boma and from tomorrow, when Laurie Jarrett goes to Lusaka for an interview until 6 May I shall be on my own in the office. This means that I shall be chronically overworked in contrast to the relaxing tour I have just finished.

I enjoyed the tour immensely since there were only two or three villages to count each day, the population of that sub-district being very sparse. On one of the days' marches, a small buck was espied near the path and my Senior District Messenger, Kachana, vanished in an instant into the bush. A few minutes later there was a bang- hey presto, venison steaks for supper. He killed it with a shotgun which has an effective range of only twenty or thirty yards, so you can understand how skilfully he tracked it.

On the last day of the tour, I found myself near the road where I had asked the landrover from the Boma to pick me up. So I walked to it, a mere twelve miles, and settled down to wait in a Boma camp at the wayside. The hours passed but nothing turned up.

Finally, at 7 p.m., a runner arrived to say that the pontoon was out of action, so the landrover could not get across the Zambezi to fetch me. So next morning I walked another twelve miles to a point on the edge of the plain where a wooden barge belonging to the Boma is moored during the flood season.

The day was lovely and cool, clouds overhead and a strong wind blowing. In fact, it was blowing so hard that the capitao of the barge did not want to cross for fear of capsizing. So I stayed there for the night in a Boma camp that is part of a network of such camps all over the District.

Next morning, about 6.30 a.m., before the sun had risen, we had finished loading the barge and pushed off, the men anxious to get as far as possible before the wind arose (just a day or two before the wind had capsized a canoe near this spot). So along with two other canoes we forged across the plain which is some ten miles wide at that point. Six paddlers manned my barge and they

▶

paddled like beings possessed, so we fairly sped along, now across great open lakes, now through waving reeds and grasses, their tops still above water. Occasionally we sighted a deserted village, standing on a mound in the plain, the water lapping the sides of the huts. At this time of year, the villagers are living in villages on the forest edge and will return to their villages on the plain in July when the flood has receded to plant maize which will be harvested in January/February before the flood comes again.

For the last mile of our journey my barge raced a canoe, manned by three paddlers and we fairly shot along to the accompaniment of much laughter, cheers and banter. Finally, we reached the Zambezi itself and on the far bank stood the Boma.

Poling the canoe across the flooded Barotse Plain with might and main; District Messenger sitting in state in front

You want to know more about Mongu. It is a dusty township, the European houses set far back from the few roads in the township with large, tired-looking gardens. I would reckon there are about fifty houses lived in by Europeans. How big the African township is I wouldn't know because I only skirted the outside of it.

There is an Anglican Church, a European club and a High Court where the picture show was held. The church does not have a colour bar.

▶ The club is exclusively European though recently they held a plebiscite amongst their members to vote on the following proposals: (1) That Africans be admitted as full members; or (2) That they may be admitted as guests of members; or (3) That they be admitted on important occasions – e.g. the Queen Mother's visit.

From these proposals you may well wonder: what price "Partnership"?[45] Most Europeans[46] don't want it but are forced by events to pretend they do. Also, there are a great number of Afrikaners in NR and in Mongu, too – store-keepers, artisans, etc. In fact, they outnumber those of British stock.

I don't know that there is much more to tell you about Mongu except that it has a golf course of sorts. I borrowed clubs and went out with the Cadet from Sesheke. The course is one long sand bunker, the grass on the fairways tufty and sparse and the "greens" are of sand. An essential item of equipment is a sand scraper which is used to smooth out the greens to erase the roll and plop marks of previous golf balls. Was St Andrews once like this?

Last piece of news is that I am coaching my kitchen boy to pass his Standard Six exam (the top Primary School grade). He left school after Standard Four because he could not afford to go on (over nine pounds per year in fees) and could not get a bursary. He left school three years ago but in his first day's lessons today, he did his arithmetic very well.

I was talking to the Education Secretary at the Mission here about the lad; he was quite upset to hear that he had not got a bursary despite his good marks and remarked that the local Indunas who have to recommend bursary applications often favour those related to them irrespective of the means of their parents. ▶

[45] *"Partnership" was supposed to be the main reason for the Federation's existence. It signified a collaboration between the small white population and the many times larger African one. The former was supposed to lead the other towards an equal role in the governance of the Federation but in the meantime the superior education of the whites was used as the excuse for them to run the affairs of the country. In one remark to a white audience, the Prime Minister of Southern Rhodesia likened Partnership to the partnership of a rider and a horse; his listeners cheered!*

[46] *Nowadays I would call them "Whites" because many of the "Europeans" had been born in southern Africa.*

It is also interesting to note that in country districts children are not admitted to school till they are eight years old, partly because they are slow to develop physically (malnutrition?) between the ages of three and ten and partly because they often have to walk considerable distances to school. I was told, too, that while in the past Standard Six was the key to a wide number of jobs nowadays there are so many boys passing Standard Six and more and more coming out of Secondary School that the Standard Six pupils find themselves unable to obtain a good job. This year there will be hundreds who can't get good (white collar or Government) jobs or entry into Secondary School and there will be that many more malcontents drifting round the towns.

Recently there have been strikes and disturbances in Secondary Schools, Teacher Training and Technical Colleges in NR. Some have been closed and some kept open but whole classes have been sent home, dismissed sine die. It would appear that the African political parties have tried to find recruits in the schools which strikes me as being at best unwise and at worst, completely unscrupulous.

Senanga
2 May 1960

A murderer was brought into my office, or such was the accusation at any rate. A poor broken down woman was the accused. The charge was that she poisoned her sister's husband by putting some powdered brain of a crocodile into his beer. Crocodile brain is held by Africans to be one of the deadliest of poisons though when I got in touch with the police next day over the radio telephone they told me that no toxic substances have ever been found in crocodile brain.

The Livestock Officer in Senanga, however, is adamant that there is an arsenical substance in crocodile brain. The doctor at the hospital in Senanga was unable to tell me which view is correct. However, I have some "medicine" left over from this alleged murder which I hope to get analysed. The case will probably go

▶ forward as a witchcraft offence because the woman admits that she put "medicine" into the man's beer, though the she claims it was not the brain of a crocodile.

I got a letter from Joe Chileshe last week. He has been transferred to Kitwe which he does not like as well as Lusaka. He says that he is very busy because besides being head of the Bemba language section of the Federal Broadcasting Corporation he has also been engaged on production work.

I quote from his letter: "Life in the town on the line of rail is not as pleasant as it used to be in the past. You may have heard about the terrible thing that happened in Lusaka when a personal friend of mine and his family were burned to death. It was such a shock to me that I will never forget it because Fred Mungo was not only my friend but was once my brother-in-law and came from the same village."

This refers to a recent outrage when a gang of thugs, thought to be supporters of one of the leading African political parties, drenched Mungo's house with petrol and then set it alight. Mungo and his wife and one child were burnt to death and one child is in hospital. Mungo was chief clerk in the Township Superintendent's Office and well known for his services on behalf of the African community, but was a "moderate".

In the four years leading up to Independence, which would come in October 1964, there was a battle for dominance between the two main parties: UNIP, supported mainly by Bemba speakers, and ANC, whose followers were mainly Tonga-Ila tribesmen from Southern Province. The Eastern Province was divided in its loyalties between these two parties; it was there that bitter fighting broke out between supporters of the two parties. The capital, Lusaka, where Fred Mungo was murdered was likewise a battlefield from time to time between the two parties. Mungo perhaps belonged to neither party. That would not have saved him from attack; "if you are not with us, you must be against us".

On Sunday, at church, there was a baptism ceremony at the end of the normal service. About thirty people were baptized - all adults or school boys and girls in their teens. It was quite a novel ceremony to me. First of all, they all stood and said the Creed along with the assembled congregation; then they all squatted down in a circle at the front of the congregation and one by one stood up and recited a verse from the Bible of an apposite nature. By that time, they were all standing again and the congregation joined them to sing a hymn.

Then they squatted down again and the minister moved round the circle, an African evangelist at his side with a silver-plated beaker of water and a notebook with the names of the applicants for baptism in it. The minister (one of the European missionaries) held out his cupped hands while his assistant poured a liberal libation into them. Then the minister opened his hands on the head of each one to be baptized and let the water pour over it, placed both hands on the head and said a blessing, "In the name of the Father, Son and Holy Spirit, may God keep your body and heart in his ways", or words roughly like that.

It was quite an impressive ceremony though I must say I was fascinated to see the water trickle off each head and down the neck.

Old man Harrington is, of course, invincibly opposed to missionaries and all their works, cheeky mission boys, et al. He forgets that the cheeky mission school-boy has his parallel all over the world; indeed, is not cheek the proverbial characteristic of any schoolboy? Perhaps it is true that in addition to cheek, the schoolboys in this part or the world have a streak of arrogance not so often found in their counterparts in Britain. I think this may be because these boys soon achieve some knowledge of matters which are a closed book to their parents – English, Arithmetic, History, Elementary Science, etc. This gives them early in life a feeling of superiority to their elders, something that I, for example, could not enjoy until I learned the jargon of Economics!

▶

▶ Harrington is an interesting chap, especially when you visit him on his own, as one might expect from a person with such strong prejudices as his. He is a man of strange paradoxes; in some things he gives an impression of being well informed and up to date with his information. His weekly reading consists mostly of newspapers, the "Weekly Mirror", full of pin-ups and spicy stories being his favourite, and the Government Gazette. His chief interest in this publication is the list of bankruptcies which he positively drools over especially if there are Indian-owned businesses amongst the list of failures.

He has curious blank spots where he is about thirty years behind the times. For example, he still seems to think that the League of Nations is on the go, or as he calls it, the League of Irritations (is this original?). He dislikes the Boers intensely, not for their racial policies (although he wouldn't be allowed to take an African woman as his wife in South Africa – he has got six!), but for their lack of self-restraint in shooting wild animals – they don't shoot for the pot but to slay the greatest number of beasts in the shortest possible time.

He has an engaging habit of getting peoples' names wrong; the only one I can recall at present is Mr Macmillion![47]

The Mongu Club has just voted to keep it all-white even for the period of the Queen Mother's visit. Ostriches have nothing to teach these people.

[47] In reference to the then British Prime Minister, Harold Macmillan.

THE QUEEN MOTHER'S VISIT TO BAROTSELAND

Queen Mother being welcomed to his Palace by the Paramount Chief and his wife

I have changed my abode for the time being as you can see from my address. The reason for this is that on Friday, a radio-telephone message came through to the effect that Adrian Thomas and myself were required in Mongu that day to help with preparations for the Queen Mother's visit.

I have been assisting the District Officer who is acting as Liaison Officer between the Barotse Native Government (BNG) and the Northern Rhodesia Government. In effect this means that he is in charge of all the arrangements being made at the BNG capital at Limulunga ten miles from Mongu for the reception of the Queen Mother there on Thursday morning, and the arrangements being made for the Paramount Chief and his chiefs and indunas to meet the Queen Mother aboard his royal barge at a point some miles from Limulunga near the confluence of the Zambezi and one of its tributaries.

To put you in the picture I'll give you an outline of the Queen Mother's programme. She arrives on Wednesday (tomorrow) afternoon at 5 p.m. and is driven from the airport to the Residency. In the evening there is a Ball which she might attend. On Thursday morning she sets out from the Residency and is driven to Limulunga. There she is met by the Paramount Chief and his wife and she has tea with him in his palace together with his eldest son, the Mulena Mukwae, one or two other leading chiefs, the Resident Commissioner and his wife, and the DC Mongu and his wife. Then, tea over, they walk from the Palace to the Kuta and on the way watch professional dancers and salute the Flag and the Royal Drums.

In the Kuta, the Paramount Chief's Prime Minister, called the Ngambela, reads an illuminated address of welcome and the Queen Mother replies. Afterwards, she leaves the Kuta and walks to her car which is waiting outside the Palace gate some one hundred yards away and drives off.

Shortly afterwards, the paddlers (most of them indunas) for the four royal barges board lorries and drive to the landing stage at Mongu where they embark on the royal barges and proceed along ▶

a canal till they reach the aforementioned tributary of the Zambezi. There they await the arrival of the Barotse royalty who will be taken out on a special launch after attending a Garden Party which is being held in the garden of the Residency at midday. Then follow the Queen Mother and the Resident Commissioner on board another launch. They are received aboard the Paramount Chief's barge and they all proceed downriver to an island where they have tea. Then back to Mongu and next morning the Queen Mother goes off to the Copperbelt.

Senanga
Sunday 22 May 1960

Dear Folks,

I wrote the first page of the letter on Tuesday and Wednesday but forgot to post it on Thursday because of rushing hither and thither on account of the Queen Mother's visit.

My work consisted in helping to make Limulunga, the flood season capital of the Paramount Chief, presentable for the Queen Mother's visit there. Before I arrived much had been done; the Kuta was gaily decorated with bunting, a new road up the hill from the edge of the plain to the gates of the Palace had largely been completed and loads of clay soil had been dumped and spread over the sand in front of the Palace and the Saa-Sikalo Kuta (the Court House where the councils of the Barotse nation meet) so that the spectators, dancers etc. would not create a terrific dust cloud with their dancing and foot-stamping.

I was engaged in putting the finishing touches to these various jobs – mostly supervising the laying, spreading, breaking, smoothing, pounding and watering of the loads of soil brought up from the plain and dumped on the road and the surrounding area in front of the Palace and the Kuta. Also, I had the road up the hill lined with whitewashed bricks and also the path from the Palace to the Kuta.

I also had to make an enclosure for the Press and finish off the work in the Kuta, putting rush mats round the roof-supporting poles and getting the floor re-smeared. All this may not sound much but it kept me fully occupied.

On the Sunday, four days before the QM was due to arrive, a full scale rehearsal was held and some of the cars got stuck in the soft soil in front of the Palace. The road had to be realigned and frantic work done on it. I was supervising a gang of about thirty men and twenty women. My chief headache was trying to get them to work steadily for more than ten minutes without them stopping to chat, an occupation which seemingly needed all their energies and attention.

On my first day at Limulunga I was introduced to the Paramount Chief by Mr Fisher who is a District Officer in Mongu and in charge of the arrangements at Limulunga. The PC was very pleasant, asking me where I was from, what the road from Senanga to Mongu was like, etc. His Palace, which happens to be the only two-storied building in Barotseland, was built in Portuguese style by the Paris Mission Society. It's quite an impressive building.

I went inside the Palace to help Mr Fisher with some curtains and then to unpack some new furniture that had arrived from Livingstone. The furniture was lovely – four armchairs, two sofas, a table, an occasional table and a nest of tables. The Paramount Chief's son had gone to choose them in Livingstone. His choice showed excellent taste.

It was fantastic to see Mr Fisher beetling from room to room in the Palace making plans for redecorating the walls, rehanging the pictures etc., with the Paramount Chief padding along behind and nodding his head in agreement as the District Officer put forward each suggestion for his consideration. I had the feeling that the Paramount Chief was being bowled along by the energy of the European, quite helpless to affect the direction of the proposed changes. Actually, the Paramount Chief has the reputation for being a wily old bird and was probably quite content to let his European advisers do all the work and worrying because there was nothing really important at stake.

On Wednesday, the preparations at Limulunga were completed. In the afternoon I had to supervise the departure of some two hundred indunas and other Africans aboard a fleet of ten lorries. They were going into Mongu to be part of the crowd which was collecting to meet the Queen Mother on her arrival at the airport. I followed behind them to make sure that none of the lorries broke down en route.

After arriving at the airport I had to rush home, bath and change and then hare back to the airport. A little later, the QM's plane appeared in the sky. It swooped down and caused a gasp from the large crowd because of its bright crimson colour. The QM received a formal welcome from the local dignitaries – Paramount Chief in green frock coat and top hat, Resident Commissioner, DC, and their wives and a bouquet from two small girls, one black, one white.

Then she received a welcome from the indunas – the royal welcome, when they get down on their knees and clap and then stand up and fling their arms forward chanting "Yo-Sho, Yo-Sho". Then the QM walked across to the VIPs enclosure where mostly Europeans were standing and came to within five yards of the crowd, smiling and waving her hand. Then into her car and away.

That evening, there was a Ball in the Mongu Club and at about 10.15 p.m. the QM arrived and walked slowly across the room between the parted ranks of the dancers and passed within a couple of feet of me. She mounted the stage and after the National Anthem was played she danced with the Resident Commissioner (RC).

The music stopped and I moved off to a room abutting the main hall where tables were set out for people to sit at. I was standing at the doorway chatting to one or two friends when hey presto, in comes the QM with the RC. I was not more than a yard from her and as she kept looking in my direction and giving a regal smile I felt compelled to bow from the waist each time murmuring inanely "Yes, ma'am", the while. I felt a proper Charlie I can tell you and naturally when she had moved off, the chaps who had been standing behind me had a fine old time ribbing me about it. She stayed at the dance for about an hour and quite a number of people were introduced to her.

Next morning, despite getting to bed at 3 a.m., I had to be at Limulunga shortly after 8 a.m. to see that all was well. By the time I got there, large crowds had already assembled. Photographers, television men and plain reporters, as well as Audrey Russell from the BBC, were milling about mostly taking photographs and recordings of the groups of dancers who were beginning to perform in front of the crowd in the space in front of the Palace.

All was noise and confusion; drums beginning to thrum, gaily decorated "makishi" dancers beginning to stamp and twirl in groups of three or four, each inside a ring of chanting, clapping, swaying Africans. Inside the Kuta, two hundred chiefs and indunas were already seated and around the area between the Kuta and the Palace stood a great throng of Africans six-deep all the way.

It was a very exciting scene and very colourful. All the women were decked out in their best dresses of brilliantly hued cottons. As word passed around that the QM was on her way, the hubbub increased and when the Paramount Chief and the Moyo, his leading wife, appeared at the gate of the Palace all the drums apart from the special Royal Drums beat out a tremendous welcome. It was then that the QM's car hove in sight and seconds later she was stepping out of it at the gate of the Palace and shaking hands with the Paramount Chief. He was resplendent in uniform. She herself had on a lovely white dress and as I was standing only five yards away I had an excellent view.

A Likishi dancer performs for the crowd

With the Paramount Chief she walked towards the Kuta and stopped some twenty yards from it to receive the Royal salute from the chiefs and indunas who had come forward to greet her. In the background the women kept up a continuous shrill of welcome.

The QM turned and walked the fifty yards or so back to the Palace gates where she disappeared to go and have tea with the Paramount Chief. Inside the outer enclosure surrounding the Palace the wives of the chiefs and indunas danced their welcome, the dance consisting of shuffling and swaying in a large circle.

Twenty minutes later The Queen Mother appeared with the PC and their party (RC and DCs in white uniforms with white pith helmets) and mid-way between Palace and Kuta she stopped before the flagpole where the Union Jack fluttered in the breeze. Beside the flagpole the "Maoma", the three Royal Drums, were drawn up. The party came to attention. Silence: then two thuds on each drum by each of the three drummers. Then the chief drummer took over, beating slowly at first and gradually working up speed. He was joined by the others and they thundered a glorious salute with a great, deep, quite distinctive note only obtained from huge drums, decades old such as these.

The Queen Mother and the Paramount Chief in procession to the Kuta; the Maoma are in the foreground with the drummers in red berets

The Saa-Sikalo Kuta where the Queen Mother addressed the Barotse National Council

The procession continued into the Kuta preceded by a man playing a traditional xylophone made of gourds with a wooden key across the mouth of each one. There, an address of welcome was read which stressed the loyalty of the Barotse people and their reliance on the preservation of the existing treaties. The Queen Mother replied, each phrase being translated into Lozi by an interpreter. She closed by saying "Stay well" in Lozi which, of course, brought the house down.

That over, the makishi dancers came forward with their attendant dancers and drummers and proceeded to dance, stamping and twirling, enacting various traditional themes, the best known being one where two cocks fight for the attention of the hen. This went on for close on half an hour, much longer than the official programme had allowed for, which shows how fascinated the QM was. Then she went back to her car and was driven off.

I had then to supervise the loading and despatch of one hundred and fifty paddlers for the royal barges and of another fifty or so garden party guests into Mongu. I got them all away with reasonable speed and took in Mr Mulonda and his wife in my landrover, he being the member for Barotseland in the NR Legislative Council.

I did not have time to go to the Garden Party because I was late in getting into Mongu and had to change out of my suit into less formal attire to set off quickly with a couple of other Cadets and the Ngambela, the Paramount Chief's Prime Minister. We were the communications launch and also supposed to land on the island immediately after the Paramount Chief's barge, the *Nalikwanda*, to disembark the Ngambela who had to be there for the tea party.

So we set off to join the barges which had already left and to see that all was ready at the island for the tea party. We motored from barge to barge passing on instructions from Mr Fisher and the Paramount Chief who were both on board the *Nalikwanda*. The Queen Mother set off from Mongu in a motor launch and transferred to a paddle barge about a mile from where the four royal barges lay. These were the Paramount Chief's, the Mulena Mukwae's, the Mulena Mbwanjikana's (the chief of Kalabo District) and the Moyo's (the Paramount Chief's wife) which were drawn up in the reeds at the side of the river. The Queen Mother swept up in her paddle barge at a tremendous rate and came alongside the *Nalikwanda*. She and the Resident Commissioner and his wife stepped aboard and all the royal barges, the Queen Mother's barge (now only carrying her ADC, lady-in-waiting, etc.), the District Commissioner Mongu's barge and a host of boats and motor barges carrying spectators proceeded up river. The drums on the *Nalikwanda* were beating and its paddlers were attempting to paddle and swing to the drum beat at the same time - with the result that the *Nalikwanda* made pretty slow progress.

The QM was obviously enjoying herself and certainly it was a splendid scene – brightly coloured barges with paddlers stripped to the waist and wearing, in the case of the *Nalikwanda*, skirts of leopard and lion skins with red berets on their heads. On the Mulena Mukwae's barge they wore on their heads a tuft of lion's mane.

I had an excellent view of all the proceedings from the launch I was on because we had to stick close to the *Nalikwanda* so as to land the Ngambela on the island immediately after the VIPs on the *Nalikwanda*.

Next day, I was at Limulunga by 7.15 a.m. to see the paddlers and indunas onto lorries to go to the airport to say farewell to the Queen Mother. Quite a crowd was there; she again got the Royal Salute from the indunas and three rousing cheers from the Europeans.

PS - Everyone in Mongu, South Africans and all, is a confirmed Royalist now!

The Queen Mother on her way to her rendezvous with the Paramount Chief on the Zambezi. The Queen Mother is in the front row under the canopy

The Nalikwanda with the Queen Mother and Paramount Chief on board. Note the Paramount Chief's flags, one with a white elephant at its centre

Shekela again

Shekela Kuta
Tuesday 31 May 1960

Well, here I am on tour again and enjoying myself hugely, though I have just completed today an exhausting eighteen or nineteen mile hike from my previous camp. This is my last night on tour and besides getting this letter written, I hope also to finish off my tour report.

I took a lot of trouble on my last tour to explain the fairly recent law on the building of decent huts. This tour has been fairly encouraging; well-nigh every man in every village, has started on a new hut and a good proportion have been completed. Moreover, they have not stuck to the minimum fixed by law but have usually exceeded that size quite considerably, perhaps feeling that if they have to build a good house, they might as well make a thorough job of it.

Of course, in some cases, the villagers stick their framework of poles into the ground and are prepared to leave them like this for years, as a sop to succeeding generations of touring officers; but I have told them that I will be returning in September with the Indunas and that if they have not completed their huts by then they will be fined five pounds or thrown in prison if they fail to pay.

Actually, I don't mention the sum of five pounds but content myself with saying they will be fined. The fiercer threats come from the Induna and my District Messenger who seem to have settled on this sum as being the minimum threat needed to produce the proper activity from the villagers.

The villagers take all these threats quite good-naturedly and with a large pinch of salt just as we in our turn treat with disbelief the various excuses, disasters, etc. that have prevented the completion of the new huts. When September comes, no doubt the most flagrant offenders will be fined anything from five shillings to one pound.

▶

▶ I have also been trying to encourage people to grow rice. However, this is rather a difficult task because the people have had very good crops on the whole in this silalo this year and see no point in expending more energy on growing rice. Moreover, they don't recognise the possibilities of selling their surplus food partly because, in fact, they are limited. The market near at hand is not a good one for selling rice.

However, a navigation canal is due to be dug across the plain on this side of the Zambezi and it would be reasonably close to Shekela. Sacks of grain could be pulled to it by oxen on sledges and thence transported by paddle barge to Mongu where there would be a substantial market for rice.

Rice is a very useful crop. It can be planted before the rains come in permanently damp soil in the depressions (pans or dambos) which flood in the rainy season. The flood does not harm the rice because the higher the water rises, the taller the rice grows. In fact, it grows just fast enough to keep the ears above the surface of the water.

The problem with maize is that it has to be planted before the rains and the people, not knowing whether they are going to be light or heavy may find they have planted too far from the centre of the pans, in the case of light rains; the maize withers from too little water and too much sun. Or if the crop is planted close to the centre of the dambo heavy rains may flood it to a considerable depth and ruin the crop.

PS Last week I received in the office a comment from the Ministry of Native Affairs in Lusaka on my first tour report: "The officer is to be congratulated on writing an interesting and optimistic tour report."

This was in contrast to the only comment from the Resident Commissioner, Gervas Clay, to point that I had added up the numbers of women in the villages of Shekela incorrectly. I was only one out. I was dismayed by the RC's abrupt dismissal of my report because I had put so much thought into it, especially my suggestions for improving the cash earning possibilities of the silalo." Old timer cynicism", I told myself.

Return to Sitoti Bushanjo

Senanga

7 June 1960

Tomorrow, I set off once more on tour, returning about the 22nd or 23rd of the month. I am going to Sitoti-Bushanjo, part of which I toured at the height of the hot season last year.

I have to return to Senanga for a District Bursaries Committee (as Chairman) and then I shall return to finish off my tour. Breaking up a tour like this is quite a good idea when the tour is one of more than three weeks because at the end of a fortnight one is beginning to look forward once again to the amenities of civilisation, especially a decent bath and an armchair.

Mutomena's Camp

Sitoti-Bushanjo Silalo

12 June 1960

This is an area of wide plains broken up by patches of woodland, the plains covered at this time of year with waist-high grass that is now burnt brown with the sun. In the weeks to follow, the villagers will set fire to the grass in the belief that this will help the first flush of new grass that comes up in October-November.

I and my Messengers have taken bicycles this time in the belief that the flat plains with their fairly firm soil would be ideal for cycling. Unfortunately, I think I have miscalculated in this matter. Although the soil on the plains is for the most part fairly firm, it is not so firm as to prevent the paths that run across them from being made soft and sandy by the passage of innumerable feet, day in, day out.

I tried out the bicycles on Friday for the first time and found that I spent three-quarters of the time pushing and the rest of the time making very laborious progress cycling. Perhaps the area to the north of this camp to where I shall be moving tomorrow will be better suited to cycling.

At my first camp I met Induna Imukondo; he has the face and body of Mussolini. Next morning, I censused four villages, visited two close by the camp on foot and the other two by lorry because they lay on the route to the next camp, about twelve miles away.

From there the lorry continued back to base while I turned north having reached the western boundary of the silalo at that point. I censused three villages there and next day, Friday, set off by bicycle to visit them and four other villages that lay along the way to the next camp. We travelled about 20 miles and pretty tiring it was especially as my water bag[48] had got left behind in camp so that I was eventually reduced to drinking some of the raw stuff in one of the last villages we visited before reaching the camp. I reached the camp at 2.30 p.m. having set out at just before 7.30 a.m.

I had some food, a rest and then at 4 p.m. started censusing the villagers who had come in from the surrounding villages. This took me until dusk to complete – i.e., until just after 6 p.m. and afterwards I had to do some homework on the figures getting them noted down and added up.

Next day, yesterday, I set off to visit some of the villages censused the afternoon before. It was a very pleasant day because the villages lay only about two miles from one another and women folk from the village would walk with us singing and dancing to the next so that we walked all day, fourteen or fifteen miles, to a musical accompaniment.

In one of the villages I was offered "tea". I accepted the offer and a few minutes later the headman proudly presented me with a teapot full of, not tea, but boiled milk! Nor was there a cup to pour the milk into so, not wishing to embarrass my host, I drank the milk straight from the teapot, taking off the top to do so.

In that village lives the Paramount Chief's hunter. He showed me into a little hut where he keeps his trophies until the Paramount Chief sends transport to collect them. Inside the hut were four elephant tusks, and one, when set on its end reached up to my face. This tusk must have weighed a hundred pounds (it was almost too heavy to lift single-handed).

[48]*My canvas water bag always contained water which had been boiled by my cook first thing in the morning, thus ensuring that it was safe to drink.*

It is unlikely that the Paramount Chief would have sold all the ivory although he might have sold some of it to augment the Royal Treasury. Instead, he would have had it carved into ceremonial fly whisks and other artefacts which he could use or give as presents to distinguished visitors. He would often carry a beautifully carved fly whisk as a symbol of royalty.

Iain Stuart reminds me that the hunter's elephant rifle was a formidable one made by Cogswell and Harrison, famous sporting gun makers of London "with a bore as large as a cannon's". It would have been paid for by the Paramount Chief.

Liwangu Camp
Sunday 19 June 1960

This tour has been enjoyable. The weather is very much cooler[49] now and except when attempting to cycle, I haven't raised a sweat at all. So far, I have been able to cycle about one mile in every three or four.

At this point I have been interrupted by the arrival of a landrover, specially sent out by the District Commissioner to carry here a friend I met on the boat, David Radcliffe, a teacher at a Methodist Senior Secondary School near Lusaka. You could have knocked me over with a feather when he stepped out. He got the chance of coming to Mongu on a new landrover that was being driven there from Lusaka by Peter Wilson[50] who, having been stationed at Ndola for a couple of months since his return from leave, was on his way to Kalabo which borders Senanga to the north.

David arrived in Senanga on Friday having covered the last part of his journey from Mongu to Senanga on a WNLA lorry. He stayed at Senanga on Friday and Saturday and today the District Commissioner gave him a landrover to come out and join me for the remaining days of my tour. He is lucky because there is a big dance planned to take place here tonight.

As in Shekela, I have been concentrating on putting over the idea of bigger huts. I could tell the Induna to prosecute each person found offending the law which lays down minimum standards but I ▶

[49]*It was the middle of winter NR being south of the Equator.*
[50]*Whom I had shared a house with for a few months shortly after I arrived in Senanga.*

don't think this is the best way of getting new standards accepted, even if it is the quickest. So I have given them all another 3 months to get their new huts finished, just as I have done in Shekela.

Actually, as in Shekela, my last visit seems to have had its effect for in ninety percent of the villages visited (in Shekela it was well-nigh one hundred percent) the people have at least made a show of putting up new huts; ie., they have cut the basic poles and stuck them in the ground.

Also, in the past week, I have bought a couple of beautifully decorated reed mats and two karosses or skin blankets which will be useful for providing me with additional floor furnishings.

Senanga
Tuesday 28 June 1960

I am now back from my tour for a few days. Tomorrow, I leave with the DC to go to Mooyo, where the Mulena Mukwae's flood-season capital is, to do a surprise check on the Treasury Clerk's books and cash and apprise the departmental Indunas of the money at their disposal during the present year and set them to work on using it.

I left off last week's letter rather suddenly if you remember. When I was in the middle of it, up popped this chap, David Radcliffe.

On the afternoon of his arrival, some villagers arrived to dance for us. The principal dancer is always a man and dances in the middle of a circle of women who sing and clap their hands. He is also accompanied by drummers. The dancing is of a spasmodic, jerky nature- ie. the dancer twitches first his shoulder and arm muscles and then starts twitching and jerking all over, with variations to imitate different sorts of animals.

The spectators show their approval by coming forward and crossing his palm with silver (usually a silver three pence piece!) and there is also an assistant who comes after a discreet interval to collect the money from the dancer lest the weight of it interfere with his movements!

▶ Next day, we set out on a visit to a couple of villages involving an eight mile walk; a mere flea-bite for me but on our return David took to his bed exhausted. In the afternoon, I had to visit another village involving a walk of about six miles and this time David preferred to stay in camp to husband his strength for the next day's journey.

I saw quite a lot of wildebeest, tsessebe and zebra close at hand. David was also there so he, too, shared in this not so common sight.

An addition to my party arrived the day before David – Induna Akawi, the Health Induna for Senanga District. He has a great line of patter about the dread results that befall any who live in bad houses – diseases, fines, trouble for everyone etc. He himself lives in a sub-standard house in Nalolo, though he says his house at Mooyo is up to standard!

On the second last day of my tour, the two Indunas came to tea. The third Induna had been left behind to superintend the completion of two houses for teachers at a Lower Primary School near the Kuta being built by voluntary labour. Induna Imukondo, the President of the Sitoti-Bushanjo Kuta, said how much he appreciated the trouble I was taking on tour to encourage the people to improve their standard of living - no previous officer had ever taken such trouble. Shucks!

One interesting thing I saw on this tour; many of the women have tattoo marks on their faces and sometimes on the small of the back and on the chest. The induna told me that the cuts are made with a razor blade and a paste made from a certain tree root is rubbed in so that when the wound heals, a scar darker than the surrounding skin is left. The paste "hurts like fire" so said the Induna and I saw one girl's face scored with fresh fiery scars – she, obviously, had just received the "beauty" treatment.

Letter from Sitoti Silalo – the land that borders the Zambezi

Matabele Causeway Camp
Near Sitoti,
4 July 1960

I am on tour again, finishing off the Sitoti-Bushanjo tour which I had to break off to attend a District Bursaries Committee meeting. This was last Monday and over the weekend I took the trouble to vet all the bursary applications dividing them into various categories of academic merit for the most part. It is just as well I did for it saved a lot of time by getting rid of the certainties for bursaries, and the certainties for not getting them. This enabled us at the meeting to spend most of the time discussing the border-line cases.

There were three others there: the second most senior Induna from the Nalolo Kuta, the Education Induna for the District, and a member of the public, a retired Inspector of Schools. The meeting lasted all day though I could have made it shorter if I had tried to ride roughshod over the other members of the committee.

On Wednesday, I went to Mooyo with the DC to check the Treasury Clerk's books. When we reached there, we found the Mulena Mukwae had just returned from Limulunga where she had been staying since the Queen Mother's visit, a period of some six weeks. With her were some one hundred paddlers who had paddled her and her retinue to Limulunga and who were also required to paddle her back. But instead of being sent home, to return at the end of the six weeks, they just stayed on, doing nothing, no one thinking of sending them away.

Ladies in their finest dresses celebrate the return of the Mulena Mukwae to Nalolo (photo: Rev JL Baumgartner)

During that visit with the DC, David Acheson, to Mooyo we stayed a couple of nights in the Government rest house. I remember standing outside the rest house on a beautiful evening when I was suddenly minded to ask David a question that had been on my mind ever since my first visit with him to Nalolo the previous August.

"David, why don't you ever shake the hand of an African?" He paused and then astonished me with the frankness of his reply. "It's because I feel a physical revulsion at doing so. I know that it's wrong but I can't help myself".

David was brought up in Northern Rhodesia and I think that unless one's parents have taught one otherwise, one is bound to acquire deeply held racist attitudes in a racially divided society where one group regards itself as superior and persuades the other group that this is so.

> On Friday, I set off on a tour of Sitoti and reached my camp after a journey that took only one and a half hours. This camp, I am still at it, stands close to the main road from Senanga to Livingstone on a hill overlooking an inlet of the Zambezi. The view is beautiful looking over water, forest and plain. There are thirteen villages close to the camp because there are fish aplenty in the afore-mentioned inlet as well as good soil on its sides.

> On Sunday, I took a day off and in the afternoon set off in a dugout canoe with Kachana,[51] my Senior District Messenger, and a villager to hunt for birds along the inlet.

> We paddled quietly up the inlet, the dugout rocking with such an irregular motion that I had to squat amidships till I got used enough to its motion to be able to stand up. After a short while we rounded a bend in the inlet to see a flock of herons on the edge of the water some distance away. The two paddlers immediately crouched down and very softly we slid along by the side of the reeds until we got to within about twenty to thirty yards. Then I fired into the middle of the flock. With a great beating of wide black wings, the birds took off leaving six lying dead or mortally wounded behind them. My companions were highly delighted, the >

[51]Kachana, my Senior District Messenger, always took the lead in these hunting expeditions. Before setting off he would always remove his boots and go barefoot. He moved absolutely silently and I tried to do the same. Although he always had his shotgun with him he was happy to let me do the shooting with my gun because he wanted to conserve his own expensive ammunition.

heron being a very favoured relish and surprised, too, at my expertise and pleased at the economy of cartridges – Africans are not at all "sporting" when it comes to hunting.

While a European will not normally hunt for heron, an African will because they are usually less timid than ducks or geese. The European, too, when out shooting ducks, usually tries to get them on the wing. To the African this is sheer foolishness; he finds out where they are sitting and then wriggles up close and lets off his shotgun into the middle of the flock, bagging as many as possible with one cartridge.

So we hoisted the herons on board and set off once more. We saw plenty heron, but they cleared off before we could come close enough. At one point, some women were grubbing in marshy soil by the water's edge. I stopped and found that they were digging up small bulbous roots; I ate one and found it to have quite a nice flavour.

Eventually we came to the end of the inlet where we disembarked and struck overland to some pans (dambos) about a mile away where we hoped to find some duck and spurwing geese. Sure enough we sighted a fairly large flock of small duck – red-billed teal – and, when within about a hundred yards, dropped onto our hands and knees in the long grass and crept stealthily, Indian fashion, towards our quarry.

We reached the edge of the grass bordering the pan, the ducks some thirty yards away, but alas, before I could raise my gun they sensed us and took off. Luckily they did not go far, merely circling and landing on another pan nearby. Again we made towards them and crawled the last one hundred yards or so, and again, just as I was raising my gun, the birds flew off. Some of them returned to the same pan as before so we made our way back and again did our Davy Crockett act. This time I actually got my gun to my shoulder and took aim when the birds started to lift from the water. Deciding it was now or never, I pulled the trigger, and hit four of them. We raced into the water... but caught only three of them. The other, being only slightly hurt, was able to wing away. So that made a bag of nine birds, ample to supply me, my messengers, indunas (three of them), cook, kitchen boy, court clerk and veterinary assistant with meat that night and the following day.

On the way back we saw a couple of white-breasted storks, huge birds with scarlet bills and scarlet tips to their leg and toe joints. They were a beautiful sight and I said so to Kachana. He however took it to mean that they were beautiful because they are good to eat (!) but I refused to shoot them.

Today I visited a school run by the Seventh Day Adventists. There happened to be two Europeans there from their central mission station in Barotseland which is in Kalabo District to the north of this one. They were in the middle of a pep-talk meeting with their African teachers in this District when I arrived. The silalo Induna knocked on the door of the classroom where the meeting was being held and an African teacher stuck his head out to see what was the matter.

He looked gratifyingly startled to see me standing there and with alacrity (what a big head I am!) one of the Europeans left the meeting and came to find out the purpose of my visit. I may add here that any officer from the Boma is exceedingly big cheese in his District because the centre of power is still very much at the Boma despite the fragmentation of responsibilities in recent years – e.g. the growth of PWD, Education, Health and other departments.

In fact, all I was doing was making a routine visit which is expected of a touring officer. The European and the chief African pastor showed me round. Some buildings (two new classrooms and houses for the teachers and the pastor) were new and in excellent condition but the walls of the old classroom block were ominously cracked. It is high time they were mended and I told the missionary so, tactfully.

Then I informed him that I had been told by the villagers who sent their children to this school that they were dissatisfied because theirs was the only mission agency in the District that did not provide Standard Six education. Their only Standard Six school is in the Kalabo District, 140 miles away to the north.

The missionary rather hastily said that indeed they were talking about this in their meeting and had resolved to make a Standard

▶ Five at this school next year and a Standard Six the year after. I asked if this was definite and he replied it was, barring catastrophes. However, when we returned to the new classroom block where the meeting had been in progress we met the other European. He gave me a handshake favoured by many ministers: a very firm squeeze in two parts, the second part squeeze I suppose to emphasize that we're brithers a'.

I told him how pleased I was and how pleased the villagers would be to hear that there was definitely going to be a Standard Five at the school the following year and Standard Six the year after.

Missionary No. 2 looked rather startled at the news and No. 1 looked just a little abashed.

"Well", he said, "I think we can confidently expect to be able to start Standard Five here next year" and so he repeated himself in such a way as to wriggle out of his earlier firm statement. It was rather obvious that the matter had only been discussed in committee, if that, and no firm decision taken and (more important) no money allocated for the project.

The SDA is an American outfit and I can't say they have much of my sympathy. They complicate a missionary situation already complicated enough without their esoteric, crack-pot beliefs (no meat, fish, coffee, tea, etc. in their diet); also they refuse Government aid and so require bigger fees from their pupils and more communal help on their buildings. They say that thereby they can take a more independent line with Government should that ever be necessary and that it encourages people to put a proper value on education. Naturally this last point does not have great popular appeal, not with the Lozi at any rate.

Indeed, the SDA influence is gradually diminishing in this District. One at least of their schools has been taken over by another agency and they will gradually be squeezed out as the other agencies with more money (especially the RCs) expand their education provision.

At this distance it makes me blush to recall my shooting of the herons. My defence is that it was done to provide food for myself and my companions on tour – it certainly was not killing for killing's sake.

Let not this week's address make you think that I have been transferred. Just the opposite; a couple of days ago or so, the DC confirmed an earlier rumour that I shall be staying in Senanga for another year. Needless to say, I am glad to get this news because it will enable me to get to know this District reasonably well and perhaps enable me to get some things accomplished that otherwise would have been impossible – e.g. good house-building, follow- up tours etc. Also, it defers the day when I shall have to pack all my goods which is not something I relish.

Hollowing out a dugout canoe (photo Rev JL Baumgartner)

Last week I finished off my Sitoti-Bushanjo tour. Very interesting this last week was because I was visiting the villages along the bank of the Zambezi beside which runs the road to the south to Sesheke and then to Livingstone. In this stretch of country there are two mission stations, two migrant labour depots (one abandoned), "teashops", stores, coloured (mixed race) farmers and so on.

Between the two missions (SDA and Capuchin Fathers) is a WNLA labour depot where recruits for the gold mines stay overnight on their way from Senanga to Katima Mulilo, some eighty miles or so the south. There they get onto aircraft to be flown to the mines.

Beside the depot are two stores and three tearooms; two of them sell tea, bread and scones and the other which is rather small and dingy is mainly into mending chairs, tables and the like. In fact, there are two or three carpenters in this area selling planks for house-building and chairs, stools, sieves for flour and so on. This area is, indeed, fairly wealthy because many men are able to find employment on the road gangs and as labourers at the missions. There is also a handful of teachers.

There are three coloured families in this area. One operates the motorized pontoon that crosses the Zambezi at Sitoti and the other two live together being brothers descended from a Canadian ornithologist. He came over to do research but so liked the country that he stayed on and spent the rest of his days here making his living off a small farm.

On one day, I had to visit some villages on a large island on the Zambezi. In the course of the morning, the Induna, myself, my Messenger and the Veterinary Assistant who were the only ones in our party to have bicycles got separated from the rest of the party and got lost, largely because it had been nearly two years since the Induna last visited this island.

The Induna eventually decided to retrace his steps alone while the rest of us pushed off in the general direction of the village we were looking for. Eventually we stumbled onto the right path and made our way to the village. The village women, noticing the absence of the Induna began to make up songs about it as we walked on to the next village. Just as we were setting off again the Induna appeared, panting. The women often make up songs on the spot about their important visitors. In one village they sang about my long neck and in another that I had a neck like a bottle!

Also, of course, they sing songs of elaborate respect: "Welcome, Lord!", or "We thank the District Officer who protects us", no doubt to show that there are no hard feelings!

It happens thus with the traditional rulers as well. At the feast held when the Paramount Chief moves from Lealui in the Plain to Limulunga on the forest edge, the makishi dancers[52] who, on these occasions, play the role of court jesters, tell him in impudent fashion that he had better bring good rains lest there be trouble for him. ▶

---

[52] *The Makishi dancers were actually associated with initiation ceremonies for boys of the Mambunda and other tribes from eastern Angola/southern Congo. During these ceremonies which last from one to three months, boys of between 8 and 12 years old are taken to a camp in the bush near their village where they are taught the traditions of their tribe and undergo circumcision.*

"Two years since the Induna had visited". That sums up why I was so thorough in visiting every one of the villages in the silalos that I toured. Were their crops sufficient to last them until the next harvest? Were their cattle healthy? Were their children able to get to school? Above all, I suppose these visits were to demonstrate that each village mattered to the Government and to the Mulena Mukwae and her local Indunas. I sometimes asked myself as I trudged along a sandy path in the midday sun why I was bothering to visit some distant, disregarded village. But the reception we received demonstrated that the people regarded our visit as a very special occasion to be celebrated in the way they excelled in, their communal singing.

▶ I came back from tour on Friday and on Saturday (my birthday - two dozen years already, alas) I left to come up to Mooyo to check the books of the silalo Court Clerks (twelve in all). I stopped only briefly to dump some goods at my camp there and then pushed on some seven miles further to Namushakende where plans for the development of the Protectorate are hatched. There is a Training School for village craftsmen and a Cooperative Society which markets carvings and basket work.

I have come here to spend the weekday evenings and also Rhodes' Day with David Salmon. Tomorrow I shall go back to Mooyo and start work.

You will have heard the Congo[53] news. It is very disturbing. Believe it or not, some Europeans are rather gloating over all the commotion and bloodshed, saying "I told you so", etc. Pretty ghastly and goodness knows if the Africans are also rubbing their hands, though for a different reason of course.

There are no refugees coming this way, but where Gus[54] is, in Fort Rosebery, the wireless reports refugees coming in by the hundreds and in Northern Province as a whole several thousand refugees have arrived. These happenings may well strengthen the hands of the reactionaries though of course the real lesson is that the sooner we press ahead with African advancement in the civil ▶

---

[53]I was referring to the chaos which broke out in the Belgium Congo after it became Independent on 30th June 1960. Different political factions led by inexperienced leaders fought amongst themselves for control of the country.
[54]My friend from university days, Angus McDonald.

▶ service, mines, local govt, etc. the better, so that there will be a sufficiently large cadre of responsible and experienced Africans to ensure stability and good government when African self-government comes.

Senanga
19 July 1960

Exactly a year since setting out from Southampton on the *"Winchester Castle"*.

The last week has been extremely enjoyable. Last Wednesday and Thursday were spent in camp near the Native Authority capital at Mooyo checking the tax receipt books of all the Court Clerks in the District - twelve in all. This also involves reading through the Case Records of each of the silalo Kutas to endorse each sentence and to check that court fines have been paid and tally with the receipts issued.

The Kutas hear cases relating to truancy, felling trees in forest reserves, village hygiene, assault and theft. But the cases most often heard relate to adultery, cursing and land and cattle disputes.

Adultery is very severely punished; in the old days the guilty party might have been speared to death. Nowadays, he has to pay compensation of five pounds (ten pounds if a member of one of the Royal families is involved either as the guilty or injured party) and a fine of one pound to the court. If a man runs off with someone else's wife and is caught, he has to pay ten pounds' compensation to the injured husband and a two pound fine, on grounds of abduction, and five pounds' compensation and the one pound fine for adultery: a total of eighteen pounds.

This is an astronomic sum to pay by local African standards. Labourers are paid two shillings and four pence per day (Three pounds per month approx.) and most men do not have paid employment at all. Despite the penalties, at least thirty percent of all cases heard in the Kutas concern adultery.

After that the most commonly heard cases concern cursing. Women are usually the guilty parties and usually the injured ones as ▶

well. To curse another is to injure him by making him unhappy – so the Clerks explain to me. Depending on the venom and outrageousness of the cursing, varying amounts of compensation are awarded, most commonly one or two pounds.

If the cursing takes place in front of a large company, the fine may be as much as five pounds or three months IHL (imprisonment with hard labour) if the fine is not paid. It's the equivalent to our charge of criminal libel though a good deal wider in scope. Thus the law states: "The use of abusive language is forbidden".

Thirdly, land disputes often arise. Usually these occur in the silalos that border the plain where the population is densest, the land very fertile and so the gardens relatively static and highly valued. In the hinterland, however, such cases are hardly ever met with because the soil is infertile and the people practise shifting cultivation. But on the edges of the Plain, gardens are handed down from generation to generation and disputes often hinge around what happened two or three generations before.

Cattle, too, are the subject of many disputes: non-payment of herdsmen, death of an animal while in the herdsman's care – did it die naturally or was its throat cut to supply a hungry herdsman and his kin with sorely needed meat?

These case records hold the key to the understanding of much of the Barotse way of life and way of thinking.

On Friday I called into Mongu and made a courtesy visit (obligatory) on the Acting Resident Commissioner[55] – the previous Resident Commissioner is due to return at the end of his long vacation leave. He was very pleasant and invited me to lunch, something that would never have occurred to his predecessor.

So I rolled up to the Residency, quite a handsome white walled building. Inside, I was introduced to Mrs Acting Resident Commissioner, a very pleasant person. After lunch a record of Kenneth McKellar was put on and everything was very chummy.

[55] Mr FMN Heath.

▶ My opinion of the Acting Resident Commissioner went up again when I returned to Senanga to find that his comment on my last tour report was "Short but practical and makes good reading", while his comments on the one or two suggestions I put forward were complimentary.

On Saturday I set off for Mooyo with a sack of rice seed and some coffee beans for Induna Imutulo of Shekela Silalo who is a keen farmer. Imutulo is a rarity; someone in the Lozi hierarchy who is innovative. In his case, as I've mentioned, he is growing rice at the Kuta in Shekela, showing the school staff and pupils how to do so and encouraging others in his silalo to follow suit. We had also talked about the possibility of him trying to grow coffee which is why I was taking coffee beans to him.

We stopped in a village where we knew potatoes are grown. There were none ready at the time; however, the villagers gathered round and gaped as the radiator was topped up with water. Good natured banter passed back and forth between my Messenger and my cook, Jameson, on the one hand and the villagers on the other. Someone made a joke which I understood and the villagers rocked afresh when they saw that I, too, was sharing in the mirth. One toothless old woman came forward to say that she was the mother of District Messenger Mundia and I replied *"Bome, mu na ni mwana wa mushimani yo munde ahulu; ki masinja yo munde ahulu-hulu-hulu!"* (Mother, you have a very fine son; he is a very, very, very good Messenger). This was said half in jest and the villagers clapped in appreciation of this and of my Lozi as they like to hear a European speak their language, however badly; and the old woman beamed. Everyone was in a high good humour as we drove off exchanging "Stay wells" for "Go wells".

SENANGA YEAR TWO

Letter to Willie Farquhar

Senanga

30 July 1960

Dear Willie

It is just about three months since I last wrote and exactly a year to the very day since I first set foot on the Continent of Africa.

Since I last wrote I have been on tour for a considerable part of the time. I am glad to say there were no encounters with crocodiles or lions though one day we killed a mamba which was in the process of crossing our path. Another day, walking through thick forest, Kachana, my Senior District Messenger, walking a couple of paces in front of me, suddenly hurtled himself into a thorn bush at the side of the path. A foot or two in front of me was a snake dangling from the branch of a tree; my Messenger must have been within an inch of it before he saw it. I and my companions all had a hearty laugh at him. He had just escaped a venomous snake bite at the price of a momentary loss of dignity. Jokes and jibes were bandied back and forth for Africans have a pretty robust sense of humour. Back in camp, my Messenger could be heard enlarging on the episode in the midst of all the carriers and cooks.

The Congo has provided us (the Europeans) with plenty to talk about but most of the talking is rather facile. Some are rubbing their hands in glee as reports come in of women being raped, soldiers mutinying, tribes scrapping, mobs looting and so on. It is really rather ghastly to hear such attitudes being expressed. Usually I just keep my mouth shut but last week I startled the company at the D.C.'s house by following a remark of the DC's to the effect that "The Colonial Office should get out and leave us to run our own affairs" by saying "I disagree!". Sudden silence fell and then followed a very reasonable argument amongst us all apart from the DC's wife ▶

who is a Rhodesian like her husband (who is highly intelligent and willing to listen to views that don't agree with his) and who kept saying "Oh, Malcolm!" and "You can't believe that!" Her solution to the Race Problem is "Before we can let them have more power, they must practise birth control." Since she and her husband are Roman Catholics and by the rate at which they are producing children are not exactly a good example to their black brethren, I felt like suggesting that the activities of our local Capuchin Fathers be stopped forthwith - but my famous tact got the better of me.

It is now almost a year since I received my first airmail "Manchester Guardian Weekly".[56] You can't possibly know what a wonderful boon this has been especially when my wireless has been out of action.

Senanga
2 August 1960

I have not been on tour for the past three weeks but next week I shall be starting out on my travels again. I think I'll be going to the western boundary of the District. Across this boundary is Angola (Portuguese West Africa). Tsetse fly are encroaching along this boundary and already some cattle in the District have died of sleeping sickness which is transmitted by tsetse. Since there are about one hundred thousand cattle in Barotseland and because this District is one of the most important cattle areas, urgent steps are being planned to prevent sleeping sickness from spreading.

One measure will be to cut a track parallel to the boundary, about ten miles inside Senanga District and mount a strong guard on it to prevent cattle movements across it. It is likely that I shall be given the job, together with the Livestock Officer, of supervising the cutting of this track. It will be at least eighty miles long, nobody knows exactly what the terrain is like and it may take a considerable time to do.

It is also planned to build permanent Boma camps out on this boundary to assist the Native Authority which is likely to agree to set up two silalo Kutas in the area which is at present a no-man's ▶

[56] *I received a year's subscription for the MGW from Willie -see page 63.*

land, favoured occasionally by a visit into Northern Rhodesian territory by a Portuguese tax collector.

The new DC arrives on the 10th August and it may be I won't be able to go on tour before he comes. The present DC will stay on for a few weeks to show the new chap the ropes.

A new District Commissioner

Nangweshi Rest house
Senanga
15 August 1960

The past week has been very hectic. I've been packing up all my worldly possessions (they are slowly multiplying) and getting them transported over to the present DC's house. Also, I have had to pack my touring boxes for once again going on tour. I'm exhausted at day's end.

The new DC arrived on Saturday at 6 p.m. after a rather harrowing journey with his wife and three children from Livingstone – a three-day journey on a timber-carrying train and then a rackety ride from the rail head over a terrible road, even by Barotse standards, to Sesheke.

By the time he arrived here his (previously our) house had been scrubbed, polished and dusted, beds made, a meal prepared; all this thanks largely to the DC's wife who worked like a Trojan to get everything shipshape besides getting on with her own packing and keeping tabs on her own three kids.

After I moved out of my house, I stayed with the Achesons while Adrian stayed with the Jarretts. The DC and his wife are very easy to get on with and they just left me to look after myself.

Before I give my impressions of the new DC I might say something about the one I have worked under for the past year.

He is young as DCs go; he is now thirty-two and when he was appointed he could only have been about twenty-nine. He is a Rhodesian as is his wife and they are both very conscious of the fact. As I have said before, they are a friendly couple and not at all snooty as some DCs and their wives are said to be in their dealings with members of other less classy Departments.

I have always remained friendly with them but never very close, partly because I like my own company too much and partly because I have been even friendlier with the Jarretts and to a lesser extent the Livestock Officer and his wife (the Farrans).

Unfortunately, relations between the Jarretts (and the Farrans to a lesser degree) and the Achesons have not always been particularly cordial, partly because the Achesons are touchy in some things and are apt to read anti-Rhodesian settler feeling into any everyday sort of dispute and partly because the Jarretts and Farrans as well as myself are suspicious and a bit contemptuous too about Rhodesians, their hard drinking and their lack of culture!

In fact, I think it is because I felt I could not air my political views in the DC's house without being dubbed an "Enemy of the People" that I visited his house comparatively infrequently and had few conversations with him.

However, as I may have told you, about four weeks ago, in an after-dinner discussion at his house, with the Building Foreman and his wife (English but reactionary) present, with Macleod et al being slanged, I decided that silence was no longer worthwhile and gave them a good dose of "Fabianism". To my surprise David Acheson not only gave my views a hearing and argued cogently against them but also jumped to my defence when his wife started getting angry with me.

Since then, I have had some very interesting talks with him. He is very well informed on the contemporary situation in Rhodesia, though he interprets it differently from me. I think he is striving as hard, if not harder than the liberals inside and outside Africa to reach an honest and workable solution to the Central African situation.

As you may have gathered, Mrs Acheson is not as calmly reasoned as her husband. In her and in some other Rhodesians I have met, the instinctive reaction to criticism of white rule has become a blinding emotion and it is both depressing and hopeless to argue politics with her or her kind. At the moment she is quite pathetically bewildered by what is going on and does not realize the forces that are fast pulling her world to pieces. The result is that an argument that goes against her established way of thinking drives her furious because her brain just can't keep up (I imagine the bull feels angry with the matador for much the same reason).

Mr Acheson has allowed his work to get on top of him during the past year as he himself told me earlier today. Partly to blame may be the fact that he has never had an experienced man underneath him to shoulder some of the responsibilities. In his three years, his most senior officer has been a Cadet, and never one of more than one year's experience. After that, they have been transferred just when they are beginning to know the ropes and be useful.

Also, and this may explain what has gone above, the Resident Commissioner,[57] presently on leave, has been the reverse of helpful. The RC is the longest serving officer at present in the Provincial Administration and maybe he is embittered at not getting further promotion. Anyway, he is a stiff, unfriendly type of man.

He has had it in for our DC from the beginning. Seems crazy to me; you would think that a man such as Mr Acheson given so much responsibility so young would need all the encouragement and friendly advice that the RC could give. I suppose that if the DC had been of tougher fibre he could have withstood this but instead he is a person who will do anything to avoid a scene – I have very seldom seen him lose his temper.

The result was that the DC became lacking in determination and drive and I just could not understand how Jonathon Cole, the first cadet to work under him, had such a high opinion of him. However, since his three-week holiday and the arrival of the Acting RC (I hope he becomes permanent) the DC has bucked up considerably and it is like working for a new man.

[57] *Gervas Clay.*

▶ The new DC, Ian Edye, is about thirty-eight to forty years old I should think and at first meeting, extremely pleasant. I think I am going to enjoy working for him. He is English and his wife is a New Zealander. She, too, seems pleasant though I have seen less of her. They have two boys aged five and seven, and a girl aged nine.[58] Very nice kids.

Letters from Lumbe Silalo, the remote Land

Lumbe Silalo
Senanga
21 August 1960

It is now the end of my first week on tour in this silalo and just another four to go before I finish. So far, the time has passed very quickly except this afternoon when I have been waiting rather impatiently for the arrival of a runner from the Boma with my mail. He should have arrived yesterday but in this country you always allow an extra day for unforeseen contingencies.

Early on Tuesday morning I left Nangweshi Rest House and drove in the Boma lorry twenty miles south to the point on the Zambezi where there is a Government ferry.[59] The ferry was just reaching the bank when I arrived, packed with small children coming over to the nearby mission school from the other side of the river. About twenty got out and when they had, my goods and chattels were on-loaded. Quite a load they made, too; a large tin box, a small tin box containing tax registers and writing materials, three wooden boxes containing blankets, cooking utensils and tinned foods, a tent, two groundsheets, a tin of paraffin and a box lavatory seat and various other odds and ends – enough to supply each of sixteen carriers who carry them from camp to camp with a fair-sized load.

▶

[58] *The Edye children spent most of the year at boarding school. They only spent the school holidays in Senanga.*
[59] *The ferry or paddle pontoon was a broad flat bottomed barge which could take one vehicle at a time. It was powered by up to 12 paddlers.*

One of the Boma's rickety paddle pontoons capable of carrying a vehicle

The carriers move along as fast as they possibly can to reach their destination, their aim being to off-shoulder their loads as soon as possible. The bigger boxes are slung on the middle of a pole and carried by two men. Lighter loads are managed by a single man and distributed so that he has an equal weight on each end of the pole. Instead of the pole resting on his shoulder, the carrier has a stick in his hand which he inserts between the pole and his shoulder, so taking some of the weight on his arm as well as on the shoulder.

For their exertions, the carriers are paid two shillings and seven pence[60] per day whether they are working or not. Between now and the end of the tour they will have about six days when they will remain in camp while I am either resting or touring villages near the camp.

Wednesday was a day of routine visiting of villages. In one, as we approached, a dreadful wailing was heard. We entered the village and were told that one of the men had died during the night. His womenfolk were leaning against the "lapa", the fence around the house and the small yard, lamenting not with tears but with wails. Two days later, when I passed through this village, life had returned to normal and the women sang a welcome. However, a hole had been made in the thatch of the dead man's hut to let out his spirit and all his goods had been taken outside.

[60]*14 pence in modern UK currency; multiply probably by about 50 to arrive at present-day spending power, ie £7.00.*

Allotment of loads to the carriers by the District Messengers

On Thursday I visited the Sioma or Ngonye Falls, the biggest on the Zambezi above the Victoria Falls. At present, the middle of the dry season, the river is comparatively low so we were able to clamber over great iron-stone slabs of rock at the edge of the large Falls and come up close to the really large cataracts. There, in a semi-circle, the Zambezi thunders over the edge of the precipice to create a monstrous, heaving white and yellow maelstrom below. White spume thrown up from the plunging waters drifted over us and provided a cool shower bath.

I had my camera with me and was able to take a few photographs. Reluctantly I came away and we picked our way back over the boulders. The Zambezi in the few miles above these Falls is much like a Scottish river being shallow, tumbling over rocks and stones in a most attractive way between banks that are also fairly steep and quite beautiful.

On Friday I shifted camp some eight miles north, close to a village which has just come to this silalo from another part of the District in search of better gardens. From there I had to walk six or seven miles to another village, also newly arrived, and also in search of new and better gardens. There was no path to the further village ▷

and we were guided through light forest by the headman of the closer one. After five miles or so we struck a path leading to the village we sought. At present it is on an island on the Zambezi but there were two villagers waiting with a large canoe to take us across.

Down river some herons were perched on a rock and my Messenger asked me to try a shot because everyone was in need of relish. So when the rest of the party had landed on the island my Messenger and I in the big canoe paddled by two villagers went downstream as slowly as the fast current would allow us towards where the herons were perched.

On both sides of the heron for some distance the water was shallow, running very fast over stones and rocks so when I fired it was from at least fifty yards. The result was that I only hit one which was quite good really. Unfortunately, I did not kill it outright and as we edged across the fast current towards it, it flopped into the water. Luckily the current took it into our path and the paddler was able to knock it on the head with his paddle and haul it on board.

On the way to the village our guide had found difficulty in finding the crossing place across a marshy valley. Eventually we did find it and having crossed he blazed a tree to show us where to cross on our way back. When we left the river on our return journey he decided not to follow the path along which we had walked for the last two or three miles but to cut across country which however was quite pathless. Believe it or not, we emerged from the light forest right at the blazed tree that I mentioned – surely evidence of his amazing sense of direction.

I was rather footsore and weary by the time I returned to camp having had a small blister on each foot from the beginning of the day and walked twenty miles or so into the bargain.

Today is Sunday so no work. But because the Falls are only three miles away I decided to go and visit them again. A very old man from a village near the Falls guided me across the rocks to the main Falls. Half way there when I felt I knew the rest of the way I thanked him and told him he could go home. He would not hear of this; he could not leave the "chief" to go on his own. So he hobbled along in ▶

front as before. At the Falls I sat on a rock, two or three feet from the edge of a drop into the boiling waters below, an action which made the old man fairly apoplectic with apprehension.

The old man guiding me to the Sioma Falls

On our way back we met a Kapasu whom the Induna had sent out to find if I was safe and two other villagers also come to see if I was safe. Very touching! The old man proceeded to tell them how I had wanted to go on by myself and how I had sat near the edge of the precipice to view the Falls and how he was frightened because if I fell over he would be blamed and put in prison! Great laughter from all.

I found out from this man that he remembered seeing Paramount Chief Lewanika passing by on his way up river and he pointed out the course of a canal that Lewanika had made around the Falls, along which his canoes could pass. This canal is about three miles long, cut through ironstone – very difficult to dig, my companions asserted.

Just to the north of my camp is the site of one used by Lewanika. The young trees that had been planted around it to form a fence are now huge trees, fifty to sixty feet high.

> Back in camp, I gave the old man five shillings, at which he was greatly delighted and proceeded to give the Royal Salute which I found embarrassing as I am pretty certain this should only be made to the Paramount Chief and a few senior chiefs e.g., the Mulena Mukwae, closely related to him by birth.

Lewanika was King of Barotseland from 1878 to 1912. In the 1880s he welcomed the first European missionaries to his country and in 1890 and 1900 he signed Concessions with the British South Africa Company. In these, the King exchanged mineral rights over his lands and the lands of chiefs who paid him tribute, for the protection of the British against his enemies both African and European. The old man must have remembered a journey that Lewanika made through this area some fifty or sixty years earlier.

Samwinga Camp
Lumbe Silalo
27 August 1960

It's Saturday evening and I am beginning my letter now. Will finish it tomorrow and send it off on Monday morning so that it should catch the Wednesday morning plane.

My mail brought me my Manchester Guardian Weekly and my latest order of books from Foyle's.

This last lot of books consists of three rather expensive tomes; I hope Foyle's forget to send the bill! They are Bullock's "Life of Bevin" Vol 1 (fifty shillings,), Schlesinger's "The Age of Roosevelt" Vol II (sixty-three shillings,) and Berenson's "The Italian Painters of the Renaissance" with four hundred plates (thirty-seven shillings and sixpence, a mere flea bite). Anyway, I won't have any lack of reading material on this trip.

The tour is continuing to be very enjoyable though it promises to be even longer than I expected at the outset and my feet have been giving me a bit of trouble. I rested yesterday instead of today

(Sunday) in order to give them a proper chance to heal and today they gave me no bother at all during my fifteen mile walk.

On Thursday I visited a Lower Primary School; as I hove in sight the whole school, lined up for my coming, marched toward me singing a lusty hymn. Just when I thought they were going to trample me underfoot to the strains of "Onward Christian Soldiers" they did a smart right wheel and their head teacher came marching forward to shake my hand.

There followed marching and counter-marching, the children singing lustily the while, exhorted by their teachers with the head teacher keeping them in step and his eye on them by walking backwards in front of them while peeping on a referee's whistle.

The culmination to all this occurred in front of the flagpole where more hymns were sung, finishing with a song entitled "Welcome to the District Officer". I doubt if I, standing before them all, provided a really satisfactory rallying symbol of Empire. For one thing, I was very conscious of the fact that I had forgotten to comb my hair before leaving camp that morning; for another, I was extremely dusty after walking ten miles along sandy paths and finally, my expression of thanks was expressed in extremely imperfect Lozi.

It is a funny (peculiar) thing that sometimes I can speak the Lozi language not too badly but on other occasions my brain just refuses to click.

Synchronised dancing led by the head teacher

Well, I have now completed the third week of my tour and there remains just over two weeks to go. I am afraid the writing is going to be worse than usual this week because the mosquitoes have driven me to take refuge under my mosquito net.

The tour continues to be most enjoyable and during the past week my feet have given me no trouble at all. In this silalo, many of the villages have two or more parts, each inhabited by a different tribe. Within these tribes there are two main groups. One, the original inhabitants of this area, are called Makwandi, Makwangwa, etc. and are essentially offshoots of the Lozi people. They live on the river and stream valleys and grow maize and sorghum and keep cattle.

The other group, the main tribe of which is the Mambunda, consists of tribes who came to settle in Barotseland thirty to forty years ago. So after leaving a village or approaching your camp you are liable to be accompanied by Makwandi and Mambunda women, one group on your right and the other on the left, each singing their traditional songs which are quite different in time and rhythm. As each group tries to out-sing the other the most tremendous cacophony ensues and my poor ears are close to bursting.

The Mambunda are less sophisticated than the Makwandi but despite that they are the more enterprising and it is they who are the store keepers and hawkers of the area.

In this silalo their enterprise extends to selling their wives to migrant workers who pass through their silalo on their way south to the large sawmills in the adjoining District and to Livingstone. The women accompany these men until they reach their place of employment and pick up men who are returning to their villages, so that they find employment both coming and going!

Nowadays much of the migrant labour travels to its destination by truck so one or two Mambunda villages which formerly resided close to a labour rest camp in this silalo have moved south into the next district and resettled close to the sawmills so that the women ▶

can find clients. Perhaps because of this immoral way of life, the Mambunda have very few children and in the next decade or two their numbers will decrease considerably.

The Mambunda, for all their immorality, are a very gay crowd. When they sing they dance and jig alongside you as well. Yesterday, a great crowd of them met me about a mile or two from camp and as we walked along they sang and every now and again rushed forward in front jigging and dancing. At camp they started up a dance while the Makwandi women stood by watching rather disapprovingly. I went and got my camera and took one or two photographs of the dancers. They were not a bit abashed but danced with even greater zest.

At my camp with Induna, his two kapasus, my Senior District Messenger, Kachana, and a merry chorus of local ladies

Outside some Mambunda huts are to be seen short poles, about two feet long, stuck in the ground. Sometimes these poles are painted but usually are just plain wood. Each one stands for a different ancestor spirit. When illness or some misfortune strikes at a man he consults a witchdoctor who divines who is responsible by throwing about a collection of sticks and boxes inside a basket. When he finishes, the pattern of sticks and boxes reveals the ill-disposed person or spirit. If a spirit is responsible, an offering of beer is placed on the appropriate pole.

The memorials to a Mambunda family's ancestors – equivalent to our tombstones (Photo: Rev JL Baumgartner)

In another Mambunda village I saw two poles, one wrapped round with rags, the other with a goat's skull on top: this marked the hut of the late headman. Today I visited a Mambunda village about four miles from camp. Just outside the village, in the forest, was a blackened ring of poles. This was what remained of the shelter where boys, when they have been circumcised, are put and must stay there for a month without stirring beyond it and no one can come to visit them. Two men guard the shelter. At the end of the month the parents of the boys come and set them free and a great feast is held, poor men bringing a hen and rich men either a goat or a cow, and the boys' shelter is burned down.

Some Mambunda collect honey by constructing drums made of bark, covered at the top with grass and with a piece of wood covering the bottom with a small hole pierced in it to allow the bees to get in and out. The drum is about four feet long and a foot in diameter and is placed horizontally on a branch high up in a tall tree. The honey is used as a relish and also in beer making.

The Watchtower Church is quite strong in this silalo and yesterday I passed through a village where they have built a church. The men clapped their hands in the traditional manner but the women refused to sing. I can't say that this upsets me but when it comes to refusing to take a share of compulsory communal work such as the repair of school buildings and boma camps then action has to be taken. Four men are languishing in Senanga prison at this moment for refusing to carry out the order of the indunas of this silalo to help repair the local school. Apparently, part of the Watchtower doctrine is that since all men are created equal, no man can be the servant of another, especially if he is not being paid to serve. For this reason, too, in certain areas they refuse to pay the traditional respects to chiefs and Provincial Administration officers.

Iluya Camp
Lumbe Silalo
10 September 1960

There was one day (Tuesday) this week when I was feeling off-colour and I trudged disconsolately along, half dead with the heat and every minute an hour. But the rest of the time my feet have had wings, the heat has bothered me very little and the hours spent walking seeming quite short.

On Friday we had to cross a bridge over a fairly big stream on our way to visit a couple of villages. On the return journey when we arrived at the stream the Indunas announced that this was a favourite bathing place of officers on tour. Being informed that there were no crocodiles nearby I needed no second invitation to strip and enter the water. Most of the Africans with me followed suit. They don't have strokes like the breaststroke or the crawl and use instead the doggie's paddle. However, they can submerge for a fantastically long time though my admiration of this feat was at least equalled by theirs' of my swimming ability as well as my daring in using the bridge as a diving platform. It really is a terrible pity that in such a hot country as this bathing should be fraught with danger from crocodiles in so many places.

There seem to be far more disputes and complaints discussed in my presence on this tour than on previous ones. Such things as the appointment of headmen, postal runners, schools, land and marriage disputes, etc. arise nearly every day. Maybe this is merely ▶

> by chance, maybe they feel that now that I have been in their country longer they can expect me to suggest an intelligent answer to their problems and maybe it is because my questions are more relevant to their problems.

Well I'm tired of writing and I see my District Messenger coming with some people who want to speak with me about matters that concern them.

A very sad death in Senanga

Senanga
22 September 1960

Well, I'm safely back from tour and my nose is at the grindstone for the new DC is making the tempo of life really speed up. It is now Thursday and I have been so busy since I came back on Sunday evening that I just have not found time to write. It is now mid-morning, the DC left yesterday to go to a conference in Mongu, I have got through the backlog of pressing work, so I am taking Govt's time to scribble a note before the plane leaves at midday.

Yesterday, Laurie and Sheila Jarrett left with their baby on the long way home. I was sorry to see them go as they were good company, though the new cadet and his wife who have just arrived seem very nice people. The new cadet is from Inverness, educated at Edinburgh University and possessed of a good Scots accent.

On Tuesday evening I was called out by an agitated hospital assistant who told me that the dresser at the Govt. dispensary in Senanga was very ill. There being no driver about I went and got a landrover and drove to the sick man's house. He had fallen ill at about 6 p.m. and by 7 he was delirious. When I reached his house at about 8.30 p.m. he was in a coma. At the hospital the sister in charge, Lucette Tholozan, tried to revive him with the injection of a stimulant but it was to no avail and he died at 10 p.m.

After he died I took back to his house four of his friends who had come up to the hospital. They and I were quite numb at his sudden ▶

death and when we reached the house one of them let out a terrible wail which was taken up by the considerable crowd of men, women and children who had gathered at the house. It was really quite heart-rending.

The European community, too, was greatly shocked for this man was well known. He was constantly coming to one of the District Officers at night to report a sick case requiring transport to hospital and he was perfectly well on the day he died. At the moment there is no doctor in Senanga so we have had to send his body to Mongu for a post-mortem. From the description of the illness that I passed over the radio-telephone, the MO in Mongu surmised that it might be methylated spirits poisoning – the poor chap might have decided to have a swig out of a bottle of the stuff in the dispensary.

I think the new DC will be good to work with; he is pretty tough in a gentle way and if I have any sense I shall learn a lot from him.

Senanga
26 September 1960

At the moment I have developed a yen for gardening and have indulged in a frenzy of pruning, transplanting and watering. Of course, at this time of year the thing that most needs doing in the garden is watering. I usually commence my labours at about 5pm when the sun has lost most of its heat until the back of 6 p.m. when dusk begins to descend. The temperature at this time of day is ideal, about seventy-five degrees I should say, and carting watering cans around the garden is good exercise if nothing else.

I went down to Old Man Harrington's on Saturday, the first time I had been there for about six weeks because of being away on tour. I must say I get on quite well with him. He has come to accept that although I'm a Scotsman I don't like whisky and that I don't see eye to eye with him on political matters. On Saturday, he excused me for my opinions by saying that of course the Government made me hold them!

He was speaking about his early days panning for gold in Southern Rhodesia and of one occasion when the tribesmen rose up in revolt near where they, a mere handful of Europeans, were miles from the nearest township. One man rode off for aid while the rest formed their wagons into a laager. The Africans came down, killed their donkeys and wrecked their equipment but did not try to kill anyone and at last a detachment of British South Africa Company Police arrived and relieved them.

"It was quite exciting", said the Old Man. "In those days they did not give a damn about partnership; the only things they asked of prospective settlers was that they could shoot and ride a horse."

Arthur Harrington with Flip Paterson[61] (photo: Ranald Paterson)

---

[61] *The wife of Ranald Paterson, the Cadet who replaced Laurie Jarrett.*

Gosh, it is hot! So much so that I am squatting on the steps in front of our house because inside the Tilley lamps make the temperature uncomfortably high. Maximum day temperatures have been hovering between ninety-seven and one hundred degrees[62] for the last fortnight, the skies devoid of clouds and little breeze to stir the leaves. I was quite fortunate in finishing my tour before the hot season, late this year, really got under way.

There is little news except that I continue to work like stink under this new DC; he certainly finds plenty of work for us to do. Of course, having more experience now I am able to take on more responsible tasks. For example, I have been given the task of preparing the draft Estimates of Revenue and Expenditure of the Nalolo Native Treasury for 1961 for presentation to the Saa-Sikalo Kuta[63] and the Mulena Mukwae when the DC and I go up to Nalolo in about a fortnight's time.

On Thursday, the Head Clerk, Mr Nyumbu, and his wife are coming over for dinner. He is housed in a new "superior" type of house for senior African civil servants which stands in lofty isolation about half a mile from the African compound and about two hundred yards behind the main row of European quarters. His position is a lonely one, betwixt and between, as he remarked to me this evening when I stopped to speak to him in his garden but he consoled himself that this was to be preferred to living with the plebs "for it is nicer to be near good company"!

His wife cannot speak English and probably has never sat down at a European table before. Anyway, it should provide me with a good chance to brush up my Lozi.

The DC goes on tour tomorrow, so I shall be Acting DC.

---

[62] 41°C – 42°C.
[63] *The most important assembly within the Barotse Native Government in Senanga District which was both the supreme court and the advisory council to the Mulena Mukwae.*

Letter to Christian Fraser

Senanga
8 October 1960

My dear Christian

Thanks very much for your last letter which reached me on the second last (thirty-fourth) day of my silalo tour.

May I anticipate a Christmas present from you and name it too? I would very much like a photograph of you; I have a very poor visual memory and in your case I would wish it to be refreshed.[64]

On these silalo inspections, apart from counting the people and their livestock, I listen to their grievances about the Government and then go back to the office and try to get the wheels turned so that some of these grievances may be redressed. For example, in one silalo that I toured this year the villagers complained about bad drinking water. They live in the savannah far from running water, finding their water from shallow wells which they dig in the sandy soil. These wells are very short-lived. Wind, rain, people and cattle all conspire to break down the walls and eventually the wells fill up with sand. Cattle and wild animals, besides slithering in for a drink also pollute the water.

To cut a long story short, voluminous correspondence between our office and the Provincial Health Inspector has at last resulted in the appearance of a couple of sets of well moulds and ten miners' helmets. When another six sets of moulds arrive plus a gaffer who knows how to make and site wells, the people of this particular region will be in sight of having better water.

You will note that the keynote is sand. Barotseland is on the edge of the Kalahari Desert and were it not for the numerous streams and rivers flowing into the Zambezi, this country would indeed be a desert.

▶

[64] *This was a rare insight into my thinking about Christian. She meant much more to me than a mere correspondent. I felt an emotional need to have her photograph by my bedside (there was nothing wrong with my visual memory!). She took about six months to send it to me, probably because it meant having to go to a photo studio to have her photo taken by a professional. She did not have a camera of her own; she is and always has been technology-averse!*

> The Monckton Commission Report is causing a considerable stir to say the least of it. The night before last, Welensky made a very truculent broadcast in which he endeavoured to minimize the importance of the Report, "One of many documents that will have to be considered at the Review Conference". He also tried to push the Report's other recommendations on the franchise and legislature, etc., to the background by protesting about the breach by the Commissioners of their terms of reference in considering the possibility of secession of member states from the Federation.
>
> It is surprising that some of the European newspapers, usually monstrously pro-Welensky, have come out against him on this point. It may be that the Europeans are beginning to realise that come what may, Nyasaland and Northern Rhodesia will secede unless something drastic is done to change the present Federal set-up. It is quite impossible to say to Dr Banda, leader of the main political party in Nyasaland, that he will not be allowed to secede if he has already made up his mind to do so.
>
> Yours
>
> Callum

The report of the Monckton Commission published a few days before my letter astonished the people of the Federation, and caused dismay amongst the European population of Northern Rhodesia and the royal elite of Barotseland.

In spite of the conservatism of most of its members the Commission went outside the terms of reference agreed between the British and Federal Governments which excluded the consideration of secession from the Federation of any of the three member countries. Instead, the Commission concluded that the African opposition in the Northern territories was so strong that the Federation could no longer continue in its present form. It recommended that there should be parity of representation between members of the Federal Assembly elected by the higher (European) role and those elected on the lower (African) one. Moreover, it asserted that in the Northern Rhodesia Legislature there should be a majority of members elected by African voters, similar to what had already been agreed for Nyasaland earlier in the year.

Few politicians in Britain and the Rhodesias could have had any doubt that the Federation's days were numbered. Only Sir Roy Welensky, the Federal Prime Minister, and his die-hard white supporters clung desperately to the belief that the Federation could continue under white rule.

Senanga

9 October 1960

The event of the last week has been rain. For the past two days the skies have been overcast and much rain has fallen. What a difference the absence of the sun makes to the temperature. During these last two days the temperature has been cool even at midday; there has probably been a drop of nearly thirty degrees.[65]

The rain has been eagerly awaited; no doubt gods, pagan and Christian, have also been beseeched. As one village headman said to me on Monday when the skies first began to hint of rain "We pray the Lord Jesus to bring us rain". The earth exudes a rich, manure smell and the dust is laid. The people don't seem to mind getting soaked to the skin and no doubt feeling pretty chilled as well for the rain represents their salvation. Planting is getting underway in earnest so I reckon all fingers will be crossed to ward off drought. Everyone seems to be in a good humour and cheery greetings are exchanged.

On Monday at 11.30 a.m. I set off for Nalolo at a brisk pace up the Mongu road and after about one and three quarter hours I branched off the main road and set off on an old road across the plain to Nalolo. The track was difficult to follow ...Then a tyre punctured and we had to change the wheel. Eventually we reached the river at a spot about a quarter of a mile south of Nalolo. To get to Nalolo you have to cross the Zambezi by a Government maintained ferry canoe but unfortunately there was a small lake cum river stretching well inland separating us from the ferry. By this time, it was 3.30 p.m. and though I had intended staying at the Nalolo mission station that night I decided to make for Namushakende because I did not like to ask the missionary, a nursing sister whom I did not know, for hospitality at such short ▷

notice. So I sent off my Messenger on foot to tell the acting President of the Nalolo Kuta that I would be arriving next day and then got a guide to lead me on to the Nalolo-Namushakende track. So to Namushakende where David Salmon put me up for the night.

Next morning, I set off with the Provincial Water Engineer to inspect some canals around Nalolo. Just as we reached the Zambezi opposite the Nalolo mission station we saw the nursing sister being ferried across the river in her paddle barge and seeing us she turned back and invited us to cross with her and partake of tea, which we duly did.

Then on to the Kuta where the acting President and the Works Induna were waiting for us. It took about a couple of hours for them to get a canoe and paddlers ready to take us to our destination and even then we would not have set off but for my insistence that we should, come what may, despite the thunder clouds which were building up.

We set off in the canoe along a canal for about quarter of a mile until we reached the river. There we disembarked and walked along the bank for about half a mile till we reached our destination. We had inspected a dried-up channel which fills during the flood season and which it is hoped to deepen and make a permanent water course across a wide loop of the Zambezi. The PWE's Lozi is confined to one word "welcome" or "how do you do?" which he always says twice, mispronounced, for good measure. So I had to translate while he chattered on about water flows and levels and so forth.

We crossed the river again and started haring all over the Plain in the PWE's landrover inspecting present and projected canals and eventually got back to Namushakende about 5 p.m. which won me two shillings and sixpence from David Salmon, who had wagered that I could not keep the PWE, a notoriously lazy man, working past midday. My enthusiasm for waterworks and deference to his professional expertise, however, seemed to imbue the PWE with considerable enthusiasm with the result that the day's proceedings went on considerably longer than I considered desirable.

A newly dug canal. The sticks protruding from the sides of the canal show the tasks set for the diggers by their foreman

At Namushakende I picked up my landrover and set off for Nalolo. There I stayed at the mission guest house as the guest of the nursing sister at the mission dispensary.

These nurses who staff the mission dispensaries are the poorest paid, the hardest worked but the most highly respected of all the Europeans in this country. The demands of the job are so great that few manage to keep such a lively sense of humour or optimistic a view of life as she. I must say my visit there was quite a tonic.

Indeed, these nurses did the work of doctors because their isolation meant that they had to respond to all types of medical emergency.

My last visit to Arthur Harrington

> It is now terribly late because I got in late and because I visited the Old Man (Harrington), no one else being able or willing to do so tonight.

This is the last reference to Arthur Harrington in my letters. I was visiting him with less regularity largely because I was on village inspection tours so often or away from Senanga to supervise the Treasury in Nalolo and to sit exams in Mongu. It was on one of the occasions when I was on my own with him that I had the temerity to question the old man about his attitudes to Africans.

"How can you really have such a poor opinion of them when you have spent a lifetime training them in carpentry and boat building, in repairing vehicles, in having children by them and so forth?", I threw at him. He was not usually lost for words but this time he was rendered speechless by my outburst. Instead of taking umbrage he smiled, stroked his moustache and said "Mmmm".

He died on the 27th May 1961 while I was attending a month-long course in Lusaka and so I was not at his funeral. I heard it was a momentous affair and many Lozi were there to pay their respects and give him a chief's farewell.

On my return to Senanga in September 2012 I met one of the grandsons of Arthur Harrington, called William Harrington. He was a Member of Parliament and had been Minister for Tourism in the previous Zambian Government. He told me that his grandfather used to walk hand in hand with him across the family compound. He remembered the old man as a very good grandfather to him.

Which just goes to show how little I knew the "old man" although I did realise intuitively that his overt racism was partly at least to satisfy the prejudices of his European acquaintances.

I have passed the Oral part of my Lower Lozi! Thank goodness! I was the first candidate to be taken for the Lower Lozi and when they had finished quizzing me I asked the adjudicator when I would know the result. He told me to hang around outside for a minute or two. In a short while he came out of the examination room and gave me the thumbs up sign.

It is quite a relief to have passed this because it is one of the compulsory exams which have to be passed before confirmation as a District Officer at the end of my first two years' service. In fact, I have now taken and passed all my compulsory exams.

I have decided to get down to work for my Higher Lozi Examinations which come round in April again so I shall aim to sit them then. I have to pass a Higher Language exam or two Lowers in my first six years' service, so better now than later.

I have also determined to do some serious law work with a view to taking my exam next August. The DC has said he will give me what help he can but says that I am rather handicapped by being on a bush station and not being able to sit in on a High Court or oft-meeting Magistrates Court to witness court procedure and evidencing.

Last Tuesday I had a game of football for the local Welfare Association team. This was the first time the WA had fielded a team for some years and because I had been instrumental in reviving it and because it was not then known how bad a footballer I was I was picked for the team. The game was against the Trades School and I and Ranald Paterson were given a big hand by the assembled throng when we trotted onto the field.

They were soon disillusioned; Ranald and I floundered leaden-footed in our boots in the soft sand while the bare-footed Africans danced around us. Moreover, though we were fit and though it was 5 p.m. it was still darned hot. After about fifteen minutes I began to feel sick and gradually my throat became all choked up with saliva. I had to retire ignominiously to vomit in the bushes nearby. So ended my return to the world of football. ▶

> Next time I play I shall put in some practice beforehand.

The Barotse Native Government is passing through a pretty troubled state just now. It has passed an order giving it power to deport non-residents as it wills. In the past month it has been able to chuck out Kaunda and several other UNIP[66] partisans. I have just heard that the Barotse National Council has passed a resolution asking the British Crown to allow it to secede from Northern Rhodesia. The coming year looks as though it is going to be quite eventful.

Supervising the accounts of the Nalolo Treasury

Senanga
31 October 1960

No rest for the wicked – that's my motto for the past week. On Thursday after grinding away quite enjoyably for the previous few days in the office, I set off for Nalolo to talk with the Departmental Indunas and the Kuta about various items in the 1961 Estimates for the Nalolo Sub-Treasury that I was in the throes of preparing.

We bumped up the main Senanga to Mongu road; the driver drove with zealous caution with the result that it took us nearly two and a half hours to cover the first forty-five miles of our journey. Actually when he is on his own we have reason to believe that he is reckless in the extreme in his driving.

I got a bit fed up with our snail-like progress especially as going slow does not really increase your comfort except when the really deep holes in the road are encountered; then it is certainly advisable to dip in and out slowly. But the beastly corrugations that one encounters over the length of the road are best taken at speed in my opinion – i.e. the sooner you can step out of your car[67] at your destination the better.

▶

[66] UNIP (United National Independence Party) was the successor to ZANC, the party banned by the Governor of NR five months before I arrived in the country. Its President was Kenneth Kaunda.

[67] I should have written landrover. No ordinary car could have coped with these Senanga district roads.

Thus returning to Senanga, over the same distance I took one and a half hours at what on Barotse roads is the almost breakneck speed of thirty miles per hour.

To continue; after two and a half hours of enduring this wizard of the wheel I took over and drove along a side road by the edge of the Plain close to the Mulena Mukwae's flood season capital to interview an old induna about the location of a canal that we want to reopen. Then up onto the main road again which runs along the west of the forest edge that bounds the Plain and drove like the wind to Namushakende where the track to Nalolo starts. However, it was nearly 6 p.m. when I got to Namushakende so I decided to spend the night there with David Salmon.

I eventually got to bed sometime after 1 am and next morning felt dog tired when I got up at 7. By 8 I had packed my bags, put them in the landrover and set off down the hillside on which Namushakende is situated onto the track across the Plain to Nalolo. This track is pretty formidable and only a landrover would be able to get through in one piece. Sandpits, sand dunes and bridges with holes in them faced us and dared us go on but advance we did, no bother at all. The landrover may not be the most comfortable of vehicles but it must be the most nearly invincible in the face of Nature's dirtiest tricks.

So to Nalolo itself and along to the offices where the Treasury Clerk and his assistant were surprised if not delighted at my arrival. I got down to work with them until a Kapasu arrived with the news that the Indunas had foregathered in the Kuta building and earnestly desired my distinguished presence (I doubt if these were their actual words). I stuffed my papers and files into my briefcase and, preceded by my Messenger, entered the Kuta.

It was about 11.30 a.m. when we started and at 1.15 the Indunas asked if they might go and have lunch. We started again at 2 p.m. and went on until nearly 4.30 and all that time, apart from about a dozen words in English, I managed to keep going in Lozi, though three of the Indunas had a good command of English. Looking back on it on my return to Namushakende I could not help feeling rather chuffed at my performance.

▶ To be honest the matters discussed did not really require an intimate knowledge of the language, the discussion centring on provision of new buildings and repair of existing ones, digging of canals, making of roads, ordering of equipment and so on.

Next day, Saturday, I set off to Nalolo hoping to finish my work there about midday. Unfortunately, I had to slave on until after two, making the Treasury Clerk and his Assistant work like galley slaves as well. They are a most clueless twosome. The Assistant has been working about six months and has not yet found out how to enter up the Cash Books and Votes Ledger so I did my best to teach him there and then.

At one point in the morning I had to wait for the Treasury Clerk to finish off some small piece of work before getting him to work with me on some other matter. He was engaged on putting his signature and date stamp on some requisitions that I had written out and that he had then typed. To see him at it you would think he was taking a Yoga course on contemplation so long did his pen hover over the paper and with such slow deliberation did he impress the date stamp upon his signature.

It is also an education watching his Assistant adding up a page of figures. He adds the first two amounts to arrive at a sub-total, then adds the next amount to the sub-total to make a new sub-total and so on down the page. The result is that he takes about three hours to add up a cash book page of about forty entries and at the end he cannot be relied to have the correct answer!

Luckily the old man who is Treasury Clerk is good and accurate with figures, otherwise the place would be a greater shambles than at present.

From around this time I was made responsible for supervising the Native Treasury accounts at Nalolo. The DC, Ian Edye, was a stickler for detail so I had to make monthly visits to Nalolo to see that the monthly trial balance was carried out accurately, to meet departmental Indunas and to meet and brief the Mulena Mukwae and the Ishee Kwandu about topics of current interest and importance to them. By then I was the most experienced of the junior PA officers and the only one who was reasonably competent in Lozi. I was able to conduct my business without recourse to an interpreter.

Here I am on tour again, this time ensconced in a cottage tent with Ranald Paterson, the other Cadet on the station. It is nearly 9.30 p.m. and my companion is sleeping soundly beneath a pea-green mosquito net while I slouch under my milk-white one writing this letter while the wireless rattles on to provide me company.

Ranald is staying with me for the first four days of the tour just to see how to set about doing this sort of thing. He has already gone on tour for four days with the DC but obviously the DC feels this is not quite good enough and that Ranald should get the chance of benefiting from the experience of a Lozi expert!

This morning I counted ten villages. The people of one asked permission to sing a hymn to me after the business of the day was over to which I agreed. In each village I asked if they would have sufficient food to last them till they harvested their early crops at the beginning of January. Nearly all said they would be dying of hunger by December but when I looked in the grain bins when visiting some of these villages this afternoon I found there was a good deal of grain in them; in fact, some of them were groaning they were so full.

Three grain bins on stilts out of the way of predators.
(Photo: Rev JL Baumgartner)

▶ After I had finished counting the villages all the people gathered together under a huge tree while I and the indunas dealt with their questions and complaints and during which I tried to persuade them of the reasonableness of a new tax on fishing nets. They all seemed reasonably satisfied with my explanation or maybe it was just mystification caused by my Lozi which made them automatically assent to all that I said.

It was then that we had the hymn singing. The villagers formed up facing three conductors, one dressed in a pair of green furry-textured overalls and bright tie, another in black trousers and black waist coat and the third in unremarkable clothes apart from a shockingly lurid tie. The choir sang in three-part harmony, at first a trifle self-consciously and then more freely as they gained confidence from their energetic conductors who waved their arms gracefully while one made similar graceful oscillations with his feet.

The singing was beautiful, to a PMS tune I think, but sung with a wonderful rhythm half suggestive of drums and even jazz. The eyes of one fairly elderly lady standing in the front of the choir were filled with delight and she swayed her arms to and fro in time with the music, getting real hep, man.

Most of the choir members seemed to be getting a great kick out of their singing and the faith that inspired it. These people have got an innocent approach to life that puts our sophistication to shame.

For me, at any rate, it is incidents such as this that make life here so rewarding and worthwhile.

On a Silalo Tour by Landrover

Sikopo Camp,
Senanga
20 November 1960

For the past week clouds have covered the sky and for the first four days a good deal of rain fell. What a wonderful difference this makes to the temperature. The daytime temperatures must have fallen to about sixty-five degrees and in the evenings it was decidedly chilly. One immediate difference is that you no longer sweat so that your consumption of water is markedly reduced and you find, too, that you have to cut down the amount of salt you add to your food.

I have been touring in an extensive plain that cuts into this silalo starting from the Zambezi and continuing for about seventy miles till the Angola border is reached. It widens as it goes away from the Zambezi but where I was touring it had a width of about ten miles. It is called the Matabele Plain. It teems with game. On Thursday while driving across it we came close to a large herd of tsessebe and a couple of wildebeest (gnu). They let us approach to within about fifty yards and then turned tail and ran. We gave chase and what a hilarious one it was. The beasts galloped in headlong panic every now and again plunging sideways as though attempting to sidestep whizzing bullets.

The landrover's occupants were in a frenzy of laughter and excitement especially as we came to within twenty or thirty yards of the beasts with a chance of getting in a shotgun blast if one of them stumbled or was driven to a standstill. The wildebeest especially seemed to be making heavy weather of the proceedings and their heavy black flanks, black beards and flying manes were visibly dripping fearful sweat. It was a bit like giving chase to a group of bearded and venerable Divinity Professors.

Eventually three tsessebe broke away from the main herd and we gave chase hoping that away from the rest they would despair and tire. We chased on for another two miles until they doubled round on their tracks and got onto rougher ground where they left us behind and made their getaway.

▶

> The tsessebe run with a funny awkward action, knocking their bottoms high in the air with every kick of their rear legs. Their bottoms are a lighter colour than the rest of their bodies as though they had been scrubbed to the bone when young by their over-zealous mothers.

Senanga

8 November 1960

I got word yesterday that my application for local leave has been approved by the Resident Commissioner. Yippee! This will come at a very opportune time for during the last four months in particular I have been working very hard.

On this present tour there has hardly been a day when I have worked less than twelve hours a day in order to return the landrover to the Boma as soon as possible. During the past two days when I have had to take to Shank's pony for the first time on this tour I have walked close on fifty miles and in consequence felt like Shredded Wheat after the milk has been poured on it. Yesterday I was about as exhausted as ever I've been by the time I got back to camp. Though I felt stiff, sore and tired by the time I reached camp today I am now feeling a good deal refreshed with a bath and a meal behind me.

Going on tour of a silalo from village to village by landrover was quite a contrast to the foot touring I had done until then. Why the change? Two factors, I think; the first one was that Ian Edye, the new DC, would have done what he thought was best for the smooth running of his District. If that meant accelerating the speed with which the silalo tours were done so that the district officer would be available in or out of the office to do more important work, then that is what he would have decided. Around that time, his boss in Mongu, the Resident Commissioner Gervas Clay whose bright idea it was to return to foot-touring of villages, was succeeded by a younger man with much more modern ideas.

▶ Last week I told you how we chased a herd of tsessebe and wildebeest. This week we were chased by herds of women! This event took place at nearly every village we visited by landrover. As you know, the women in these parts like to sing important visitors like me off the premises. When we have finished inspecting the huts and counting and vaccinating the people against smallpox,[68] we fill the landrover to capacity with people begging a lift and chug slowly at walking pace out of the village. The women and children swarm along behind. The landrover then speeds up slightly after traversing the gardens that often surround a village so that the women are forced to break into a trot to keep up with us. We increase speed again until the women have to sprint to keep up. The Africans in the back of the landrover exhort them to keep going so as to pay their proper respects to the District Officer. They think this is all a terrific joke and for a few hundred yards we steer an erratic course because the driver is busy looking out of the window to see how the pursuit of the belles is going.

Today I visited a canal that is being dug to drain a valley leading into the Barotse Plain. It gives one quite a kick to see a positive thing like this being done and it should enable a good deal of land to be made available for maize growing.

Smallpox Eradication Campaign

[68] *This was part of the WHO campaign to eliminate smallpox throughout the world. It succeeded through the efforts on the ground of local administrations like ours.*

My tour finished last Wednesday and in the four days, Sunday to Wednesday, I walked about eighty-five miles which made up for the idleness in terms of walking of the previous days. Our work gradually brought us closer to Senanga and as this happened we came upon more and more educated Africans – i.e. those who had four or more years of primary education, and soldiers and clerks home on leave. In these villages where the new ideas, hates, and ferments are becoming visible the traditional respects are much more slackly observed.

I must say it irked me sometimes when people did not show the customary deference when I entered their village. How proud and vain you can get in this job! I am tempted sometimes to act the high Tory but luckily I usually manage to keep my annoyance to myself though I must admit to being curt with lounging youths on occasion – and to think that I am but a youth myself! Oh, the cheek and the folly of it! However, political changes are going to corrode "likute" (respect) pretty quickly so I may still be saved from overweening pride.

In the villages beside the river the people complained that a couple of hippos were destroying the growing maize in the gardens. I walked through some of these gardens and sure enough there were the massive dinner plate depressions in the soil and stalks of maize shorn off half way to the ground. The villagers want to shoot them but I told them to try and scare them off before a hunter was commissioned. Quite apart from the desire to preserve the fauna of Africa is the fact that hippos perform a useful function in this country by helping to keep waterways clear.

We reached the Zambezi just opposite the Boma and as it was near lunch time and we had one or two villages to visit some distance away I invited the two Indunas who were with me to come across and have lunch with me.

They had never handled knives or forks before and believe me the handling of these utensils is an art which long practice conceals from most Europeans. For all the contortions that the Indunas

▶

performed to cut their meat and transfer it to their mouths I think they enjoyed themselves. They had too much dignity to feel embarrassed and we did not pretend not to notice the difficulties of eating European fashion.

I come in for a bit of ribbing from some of the Europeans for indulging in this sort of fraternising; the most common jibe is that I just embarrass an African when I ask him to dine and that the experience is only a humiliating one for him. They may be correct but each person must do what he thinks right and respect the differing principles of others.

A couple of days after the end of this tour, I set out for Nalolo where I found that the Mulena Mukwae and her leading indunas had just arrived back after a two-month visit to the Paramount Chief's capital at Lealui. The day I arrived, some Mambunda had arrived to salute her and they pounded their drums while their Makishi dancers in their weird costumes and masks danced the day long. Their costumes are made of root fibres and are very tight so that it is a wonder the dancers manage to breathe.

Makishi dancers at Nalolo

I noticed that during the heat of the day, only one Makishi dancer performed at a time and only for fifteen or twenty minutes and then a helper would come and drag him away to be replaced by another. The costumes are dyed in geometrical patterns which emphasize and exaggerate the bodily undulations of the dancer. This together with the diabolical mask presents a rather horrifying sight. These Makishi dancers normally perform at their tribe's circumcision ceremonies, no doubt to instil fear and awe and a sense of mystery into the proceedings.

At Nalolo I worked with the Treasury Clerk, talked to the Kuta and had morning and afternoon tea with the Mulena Mukwae. My Lozi stood the strain fairly well. After afternoon tea the Mulena Mukwae decided she would like to go outside her palace and watch the dancers. After two indunas had crawled into our presence and removed three canvas chairs for us, the Mulena, the Ishee Kwandu and myself went out in procession with the Mulena's royal band leading the way – three drummers and a man playing a wooden xylophone with a disdainful sneer on his face.

The Mulena Mukwae's band: a xylophone and three drummers (photo: Rev JL Baumgartner)

We sat down, me in the middle with the Mulena on my right and the Ishee Kwandu on my left, flanked by Indunas kneeling on mats to the right and to the left of us in accordance with their traditional positions in the hierarchy.

Beyond the indunas a crowd of people made a circle inside which the Makishi dancers pranced and gambolled in relays of two or three at a time while the drummers strained and sweated to keep the rhythm going. Oh for a movie camera and tape recorder to have recorded the colour and movement and noise of the scene!

On the mat beside the Mulena Mukwae squatted a pair of elderly court jesters, one the wit, the other the butt, and it was interesting to see the liberties they were allowed to take – for example shouting to elderly indunas to get up and show the dancers how really to dance.

On a Crocodile Hunt

21 December 1960

I suppose that I wrote last Tuesday from Senanga. On the Wednesday, in the late afternoon, I set off for Namushakende where I spent the evening with David Salmon.[69] On Thursday I went across the Plain to Nalolo where I had to check the books of some Court Clerks and talk about some matters with various departmental Indunas.

At lunchtime that day, Trudy, the nursing sister at the Mission dispensary told me that the week before she had gone crocodile hunting with a local chief. I asked her if she could fix up a similar expedition for me.

That evening it rained and blew but about 9 p.m. the rain stopped and the wind eased. At about 10pm I was able to set off with Chief Lukama on the crocodile hunt. He formerly ruled an area in Senanga District, just as the Mulena Mukwae rules now, but his jurisdiction was removed by the Government because it did not fit into their scheme of things. He is a young man who has extensive gardens, a large herd of cattle and his own capital. People salute him as they would a full chief like the Paramount Chief and the Mulena Mukwae.

He had finished his hunting the night before and was returning home the next day but when he heard I wanted to come out with him to hunt crocodiles he agreed to stay on for another day.

His equipment was a rifle, two shotguns and two powerful lamps worked off a six-volt battery.

We walked for an hour and passing through villages we collected paddlers for our expedition. Eventually we reached a large lake ▶

[69] *I don't know how many times I turned up on David's doorstep to ask for a meal and a bed for the night. Fortunately for me David's base at the Namushakende Provincial Development Centre was close to my route to Nalolo where I spent an inordinate amount of time in supervising the Treasury and meeting with the Kuta and the Mulena Mukwae. It did not take too much ingenuity to make my travel arrangements so that, at the very least, I could call on David on the night before I was due at Nalolo and at the end of my stint there, to stay a night with him on the way back to Senanga. It was refreshing to chat with him. His political views chimed with mine and we also shared a love of football. He worshipped 12 gods – the Stoke City first team and their manager! My support for my own team, Aberdeen, was a very lukewarm thing compared with his passion for Stoke.*

linked to the Zambezi, the spot chosen for our hunting. We set off in two large dugout canoes. In the front of the first, the chief crouched with his guns resting in the bottom of the canoe in front of him. In his hand he held one of his powerful electric lamps which he swung along the opposite shore of the lake to pick up the eyes of crocodiles lying amongst the reeds.

I sat just behind the chief and behind me were two paddlers. In the canoe behind were three paddlers, their job being to come to our help when a crocodile was shot and if it was too big to take inside the canoe they would drag it to the shore.

The strong beam soon picked up a pair of red points of light in the middle of the lake – this indicated a big croc but as we paddled silently towards it they disappeared because the wind had blown our smell or some slight sound to the croc and made it submerge. We paddled on and every now and again the searchlights picked out two white pinpricks of light indicating a small croc or more occasionally a red pair but our luck was out because the wind was very variable and never steady from one direction. Again and again we came up very close to a crocodile and at the last minute it would get a whiff of us and submerge.

The chief's tactics were to approach within an arm's length of the croc and fire a shotgun at its head at almost point-blank range. This required a favourable wind and an extremely silent and cautious approach. The paddlers reversed their paddles so that it was the handles that went into the water. Our canoes moved without a splash or a sound.

During this period, we only shot one crocodile, a small one of about four feet in length. The crocodiles were busy fishing much of the time; you could see the water lilies swaying as the crocodiles swept after fish and the fish desperate to escape kept leaping out of the water sometimes vaulting our canoe in the process. One actually landed inside our canoe where it was seized by one of the paddlers and killed. You can perhaps guess how silently we moved by the fact that we passed fish that lay still in the water until the paddle actually touched the water beside them, and duck from which we were only five yards away before they heard us and flew away.

We left this lake about 3 a.m. and retraced our steps until we came to a lagoon near the mission station where I was spending the night. The chief decided to hunt here having heard that there were two large crocodiles that were destroying the villagers' fishing nets. Very shortly we picked up two red glowing embers a long way off – obviously a big croc. We slid gently forward, the light held steady on the crocodile's glowing eyes and snout which has a phosphorescent nostril which attracts fish right into the croc's mouth. The wind had dropped and as we came close we saw a huge crocodile lying comatose. We slid up until we almost bumped into it and it was not till then that the chief discharged his shotgun into the crocodile's head.

The crocodile rolled over and then sank under the canoe and came up on the other side, its white belly showing. The paddler hurled the harpoon at the crocodile's body but it failed to penetrate it. The body slowly sank and when I threw the harpoon I only succeeded in hastening the crocodile's descent to the bottom of the lagoon. We could tell its position by the stream of bubbles that came to the surface, for the crocodile has air sacks which it alternately fills or empties if it wishes to float or submerge.

We prodded around trying to drive the harpoon into its body and lift it to the surface and eventually we succeeded. We dragged it

Chief Lukama with his giant crocodile

towards the bank and then levered the huge body to the surface with the paddles. Then the chief fired two rounds from his rifle into its brain to make sure it was dead.

With one paddler grasping its tail we made for the bank of the lagoon just below the mission making laborious progress for the crocodile was fourteen feet long and as heavy as an ox. We landed it at 5 a.m. and later in the morning when it was fully light the villagers came to gape for this was the second biggest croc that the chief had ever shot.

Trudy the nurse at Nangoma Mission Clinic close to Nalolo with the crocodile shot by Chief Lukama

I must say a few words about Trudy. She was Swiss, full of joie de vivre, and good-looking. It was typical of her that she would go crocodile hunting, a night-time activity not without its perils. She was on a short term posting to the medical centre at the mission station close to Nalolo, replacing Lucette Tholozan who was also good company and always ready to welcome visitors like me to their guest house and provide a good evening meal.

Trudy visited the outlying medical dispensaries from her normal base at Lukona in Kalabo District by walking in the cool of the night from one dispensary to the next, each one being a night's walk apart. To warn snakes of her approach she would keep up a constant whistling of every tune she knew to give them time to get out of her way!

I was half in love with her and her memorable way of treating life. On that visit she set up a table and a couple of chairs on the bank of the Zambezi which flowed past the mission station, and there we ate our evening meal to the music of Edith Piaf on her wind-up gramophone.

On local Leave outside Barotseland

Fort Rosebery

28 December 1960

Dear Mum and Dad,

Well here I am safe and sound in Fort Rosebery, in Angus's house having arrived here yesterday evening on two weeks' local leave.

I have just spent a week in Fort Rosebery and how quickly and hectically it has passed! But first let me describe how I arrived here.

In Mongu I picked up the Hillman Minx belonging to the Farrans[70] which had been put into the Govt Workshops the day before for a change of oil and had been filled up with petrol. Then I remembered that I had left some car tools given to me by Kit Farran at Namushakende so I had to go back there in the Minx.

Immediately after lunch I set off for Mankoya, one hundred and forty miles away. For the first twenty miles I bowled along merrily on a smooth broad highway surfaced with laterite, a red gravelly material and then onto a dirt road which had some very bad patches on it, especially where road gangs had been laying down fresh clay and laterite for the new surface. At one point I stuck in deeply rutted earth and just as I did so a landrover approached from the opposite direction and stopped, turned round and towed me for half a mile till I got clear. This was very fortunate for me as this was the only landrover I encountered on my journey to Mankoya.

For the next seventy miles the road was good and bad with the bad predominating and midway through this section the oil-warning light switched on. I stopped the car and, looking underneath, was horrified to see oil streaming out of the sump, the plug at the bottom having fallen out.

Jameson and I searched the road for about half a mile to find this plug, but in vain. So I stuffed up the hole with a cloth and filled up with the gallon of oil that very luckily I was carrying as reserve. The oil seeped through the cloth very slowly but it served its purpose till I reached Mankoya.

[70] Kit and Lorraine Farran, the Senanga Livestock Officer and his wife.

At the same time, I had a look at the petrol tank because I had noticed that we had been using petrol at an alarming rate, even allowing for having to drive now and again in second and third gear. Sure enough, there was a leak in the petrol tank and a thin stream of petrol was spurting out. I smeared the leak with car wax polish which stopped the leak till I reached Mankoya.

Next morning, I went along to a store where I filled up with petrol, soaped up the leak in the petrol tank and fitted a wooden plug into the sump. This makeshift arrangement did the job till I put the car into a garage at Ndola.

Thence to Broken Hill, 305 miles, which I did over very good roads on the whole in six and a half hours. It was really marvellous to get onto tarmac road once again when I was about sixty miles from Broken Hill. It almost persuaded me I was home in civilised Britain!

At Broken Hill I found where the Edwards[71] were staying without much difficulty. They seemed extremely pleased to see me. First I arranged with Ian accommodation for Jameson for the period of my stay in Fort Rosebery because I did not want to drag him away up there especially as there are many Lozi in Broken Hill and only a handful in FR.

It was about one hundred and thirty miles to Kitwe where I met Joe Chileshe who was delighted to see me. I arrived at lunch time so we went out to a very well appointed restaurant (where up to six months ago Joe wouldn't have been admitted) and had a very nice meal.

I had a very interesting talk with him about the political situation. He is all for Kaunda and a unified African approach to constitutional talks and he shares with the nationalist politicians a deep and pathological suspicion of the motives of white settler politicians.

[71]*These were the friends from Aberdeen whose heavy luggage I had brought with me to NR in 1959.*

The restaurant was in the Edinburgh Hotel which belonged to the copper mining companies. They had made it non-racial in order to entertain VIP Africans from inside and outside Northern Rhodesia. Elsewhere in Kitwe, and indeed in the whole of the Copperbelt, hotels, bars and restaurants were reserved for Europeans in the centre of the main towns. This segregation had just been made illegal but it was still in operation and any black person entering a "European" establishment was liable to be beaten up. This was an eye-opener to me because I thought that in general Northern Rhodesia was a non-racial society. The copper mines were staffed in the middle management and technical positions by many men from South Africa and a lesser number from Britain. The former thought that apartheid between the races was the norm, a view shared by many Europeans brought up in Northern Rhodesia, particularly on the Copperbelt.

1961 – A YEAR OF VIOLENCE AND CHANGE

In December of 1960 a Federal review conference was convened in London. Despite events elsewhere in Africa (chaos in the Congo, imminent majority rule in Kenya and Nyasaland) or because of them, the Federal Government was adamant that political control in the Federation had to remain in "responsible", ie. European, hands. The Northern Rhodesian African leaders' response was to demand the right to secede from the Federation. The Conference broke up after a few days without hope of an agreement and was never to meet again.

At the end of that conference another one began to discuss a new constitution for Northern Rhodesia. It lasted for two months and it too ended in profound disagreement between the two sides, African and European. Where previously it had been a tactic of the Africans to boycott conferences where they felt at a disadvantage, on this occasion it was the United Federal Party representing most of the European electorate at both the Federal and Territorial levels which boycotted most of the proceedings. At the same time, behind the scenes, Federal ministers were trying to pressurise the Colonial Secretary, Iain Macleod, not to give in to African electoral demands.

Pressure increased when the European Mineworkers Union demanded that the Federal Government should declare independence. Sir Roy Welensky called up the Northern Rhodesian reservists and in February, 1961, several battalions of the Southern Rhodesian territorial army. In reply the British Government moved troops and air transports to Nairobi within convenient distance of Lusaka. It was probably a case of bluff and counter-bluff. Moreover, at the end of February 1961, Sir Roy Welensky, addressing the Federal Assembly, said it might be necessary to "fight" to protect all that the European settlers had achieved in the previous seventy years.

This was all inflammatory stuff and did not help to create a calm atmosphere for negotiating a new constitution for Northern Rhodesia. It was left to Iain Macleod to propose the outline of a new constitution. This would have had an equal number of seats going to voters on the Higher (European) roll and the Lower (African) one and an equal number from a third (National) roll whose representatives would be elected by voters from both rolls. The winners in the National seats would be those candidates with the highest combined percentage from each roll, subject to a minimum percentage from each. It was assumed that this third block of elected representatives would be from the moderate Liberal Party which was expected to back the Nationalists.

Sir Roy Welensky and his Ministers used the interval between the first mooting of these proposals for the National roll and their official publication in June to have them amended in order to make them more likely to result in a majority for the United Federal Party. This was a recipe for a confrontation between Kaunda's United National Independence Party (UNIP) and the British Government who had shown that they could be swayed by violence or the threat of it. Widespread acts of violence and destruction by UNIP members took place in July and August in the north of the country. Troops had to be drafted in and additional district officers were brought in to maintain the civil authority. That is how I came to be directly involved in that period of upheaval far from my base in Barotseland.

Peace having been restored to Northern and Luapula Provinces by September and the state of emergency having been ended in November, the new Colonial Secretary, Reginald Maudling, reopened constitutional talks which resulted in a further tweaking of the complicated regulations for the election of members contesting the National seats. The African parties believed that this would give them a fair chance of winning in the forthcoming election so they agreed to the revised proposals which were published in March 1962.

Reverting to 1961, the ruling elite of Barotseland was as alarmed as the United Federal Party at the signs of the growing strength of the African nationalist parties. In April, the Litunga accompanied by a party of senior indunas and by the Resident Commissioner, Gervas Clay, had meetings in London with the Colonial Secretary, Iain Macleod, during which they pressed him to agree to Barotseland's secession from both Northern Rhodesia and the Federation. They wished instead to become a High Commission Territory like Basutoland (present-day Lesotho) and Bechuanaland (now Botswana). Their request was refused; the British Government was not prepared to pay for the costs of running Barotseland as an independent state. The Litunga had to be content with being knighted during a private audience with the Queen. The failure of their mission to London did not resign the Lozi rulers to a future within an independent African state. Behind the scenes they continued to negotiate some form of deliverance from this fate.

Senanga

3 January 1961

A fortnight ago, almost to the hour, I met Angus McDonald[72] in the Government Rest House in Ndola so that afternoon and evening we talked and dined and wined but mostly talked.

It was great to see him especially as he is one of the few who share both the past and the present with me.

Next day we shopped in Ndola with the wife of the Provincial Commissioner. In the afternoon we set off for Fort Rosebery (FR) the administrative centre of Luapula Province. Our route lay across a part of Katanga Province that juts into Northern Rhodesia, commonly known as the Congo Pedicle. At each end of the Pedicle is a Northern Rhodesia Government and Katanga Customs Post but we went through with the minimum delay because Angus had a card identifying him as an employee of the NRG and gave the Katanga official two shillings to help arrest the latter's alleged hunger because of non-receipt of his wages.

All the same I did not like the look of the Katanga gendarme who sat by the barrier with an automatic rifle across his knees. It may have been that the chap did not know how to fire it, but it was not quite the way to say "Welcome to Katanga".[73]

On our first full day in FR we drove to a station called Samfya[74] on the shores of Lake Bangweulu which is the second largest expanse of water in NR. There is a sandy beach and excellent bathing. Though the day was cloudy the water was lovely and warm.

In places like Samfya and FR there are United National Independence Party branches in nearly every village and the ▶

---

[72] *My friend and fellow Economics graduate from Aberdeen referred to on page 7.*

[73] *This was the time following the precipitate departure of the Belgian Administration from the Congo. Civil war ensued and Katanga Province in which were located massive copper mines seceded from the rest of the Congo in July 1960 with Moise Tshombe as its head of state. There was a state of semi-anarchy there, as there was throughout the Congo. There had been an army mutiny in July, Patrice Lumumba was sacked as the Congo's first Prime Minister in September, imprisoned in December and two months later, murdered in Katanga on the orders of Tshombe.*

[74] *Samfya was the station (not a railway station but the centre of a Government District) to which I and my wife, Christian, were posted on return from leave in January 1963.*

situation gets very tense sometimes. At one point earlier in the year a Cadet at Samfya was hit across the head and the general situation was very tense with schools being burnt. Finding carriers for touring was nearly impossible. But at present everything is quiet because the orders from UNIP HQ are that violent incidents are to be avoided during the talks between the political parties and the Government.

The power of UNIP is very great and the junior PA officials that I met all said that little could be done in the way of constructive work unless UNIP support was first of all enlisted. It makes life pretty frustrating at times but after all it is the Africa that we will have to live with and little less difficult than with the tradition-bound Lozi rulers who are part of the African past. To a certain extent it makes me wish that I had been posted to a place like Luapula Province.

About sixty percent of the able-bodied men in Luapula Province are away at the mines either in Katanga or on the Copperbelt and the tendency is for them to stay away for longer and longer periods with many of them settling down permanently in the towns. Gus says it is rather depressing going into some villages where there is not a single man to be seen; where there are men, they are nearly all old.

The whole pattern of rural life is being broken up and with it the traditional system of family responsibilities. Men who go and work on the mines are often frightened to return home to their village because all their relatives will come round and expect a share of their accumulated wealth. They for their part have to maintain their families in an urban environment where they have to send their children to school and where they cannot expect their wives to cultivate a garden and so keep them and their children largely self-sufficient for food.

It was interesting to see how people are moving towards the roads to trade food etc. with passers-by. Along the Fort Rosebery to Samfya road, a distance of fifty-two miles, the villages are almost continuous and most of the huts are built with sun-dried bricks as opposed to the almost universal pole and dagga huts in Senanga district.

Beside Samfya is a "village" called Mwamfuli of two thousand people. Its existence is due to the fishing trade on Lake Bangweulu; in Mwamfuli there are two or three extremely prosperous African traders with well-stocked stores, large, well built and well-appointed houses (I was shown over one) and Chevrolet cars.

In Fort Rosebery there is an African who owns amongst other things a fleet of motor buses, lorries and a hotel catering for Africans. This hotel makes a large profit, not from its paying guests but from its public bar.

Many other traders make a sizeable profit from bottle (beer) stores throughout the District. In Barotseland the sale of bottled beer to Africans is forbidden by the Paramount Chief so that this commerce can only be conducted on an unofficial, illicit basis.

On Christmas Day I got up at 6.30 a.m. to go to Communion taken by a priest from an Anglican mission some forty miles from Fort Rosebery. At 10 a.m. we all went to church where the whole European population of FR seemed to have gathered.

At midday we went to the Provincial Commissioner's house where all the PA staff in Fort Rosebery were gathered for drinks but half of the company left about 1 p.m. leaving us cadets, two District Assistants (ex-Army majors) and their families and the DC and his wife. About 2 p.m. we sat down to lunch – shrimp cocktail, turkey and trimmings and Christmas pudding.

At the end of my holiday in FR I got a lift in a battered Ford belonging to an apprentice electrician who was going back to work in Ndola and there I picked up my car and set off for Broken Hill. About twelve miles south of Ndola I picked up an African who was making for Broken Hill. He was from Southern Rhodesia and had come up to NR to look for work. When I dropped him off in Broken Hill he was fulsome in his thanks – said I'd saved his life because he would not have had the strength to walk to BH (over one hundred miles). I doubt if many motorists would stop to pick up an African, partly because some don't like "munts", partly because they are frightened that they may be picking up a criminal on the run and partly because they are travelling so fast that it is too much bother to stop.

▶ At BH I booked in at the Rest House and then went round to the Edwards where I had dinner. Next morning, Friday, I collected Jameson and set off for Lusaka arriving just before midday; booked in at a Government Rest House, then went and booked Jameson in at a hotel near the African suburbs which takes in Africans, fifteen shillings per night bed and breakfast. This hotel is extremely well appointed and when I collected Jameson next day he was extremely bucked at having slept in a bed with blankets sheets and pillows, a wash basin with running water and at having eaten a breakfast of corn flakes and bacon and eggs.

Letter to Christian Fraser

7 January 1961

My dear Christian

I returned from local leave five days ago to find your Christmas present and card and a pile of other Christmas mail waiting for me. Thank you for the books; the one on Edinburgh is beautiful.

I hope you have received the small gift which I sent you. If it has arrived and you are still wondering what it is, it is a fly-whisk for flicking away flies and no doubt can be adapted without too much difficulty for use against midges. The handle is of ivory and the tail comes from a wildebeest, alternatively known and immortalised by Flanders and Swan as the "gnu". These fly whisks are only used by Barotse royalty, or at least the ivory-handled ones with the wildebeest tail. The one which I sent you was carved by the carver to the Mulena Mukwae. I have a switch carved by the Paramount Chief's carver which I would have sent you rather than the other but unfortunately it was too thick to fit into the cardboard tube which was the safest container I could discover for such an object. The ivory handle of your switch is very dark with age and I suggest that you dip it in ammonia to restore its whiteness.

Senanga
10 January 1961

Dear Folks,

Last night one of the African clerks came in for dinner though his wife could not come because their baby was ill, as well as Ranald Paterson and his wife. It was a very enjoyable evening especially after dinner when this clerk was prevailed to demonstrate African style jive to some jazz records that I had bought on the line of rail and Ranald and his wife demonstrated British style; I watched agape. They are brilliant jivers.

To go back to the Epic Return Journey. A week past Saturday I left the main Lusaka – Broken Hill road and set off down a dirt road to Mumbwa. There had been heavy rain since I had driven along this road two weeks earlier. The dirt road was softer and there were several big puddles. About half way along this road the exhaust came apart but at Mumbwa I went into a garage and got it fitted together again.

Unfortunately, after another seventy miles or so the exhaust came adrift. It was pouring hard and I had no coat so I got soaked and filthy scrambling and writhing underneath the car trying to fix the exhaust.

We were in the middle of the Kafue National Game Park, renowned not only for its game but also for the numerous tsetse flies. I got bitten painfully by these creatures. I tried tying up the exhaust and silencer but after another five miles it all came adrift. I tied the whole lot onto the luggage rack on the roof and roaring like a tank I set off again. Moreover, the solder had come off the petrol tank and it was leaking so every now and again I had to get out, squirm under the tank and patch up the leak with soap.

I had to reach the Kafue River before 6 p.m. in order to catch the pontoon but 6 p.m. came and I was obviously still far from the river. Finally, we arrived almost an hour after the pontoon had closed and Jameson's "This is no good car" had changed to "Where are we going to sleep tonight"?

The pontoon was at the far side of the river about a quarter of a mile away but I hooted my horn hopefully and after a short interval small figures started moving around on the far bank and soon the pontoon had been started up and came chugging across to pick us up. Later on, when people learned that I had been taken across the river outside the appointed times they were amazed; apparently this was a unique event.

When I took my car aboard and had thanked the crew for coming over to fetch me I asked them why they had obliged. The capitao replied that they had done so because it was New Year's Eve and they felt generous. So I handed him a ten-shilling note that I had been holding in readiness saying "Here is some more New Year generosity" and everybody was happy.

By the time I crossed the river the sun had set and I found myself driving along a skiddy road with very dim lights. So I drove along gingerly, swerving here and there to avoid bush pigs and stray antelope (I was still inside the Game Park) and every now and then waltzing from one side of the road to the other when we ran into a particularly greasy patch. The chief cause of delay was the fact that since the generator was not working properly the battery also refused to charge itself. This fault developed in Lusaka. When I had to stop upon the exhaust coming adrift I had to push like billy-oh and then leap inside, push the gear into first and then let out the clutch when the car was moving slowly forward.

I drove on for another hour and a half and eventually came upon a lorry drawn in at the side of the road and in the bush nearby three Africans squatting around a fire with a tarpaulin stretched out as a cover. I stopped to ask how far it was to Mankoya and to my dismay learned that it was seventy miles on. I would have gone on but just then the engine konked out and though the men pushed, the car refused to start.

I decided to stop there for the night so that Jameson could cook his food and get shelter for the night. I had no food with me other than a pot of honey but one of the men offered me cocoa and a slice of bread. This I accepted gratefully because I had not eaten

▶ since breakfast and gave the man the honey in exchange. Then I went and stretched myself out on the front seat of the car (the back seat was full of various purchases[75] made for myself and other Senanga people) and managed to get some sleep, though I had to get up several times during the night because of diarrhoea. So that was how I spent Hogmanay 1960.

Next day I got the men to push me on my way with a noise like a hundred high-powered, super-charged racing cars revving up at the beginning of a race. The road was deeply rutted in parts and I had to go very cannily but eventually I reached the boundary of the Park where the car was sprayed to kill any lingering tsetse flies.

A little later I ran into a terrible patch of road and there my gears jammed. I got out in the pouring rain and tinkered with the innards with brilliant results – I unjammed the clutch plate and set off again and at long last hove in sight of Mankoya.[76]

Luckily next day, the last of my local leave, a small plane came in to Mankoya and I was able to get on it and land in Mongu an hour later. There I met the Patersons and Mike Bircham who were in Mongu for the New Year and got a lift down to Senanga with them that afternoon so that I was able to report for duty last Wednesday as per schedule. Jameson came by bus from Mankoya and arrived here on Saturday.

My friends and neighbours in Senanga, the Farrans, were furious that I had practically wrecked their car and left it marooned in Mankoya. In response, I could have said, but was too diplomatic to say so, that it was a very unsuitable car to bring to Barotseland. It says much for their generosity of spirit that they quickly forgave me.

[75] Mostly booze.

[76] The car was left in Mankoya until the road improved sufficiently to drive it to Mongu. It never made it to Senanga because of the poor road that linked it to Mongu.

I last wrote just before setting off for Nalolo. The day I set out, I was up at 5 a.m. though it was still dark, dressed, packed, loaded everything onto a landrover and drove down to the river to off-load onto our steel longboat. By 6.15 a.m. everything was loaded and we pushed off.

Luckily, the engine for once functioned quite well and we made good time despite being heavily laden. On board were myself, a District Messenger, a driver, my cook, the Nalolo Treasury Clerk, the Assistant Treasury Clerk and one of their carriers plus all their deed boxes, cash boxes, personal luggage together with a table, a cupboard, two bed frames and two boxes that I was taking up to Nalolo for one of the Senanga missionaries who is going to live at the mission station there.

The day was cool because there was a lot of cloud and at times the wind was fairly strong and we got spattered with spray. But it was a pleasant trip and I managed to get a little work done on the Treasury ledger and on my law. However, as the afternoon wore on the clouds became increasingly ominous and from 5 p.m. one could see parts of the plain on the windward side being blotted out by rain.

About 6 p.m. the wind rose suddenly bringing with it scattered spots of rain at first and then a steady downpour. Fairly high waves got up, say two feet from crest to base, and the other occupants began to fear for the safety of the craft.

Such was their perturbation that I agreed to put into a lagoon and tie up to let the wind die down. We repaired to a nearby village and entered a hut to get out of the rain. Inside crouched a man on his haunches beside a small fire and we all squatted around to dry off. Soon my eyes were smarting from the smoke which drifted very slowly out through the open doorway and this despite standing well back from the fire. But my companions seemed not to be a whit affected by it.

▶

In winter time quite a few deaths are caused by huts being burned down by a fire setting it alight when those who had been crouching around it had gone to sleep. A number also die from pneumonia because their lungs have been weakened previously by heavy intake of smoke. I am told that post mortems especially of old people show their lungs to be coated thickly with carbon as a consequence of crouching low over fires in stuffy huts.

We stayed there for about an hour and it was nearly 7 p.m. before we embarked on the river again. It was still raining hard but the wind had slackened and the waves had diminished as rapidly as they had arisen. Soon it got dark and we were in almost pitch darkness. Thus we had to go upriver with some care. Eventually we hove in sight of the mission station beside Nalolo which is marked by tall blue gum trees but it took us about half an hour to find the small canal that leads from the river to the mission landing place. By the time we actually landed it was after 9 p.m. and I was pretty browned off.

That was Wednesday and I stayed in Nalolo till 3 p.m. on Saturday working on the Treasury's books and having cups of tea with the Mulena Mukwae. I did not manage to finish the work but since I had made arrangements to be present at the silalo Kutas that lie on the road between Namushakende and Senanga on the Sunday to issue gun and store licences, I had to leave.

I spent Saturday night with David Salmon and had a very enjoyable chat with him and the District Officer in charge of the station and then yesterday I returned to Senanga by way of the above-mentioned Kutas.

I left for Nalolo in the landrover last Tuesday at 7.30 a.m. in pouring rain and it rained solidly all the way to Nalolo.

At Namushakende we set out across the plain to Nalolo on a road which will soon be quite impassable even for a landrover. For quite long periods we ploughed through a foot of water and at one point got stuck in some mud. Landrovers can cope with nearly every obstacle apart from thick mud and then they get bogged down like any other vehicle.

We reached the Zambezi at a point where there is a Government ferry canoe, situated opposite Nalolo (which stands about half a mile from the river) and half a mile south of the mission which stands right on the bank. It was still raining solidly – you could have cut it with a knife! – but I had to get out of the landrover and into the canoe in which I was paddled upstream to the mission while the landrover returned to Senanga.

I suppose it took half an hour to reach the mission because half way there we had to put in to shore to bale out the canoe which was leaking and filling up with rain water. The water in the foot of the canoe was in danger of damaging my goods which lay beneath a tarpaulin.

Next day I struggled all day long with the books, checking the Treasury Clerk's figures and trying to reconcile a difference of seven hundred pounds between one side of his balance sheet and the other. I got it down to four pounds by midnight but since then, though I have been through the books carefully I just cannot get rid of that difference.

Next day I recruited five paddlers and had the Boma's steel longboat paddled down the Zambezi and along a canal to the edge of the plain.

When I finally reached the forest edge there was a landrover outside a nearby store and just getting into it ready to drive off was a European. He turned out to be the divisional manager of a chain of stores in Barotseland who was on his first visit to this ▶

▶ store in seven weeks. He was going to Namushakende en route to visit another store between there and Mongu. And so to Namushakende and my rendezvous with my DC.

Senanga
1 February 1961

On Monday morning I set off with the DC, Ian Edye, to Mooyo en route for Nalolo.

Upon arrival at the canal that crosses the Plain we found six paddlers waiting for us at our steel longboat, an arrangement I had made by letter to the local Induna a few days before. We set off at 4 p.m. along the canal to the Zambezi. The road across the plain from Namushakende is now flooded and impassable to all vehicles including landrovers. That is why I had to make the long journey upriver from Senanga a week ago to put the longboat in a suitable position for crossing the plain once the road was out of action.

From Nalolo to Nangoma Mission where we were to stay is a short walk. Just as we entered Nangoma we met a small procession leaving --the missionary, Jean-Louis Baumgartner, the Sambi (the Mulena Mukwae's chief Induna) and two or three of his attendants. The Sambi had just been to the dispensary for medical treatment having had a heart attack earlier in the day. He is a big, stout man between sixty and seventy years old, so this is not unexpected. When I first met him, I thought he was a terrible fat slob but having seen quite a lot of him in the last few months I have changed my opinion; he is a very shrewd old man and can act with energy if he wants to (admittedly this does not happen very often).

He was obviously very down in the mouth but our emergence out of the darkness cheered him up a bit. Yesterday he took our longboat in order to go through the canal to Mooyo and there travelled in the Nalolo lorry to Mongu hospital.

We got a warm welcome and a large meal from Mrs Baumgartner (they have just moved from Senanga to Nangoma). ▶

> Next day, the DC spent most of his time in discussions with the Mulena Mukwae while I toiled in the Treasury. We worked until 7 p.m. except for a break for lunch.
>
> Next morning, we were paddled to Mooyo in a small wooden barge. On the way back to Senanga we stopped at two Kutas and issued licences for trading stores and arms and ammunition and got back here at 6 p.m.

A Film Show: why no Charlie Chaplin?

Shekela Kuta
14 February 1961

As you may surmise from the address I am once again touring Shekela silalo, the third time in just over one and a half years. It just so happens that the timing of this tour has been advanced in each of the last three years.

The road between Senanga and here is pretty bad; it took us ten hours to travel eighty miles and it was a case of grinding along in second gear at ten mph for most of the way. We were travelling in a five ton Bedford lorry and even at ten mph some bumps shot me two feet out of my seat whence I returned with a sickening thud.

I have brought some films and a cinema projector with me to show some films about cattle husbandry and the like to the locals. I gave a free showing in the Senanga Welfare Hall a few days ago to a packed audience. They were quite interested but greatly disappointed that the programme did not include a Charlie Chaplin film. At the end of the show they chanted "Challee, Challee" but "Challee" was totally absent.

I shall certainly order some Chaplins with my next order of "educational" films. Isn't it amazing, though, that a man in his lifetime should become a legend like Chaplin has done. I would say he is the most famous man alive (or dead), certainly more widely known than Churchill, Khrushchev or Kennedy in this part of the world.[77]

---

[77] Chaplin's films were probably seen by migrant workers in South Africa.

I have now been on tour for a week. The tour is quite enjoyable because the sand has been packed down somewhat by the rain of the last few weeks so that the walking is easier than on my two previous tours in this silalo.

I sometimes wonder at the usefulness of these wearisome peregrinations that I make round various silalos but I must say that there is a marked improvement in hut-building standards since my first visit and some of this improvement is probably due to the time I have been willing to spend on previous tours on this matter as well as the worst cases being fined in the Indunas' Court.

On this tour, besides the silalo Indunas, I have had two Indunas from Nalolo - the Health Induna and the Veterinary Induna. The health merchant is an extremely glib fellow who could sell meat to a vegetarian; he lives in a dreadful hut in Nalolo.

The Veterinary Induna knows practically nothing about cattle husbandry but on this tour he has been exhorting people to take their cattle to the Cattle Sales that the semi-public corporation - the Cold Storage Commission – is holding in Senanga District at the back end of the year and about how they should improve the drying of cattle hides. He is a small man with a brush moustache and has a staccato-style delivery – looks and sounds like Clement Attlee.[78]

I am not a very popular visitor at this time of year for it is the season when the millet and maize on the ant-hills are coming to fruition and all hands are out in the fields from dawn to dusk banging away at tins and yoo-hallooing to frighten off the large flocks of birds that try to fatten themselves on the ripening cobs.

In a week or two the people will start harvesting so naturally they don't like to be hauled into their villages and made to sit around and be counted and addressed by various bods. Also it is extremely difficult to get meal for the carriers because last year's supply is either completely or nearly finished and the people are subsisting on fresh cobs of maize.

▶

[78]*Britain's Labour Party Prime Minister, 1945-51.*

▶ Last Tuesday evening I gave a film show in the local school classroom to the people of the nearby villages. The room – a very big one – was packed with people even sitting in the aisle and peering through the open doorway at the back. The films were those I had shown a few days previously at the Welfare Hall – about animal husbandry and house building plus a film about an African sight-seeing in London. This film really made the yokels gasp especially when yours truly explained what all the huge blocks of masonry represented. I told them that the Tower of London was a prison, and Buckingham Palace the home of the Queen and her family.

After I put a name to something unusual the audience would repeat it in trance-like fashion. Thus when they realized that the road that the African tourist was walking on at one point in the film was a bridge across the Thames they all murmured B-R-I-D-G-E- or rather the Lozi equivalent M-B-I-L-I-CH-I-. Statues had them foxed, buses bewildered and the sight of the African tipping a white taxi-driver delighted them. Best of all, they loved the double decker buses, and the flashes of football from Wembley (at least the men and boys did).

Again, the big disappointment was the absence of a Chaplin film. When the projector was switched on the audience broke into a chant of "Chalee, Chalee!" As with the audience in Senanga, I felt I had let them down by not having at least one of his films with me. The trouble is that they are so popular it is extremely difficult to obtain them from the Information Service film library from where I obtained all the films.

At the end of the show the head teacher of the two teacher school got up and thanked the DO on behalf of the people, the children sang a hymn and the DO replied suitably! Some of the people had walked six or seven miles so I gave them a lift back to their village in the lorry and eventually I crawled exhausted into bed after midnight.

At the end of last week, I went up to Nalolo and had an enjoyable time. As usual I stayed at the small PMS mission station close by which means that on these Nalolo excursions one enjoys excellent hospitality. NRG gives us an allowance for this sort of thing – one pound, two shillings and sixpence per night to your host and five shillings a night to yourself to cover tips, etc.

A jolly good idea, this, because it means you can eat your host's food with gay abandon without feeling a heel. I often use the five shillings to buy a little present for the hosts so as to make the system less mercenary. Last week, I brought up a bottle of South African champagne. The cork sprang out in magnificent fashion when the bottle was opened and the wine was not too bad!

On Thursday I set off by road from Senanga to the canal that goes straight through the Plain from Mooyo to the Zambezi, coming out close to Nalolo. Just as we arrived at the canal, the heavens opened and the rain fell in solid sheets and the ground shook to tremendous peals of thunder. The storm lasted just over an hour and then eased off very quickly, allowing us to get into the paddle barge belonging to the Mulena Mukwae's Second Councillor.

We made good time down the canal for it has been cleared of grass and weeds. There were eight paddlers and as often happens one of them acted as cheerleader, joke-cracker and general whipper-up of flagging energies. It is a three-and-a-half-hour journey to Nalolo and when we were about half way there, we suddenly left the canal and cut across the flooded plain keeping cleverly to the hollows and so saved quite a distance in the process.

The flood is low this year because there has been little rain but even so it is amazing how quickly the water has risen.

Next day I repaired to Nalolo and worked with the Treasury Clerk until I received a little note from the Mulena asking if I would like to have tea. As this is not a matter of liking but a socio-political obligation, I of course replied that I would be delighted. So I drank tea and later in the morning I got another little note asking me if I would like to eat lunch with the Mulena.

The flooded plain close to Senanga

Lunch was excellent – soup, duck stew and numerous veg, and miscellaneous tinned fruits.

The Mulena Mukwaes have a reputation for massiveness and this is no doubt caused by extremely good living together with a sedentary life. At present she has a salary of £960 per year made up of a Barotse National Government wage of £800 and an NRG subsidy of £160 while her husband has to be content with a total salary of £255: £160 from BNG plus £95 from NRG.

Of course, the Mulena has other sources of income for although she no longer has a multitude of slaves as in the pre-1924 days (when tribute labour was finally abolished in Barotseland) she still has extensive lands and large herds of cattle from which she must derive a very considerable income. In fact, her salary is only meant to compensate her for the loss of her slaves – to enable her to keep up an equivalent force of waged labourers.

After lunch we talked about trivialities and then I was asked if I had heard about the new constitutional proposals for Northern Rhodesia. Of course, I had heard and in reply to a question of mine they said they had not yet heard the details and would I please enlighten them on the subject (In Lozi, of course!).

▶ I was pretty certain that they knew the details of the proposals as well as I did and in fact when I got back to Senanga I found that the DC had sent them the White Paper. Anyway, I launched out as best I could – luckily I had already had to explain it to the Indunas on tour so I had the vital vocab. at my disposal. But in the discussion that followed I was quite out of my depth but as it largely took the form of a dialogue between the Mulena and her husband in which they poured scorn and ridicule upon the heads of the nationalist leaders I could safely hold my peace.

I asked them if they had heard of Lumumba's death.[79] They openly gloated. "Some chief, he – he only lasted two months!" They are more reactionary in their attitude to African popular movements than most Europeans and yet their attitude is quite understandable and has a certain justification. Were African nationalist political parties allowed into Barotseland would they make the people happier, would they ensure greater justice or greater harmony or greater wealth?

I would say that the great majority of people here are as contented with life, and probably more so, than the people of London, Paris, Berlin, New York, or Aberdeen and that on the whole they are satisfied with the conduct of their chiefs because the latter have a long tradition of regulated authority. There is, however, a growing number of people who are discontented, and justifiably so, with the present set up. These are the teachers and clerks who see the top positions in the Barotse hierarchy filled by the members of a few families, irrespective of their abilities. The number of the discontented will gradually increase and eventually the Barotse set up must either reform itself or be knocked over by a violent upheaval from below.[80]

Saturday, I worked all morning with the Treasury Clerk, apart from the usual tea break with the Mulena at which I presented her with a large tin of biscuits – I felt I should repay a few of the many that I ▶

[79] *First elected Prime Minister of the Congo, in office for two months before being deposed in a US supported military coup and later killed in prison.*
[80] *How prescient of me; in 1966, two years after Zambia became independent, the traditional Barotse structure of government was swept away and replaced by elected District Councils.*
How un-prescient of me not to foresee the continuing strength of Lozi nationalism; in 2015 there is still an active Barotse Independence movement.

have eaten in my many tea sessions with her. Then at about 3 p.m. I set off back to Senanga. When I arrived at the end of the canal I found that the landrover was waiting. I drove to Namushakende where I had to pick up the Messengers attending a course there and stayed the night with David Salmon. We played poker with some friends until 1 a.m. and then went back to his house and cooked fried eggs and chips for ourselves and eventually got to bed about 4 a.m.

Arresting Crocodile "Poachers"

Senanga
21 March 1961

You will remember that I wrote to say that next day I was setting off with Kit Farran, the Senanga Livestock Officer, to the Angola border to investigate "una grave infractione" reported by the person in charge of a big safari outfit that operates in Angola.

First we set off down the Zambezi in the pontoon from Senanga because the plain road which connects Senanga with the south is now out of action. Then we drove for about 110 miles in a westerly direction until we reached the Angola border.

Taking the pontoon down the Zambezi during the flood

▶ At the border there is a recruiting centre of WNLA and two or three stores. This place is called Shangombo[81] and stands on a high bank on the Mashi River (the Portuguese call it the Kwando).

As we drew into Shangombo there emerged from one of the stores a European with a crowd of Africans. The European came up to us and Kit recognized him from previous trips across the border as the person who had written the letter. He was a short man, barely five feet tall but his girth nearly equalled his height.

He immediately launched into an excited explanation in Portuguese of the "grave infractione". I had been informed by Kit that at the Mission across the river in Angola one of the Fathers could speak English and as there was a considerable crowd around us I suggested to the Portuguese that we talk about it in the more private surroundings of the Mission of Santa Cruz.

I got this over to him because with him there was an African trader whose home was in Angola but who traded in Barotseland and could speak Lozi. So he acted as interpreter between me speaking Lozi and the safari leader speaking Portuguese.

We went down to the river and embarked upon a motor boat which belonged to the trader who is, I am told by Kit, an "assimilado", with the same rights as a Portuguese to vote (do they ever?), and to wine and dine in "white" restaurants. The Mashi River is very marshy in these parts and its course extremely tortuous.

The journey in the motor boat took nearly an hour because we had to wind to and fro a great deal between high banks of reeds.

The Angolan side looked pretty much the same as the Northern Rhodesian one when we stepped ashore – but soon we came to an avenue of gum trees and walking to meet us was one of the two Fathers who live there. He was also on the small side, about five foot, four inches, dark and looked as though he needed a shave. He seemed fairly young and a bit soft; of course, he was handicapped by not being able to speak English! We went up to a rather seedy looking house and shortly after we entered the other ▶

[81]As a result of local government reforms in Zambia there is now a new district called Shangombo, presumably because Senanga District was considered to be too large.

▶ Father appeared – the one who was reputed to speak English. However, his English was extremely limited.

It was obvious that Kit had overestimated the Father's linguistic powers because he wanted a comfortable bed for the night and a chance to drink the Fathers' vino instead of camping at Shangombo or somewhere else on the road. In the end the African assimilado acted as interpreter from Portuguese into Lozi. I understood him pretty well and spoke quite smoothly in return – Kit was impressed.

The infraction amounted to some Europeans who were alleged to be shooting crocodiles on the Mashi without a licence, using Northern Rhodesia as their base. The Mashi is in Angolan territory and the border is often two or three miles from the river because it has been delimited along the high-water mark in 1930 on the NR side.

If the African doing the translating was an assimilado then some people are more assimilado than others because when addressing me he always knelt one knee on the floor and when this translating job was finished, he went off leaving us to enjoy our wine. One of the people said to be involved in the illegal hunting was a Portuguese who in October of last year arrived in Senanga out of the Livingstone plane with nothing but a tiny suitcase and announced that he wanted to visit his cousin whom he alleged was a priest at Santa Cruz. At that time Kit was due to visit some cattle at the Mashi so he gave the man, Barbosa by name, a lift to Shangombo.

The Fathers said that Barbosa was not related to either of them and had been pulling the wool over Kit's eyes. He had disappeared and it was thought that he had gone to Livingstone.

We got up at six next morning, bade farewell to the Fathers and set off back across the Mashi. Arriving at Shangombo we drove south for about forty miles until we came across the tracks of a landrover. We followed them and with the help of a villager we came upon the camp of the hunters. There we found Barbosa, looking out of place in the middle of the bush and a coloured hunter who operates a lot in this District called Elliott Chipman. ▶

Kit Farran laying down the law; Barbosa in background and the Chipman brothers in front of him

In their camp we found fifteen crocodile skins, two boats, three outboard engines, one rifle and one shotgun and bags of salt for preserving skins and bags of maize for feeding their African helpers. We took over the skins and guns and drove off to Senanga with Chipman and Barbosa in the back of the landrover while Chipman's landrover followed on behind with all his assistants apart from a couple left behind to look after the hunting equipment. At Shangombo I managed to persuade the Portuguese safari leader that this was a NR case and that all statements that we got from Chipman and Barbosa would be sent to the Angolan authorities to help them in their prosecution should they want to bring a case.

In fact, the DC decided not to bring a case but just to confiscate the skins until such time as Barbosa gets a licence from the Angolan authorities. The statements which I took from Barbosa, Chipman and the others involved are being sent to Angola.

This will have to be brief this week as the day after tomorrow I set off to Mongu for the Language Exam.

The flood continues to rise, but slowly. It is now well above last year's level and eating away at my vegetable garden close to the Zambezi, bed upon bed. Already I have had the mortification to see beds of young carrots and beans go under, money and labour washed remorselessly away.

Dear Mum and Dad

The past week has been about the most hectic in my life what with visiting Ministers of the Crown, parties and other engagements.

Last Thursday the Patersons were visited by a friend of theirs from Salisbury who had travelled out in the boat with them from England. This friend has turned out to be a very pretty girl of twenty-one, and she and I seem to have hit it off pretty well so far.

She has to go back to Salisbury today and I am feeling desolate at the prospect but as luck would have it, yesterday I received a telegram from Lusaka to say that I had been chosen to go on a three week course for District Officers, police officers, etc., at a Training Centre called Chalimbana near Lusaka from 25th May to the 15th June. So thanks to this happy coincidence I may be able to meet my friend in Salisbury or some other suitable rendezvous.

Her name is Brenda Cooper; she is employed as a clerk in the Federal Broadcasting Corporation. She is very, very nice and I think she likes me quite a lot. Of course, my whole attitude is no doubt coloured by the fact that for twenty months I haven't met a solitary unattached and attractive woman and I may just be suffering from a rush of blood to the head. Anyway, if things get serious I'll take some local leave and see if I still feel the same way towards her at the end of it as I do now.

On my tape-recording I think that my last words were to the effect that Alfred Gondwe (Minister of African Education) remarked after dinner at the DC's house that if an African were leader of the Liberal Party it would gain far more African votes. To which Harry Franklin (Minister of Transport and Works) made no reply which is significant I think – even liberal Europeans do not look far enough ahead.

At the moment in the Liberal Party, the Nos. 1, 2 and 3 are all Europeans, namely Sir John Moffat, Harry Franklin and the Rev Colin Morris. Gondwe comes just below this group but I should have thought that if Franklin was right and genuine in his protestations about the Liberal Party's role in politics – i.e. to fill the gap between European majority rule and African majority rule then someone like Gondwe should be appointed leader or deputy leader.

When Gondwe and I had returned home after the dinner party he told me of a meeting that he and Franklin had addressed in the Indian quarter of Lusaka. Franklin had been the first speaker and after being introduced by the Chairman he had immediately got up and castigated his audience for their lack of civic virtues, and their unreliability and stupidity in voting for the United Federal Party at the last elections. He hoped that this time they would look to both their own and the country's interests and vote for the Liberal Party.

Said Gondwe "I didn't know where to hide myself". But the meeting continued without the visitors being lynched largely because Franklin can say outrageous things in a humorous, not too stinging way.

Gondwe thinks that Kaunda is a good man and worthy to lead Africans in Northern Rhodesia but he thinks that all his leading lieutenants are a pretty scurvy bunch – they are mostly Lozis. ▶

▶ I noticed that he lacked assurance about the house. For example, after using the hand basin and the bath, he always scrubbed them with Vim. I know a) because of the whiteness of the porcelain and b) because he left his tin of Vim behind him. I think it indicates that however brave a face most Africans, even the leading ones, show to the world, they have a terrible inferiority complex.[82]

At any rate, it was a pleasure having him in the house and I think he enjoyed his stay though he remarked at one point how sometimes he wished he had never entered politics[83] but remained in his job as headmaster of the Secondary School at Fort Jameson.

On Thursday afternoon the girl I told you about, called Brenda Cooper, arrived and, what with being invited out to dinner and parties, I did not spend one evening at home for the whole week following except on the night when I gave a party, which was quite the best, of course.

Since she left, life has more or less returned to normal though a lot of social calls have been made.

The DC also dropped a bombshell by announcing that Ranald Paterson was to be transferred to Kalabo before the end of May to replace a chap whose reports while working in Barotseland were not too good. His place in Senanga is being taken by a chap called Tony Hellen whom I knew at St Peter's Hall and who came out to NR in November 1959 without doing the A Course on account of his age. In the meantime, he has married a German girl.

Today is Monday and I have just set out on tour of Lumbe Silalo. I have reached my first camp but the Messenger whom I sent out to look for carriers has not turned up. Perhaps eaten by lions. I shall be on tour for fifteen days and the main point of the exercise is to go to the Mankoya border to meet the DC Mankoya there and discuss adjustments to the district border.

---

[82] *The alternative explanation for the Vim is that Mr Gondwe thought that the wash hand basin and the bath were grubby and decided that they needed a good clean. He might have left the Vim as a gentle reminder to me and my cook that we needed to improve our standards of cleanliness.*

[83] *After the members of the United Federal Party resigned from the Executive Council on the orders of Sir Roy Welensky in February 1960 their Ministerial portfolios were given to members of the moderate Liberal Party.*

A change to the District Boundary and a very long trek

Iluya Camp,
Lumbe Silalo
7 May 61

I am now at the end of my first week on this tour and I am steadily walking further from Senanga. This will continue for the next two or possibly three days as I have to make a rendezvous with the District Commissioner, Mankoya, at a village somewhere on his side of our common boundary. No one on this side seems to know exactly where because between here and this boundary is thirty miles and more of uninhabited forest until one village is found just on our side of the boundary.

The object of this trip is to persuade the DC Mankoya to take over responsibility for visiting and counting this village and if necessary, redrawing the boundary so that it becomes truly part of Mankoya.

I am managing to keep relatively free of blisters and as the course of our march is in the face of the prevailing cool winds that blow at this time of year, the daily treks have not been uncomfortable. There seems to have been a lot of things to explain to the

Pounding maize in wooden mortars with long wooden poles

villagers on this tour: cattle sales, election of a representative to the Katengo (Commoners) Council, new taxes and so on. It is good fun though it puts hours onto your day and taxes my Lozi as well as the charity of the listeners as they hear me butcher their tongue. However, I have reached the point where I can let the Indunas do most of the talking since they have heard me put over the main points and have acquired thereby the official "line".

When last I wrote, it was from the middle of Lumbe silalo. Since then I have really moved around the world, landing up now in Salisbury, Southern Rhodesia.

The day after I wrote to you I set off in earnest for the Mankoya border walking up the valley of a small river for some fifteen miles. Then the path turned into the forest so there I pitched my tent for the night to be near water.

Next day we walked through the forest for some twenty miles or more till we reached a stream running parallel to the Mankoya border on which is a solitary village. We thought that this was the village which the DC Mankoya wanted to incorporate into his District being the only one known to us to be near the border of his District. So after counting the people and sending off a kapasu across the river to look for the DC and tell him of my arrival I settled down to wait. Next day, the kapasu failed to return and I enjoyed a day's rest, the first in the ten days of the tour.

Next morning, as I lay abed, a shot was heard from beyond the river. I thought it was the Induna gone shooting early but it turned out to be a District Messenger sent by the DC Mankoya. The news was bad; the DC was touring another part of his border some thirty miles away so I was faced with the possibility of having to change my route back to Senanga and my time and place of meeting with the landrover. So I wrote a note to my DC and despatched a runner post-haste so that the landrover might meet me at the proper place.

Then we set off across country through untrodden forests, completely pathless. We had as our guide the headman of the village that I had counted the day before and without him we would surely have got lost because the country was quite unknown to both indunas and kapasus. After walking twenty miles we chose a place to pitch camp.

▶

Next morning I was up before 6 a.m. and away from camp by 6.30 and about 10 a.m. reached the first of the villages in Mankoya District where we were informed by the headman that the DC[84] was due any minute to census them. About an hour later he rolled up with his retinue – rolled because they all were mounted on bicycles, Mankoya being fortunately clear of the sand belt. We exchanged welcomes, he then censused the people and afterwards we talked about the boundary problem.

It turned out that the village we were in was one of five lying geographically inside Senanga District but which have always been under a Mankoya induna, included in Mankoya tax registers and administered from Mankoya. This was all unknown to me and to the Senanga indunas I had with me – in fact to everyone except the DC Mankoya, it would appear. Moreover, the Senanga indunas did not want to take over their administration because it is two days' journey through uninhabited forest to reach them and the villagers themselves want to remain under Mankoya administration.

However, as the DC Mankoya pointed out, the situation may cause legal difficulties in future over the jurisdiction of the Mankoya native court if it tries, say, a political case where the accused are aware of legal niceties so he proposed the redrawing of the boundary to include these five villages within Mankoya. To this I and the indunas agreed subject to the approval of the Mulena Mukwae and the Kuta.

He then invited me to his camp but I declined because I wanted to set off back to Senanga immediately. So he pedalled away while I stayed behind and bought meal for my carriers. Then I trudged away.

As we walked along, wanting to make sure of the stages of our journey back I asked the senior Messenger where we were to sleep that night, the 12th. He told me. And the 13th; and the 14th. I then asked him where we would reach on the 15th – and he mentioned a place about thirty miles or so away from the rendezvous with the landrover, with a wide river in between.

▶

---

[84] *John Hudson, who after Independence remained in Zambia and enjoyed a distinguished career there.*

> Whereat I lost my temper with him and the induna and raged at
> them in amazingly fluent and vituperative Lozi. Which was, I
> suppose, wrong and foolish but I was exceedingly exasperated.
> I told them that come what may we had to get back on the
> 15th (I had arranged a farewell party for the Patersons for that
> evening). I had applied for a week's local leave starting on the
> 17th and though I did not know if it had been approved, if it had,
> Jameson would need a day to wash and iron my clothes and I
> would need a day to clear up with the DC matters that had
> cropped up in my absence.

Over the course of the following four days I walked nearly 150 miles. Although I was used to long walks while on tour, this exceeded anything I had ever done, or would do in future. In the latter half of this trek, I left behind all my touring companions and carriers apart from Jameson, a District Messenger and five carriers carrying light loads. In the early part of this trek one lighter episode which I describe below no doubt gave the other members of my party something to laugh about. To my great satisfaction I managed to return to Senanga in time for my party, with about an hour to spare.

> Emerging out of a clump of trees bordering a river valley we saw a
> duiker some one hundred to two hundred yards ahead of us. As
> one man we dropped to the ground and as quietly as possible I
> shunted a bullet from the magazine into the barrel.[85] I set the
> sights at four hundred yards feeling intuitively that beginners tend
> to shoot low, slipped off the safety catch, took aim and a deep
> breath and fired – and missed.
>
> The duiker raised its head and looked towards us in mild surprise,
> then resumed its serious business of eating grass. Desperately I
> ejected the spent cartridge and pushed in a fresh one. Aimed, fired
> and missed. So I reduced my sights to the minimum and crawled

[85] An officer on tour could be issued with a rifle from the Boma armoury so that while on tour he might shoot game for the benefit of the touring party. There were very few rifles, ammunition was too scarce for target practice, and the weapons - Lee-Enfields .303's – dated from the First World War, or so I reckoned. They did not have telescopic sights, they had a terrible kick, and I swear it was not just down to my poor marksmanship that I never managed to hit an animal with any of the bullets that I fired from it.

forward through the bushes and grass and when I reached the last bit of cover I stopped, put in another cartridge, tried to obey all the rules of marksmanship... (allow for the wind, take in your breath, etc.) and fired - and missed – six more times!

The duiker did not turn a hair until it heard my dog approaching and eventually it saw her and decided to scarper – to my relief as it only left me with one more cartridge in the magazine and if it had stayed on I would have fired that and no doubt missed.

My chagrin needs no imagining though my companions kindly forbore to joke about it in my presence or to show their disappointment at the loss of the first decent bit of relish they would have had for the past week, apart, that is, from the kapasu who had crawled through the bushes in my wake and as I repeatedly fired and missed pleaded with me, almost in tears, to let him have a chance. However, his stumbling and swaying on the path gave no guarantee that he would shoot anything apart from himself or me, so I refused. Earlier that day he had met some friends during a stop for food and had drunk too much beer.

Back in Senanga, Mrs Edye, Mrs Farran and John Wyatt (a recently arrived District Assistant) had got together to prepare the food for the party though the drinks were mine as was also some of the food. I must have looked a sight having gone three days without a bath or a shave, but that was soon rectified and a most enjoyable party was held.

Next afternoon I returned to the Lui River and met the remainder of the carriers and paid them off with two days extra pay. That evening I had dinner at the Edye's house with the Provincial Forest and the Provincial Veterinary Officers – very enjoyable.

Wednesday I slaved in the office, confabbed with the DC, saw off the Patersons and flew to Livingstone at 3 p.m. on my local leave which had been approved. 7.30 a.m. yesterday arrived Salisbury by bus. 8.30 a.m. met Brenda and got installed in the Grand Hotel.

Lusaka

24 May 1961

Dear Folks

I arrived early this morning in Lusaka by plane from Salisbury.

I am now penurious and womanless. The romance is at an end; we have decided that we don't and never will love one another and I don't feel like going into details!

Salisbury has some fine buildings, of the modern, perpendicular variety and the buildings of the new University College are first rate.

I met Adrian Thomas a couple of days before I left. He is getting on fine at the University. I also saw a good theatre show, and a very enjoyable football match (Leicester City vs. Southern Rhodesia – Leicester won 2-0) and ate extremely well at my hotel.

Which is about the sum total of my news for this week. Sorry.

The truth is that Brenda already had a boyfriend whom she had not mentioned during her visit to the Patersons. She no doubt never dreamed that I would dash to Salisbury so soon after her visit to Senanga. At lunch on the day I arrived she made it quite clear that her boyfriend was still in her favour and that I might as well forget any thought of romance with her.

On a Refresher Course, Lusaka

Chalimbana, near Lusaka
29 May 61

This course at Chalimbana is proving to be a grand rest cure; lectures morning and afternoon, games of tennis and squash afterwards and no essays or exams to becloud the horizon. Just like University, only more cushy!

There are eleven of us on the Course. Five are policemen – three Africans, two of whom are Assistant Inspectors and on European pay and promotion scales and a Sub-Inspector who is still on African pay scales and two Europeans one of whom is an Inspector and the other an Assistant Inspector.

There are four from the PA. I am the senior and besides myself there is a Cadet who came out about a year ago, a District Assistant and a Learner District Assistant, a studious youth who is at present studying for the Chartered Institute of Secretaries. This involves the study of economics which impels him to air dubious economic propositions at the slightest excuse. I remember enough to contradict him on most of these occasions. The other Cadet is a very nice chap, Irish, with a rare sense of humour.

There are also two Education Officers, one of whom is a Scot from Glasgow, called Alan Mclean, who teaches English at Munali Secondary School near Lusaka. He has also a good sense of humour and shares my rather bolshie attitude towards authority, a trait probably common to many Scots of our background.

The DO-in-Charge is a very nice chap of the Oxbridge school whose main fault is that he tends to be rather patronising towards Africans and a bit too ready to assume that just because Africans can sit down for a meal in restaurants in Northern Rhodesia they have very little now to grouse about.

There is another course going on here for Departmental Councillors employed by Native Authorities and one of their chief complaints is that some members of the PA, especially those in junior positions, and many European technical officers, fail to show proper courtesy to their chiefs and to them.

I am sure the DO-in-charge would never be guilty of this. One of his themes is good manners; "There is nothing worse than bad manners". "Respect" is something that is very important to the African and the councillors tell me that the most important African nationalist leaders are punctilious in observing the proper civilities when seeking an interview with and meeting a chief.

So far, we have had lectures on the history of Northern Rhodesia, the Federal set-up, the Franchise, the various kinds of land tenure in NR, the composition and powers of Native Authorities, and a morning's discussion on race relations with members of the other course.

You may not be aware that in NR there are different types of land title. There is Crown Land, six percent of the whole, which is set aside for European settlement. Most of this is on the Copperbelt and on the line of rail which extends from Livingstone to the Copperbelt. There is also Native Trust Land and Native Reserves, together seventy-nine percent of the total. Rights over this land are vested in the Secretary of State for the Colonies and are only for settlement by Africans. The difference between the two types of land is that in one (the Native Reserves) the Native Authorities have a greater say in the disposal of the land. The rest, sixteen percent, consists of Barotseland where the rights to the land rest with the Paramount Chief.

Last Friday, we visited a teachers' training college which is next door to this Native Authority Training Centre. It was to see a preview of their end of term day at which the Governor was to be present. The highlight was a wonderful choir consisting of the pupil teachers and their wives. The choir master is an African graduate of Fort Hare in South Africa. He must be a man of some considerable talent in training choirs because the final result was truly wonderful. The choir sang songs by African composers, all South African, all of which had beautiful melodies and some of which had extremely complicated cross rhythms. This choir would be a sensation in the UK. I certainly have never heard a better one.

The past week has proved most enjoyable. The Course has been chock-a-block with interesting lectures and visits to places of interest.

Of the latter, the outstanding one has been a meeting with the Chief Architect of the African Housing Board and a tour round some of the main African Housing Schemes and unauthorized settlements around Lusaka. The architect proved a most enlightened and enthusiastic fellow and really opened our eyes to the various factors that influence house design. The two main ones are the present shortage of government funds in relation to the number of houses required and the need to design houses that can be improved without major alterations as African incomes rise and the housing position improves.

We also visited the unauthorized compounds where people squat on land owned by farmers or Government around Lusaka (Crown Land). Their houses are of pole and dagga or cardboard boxes or other scrap material. Crude, but the people keep the surroundings clean. The farmers try to collect rent (five shillings or ten shillings per month) with differing degrees of success from these squatters. Government, too, has recently started changing ten shillings per month from squatters on its land.

I asked the District Assistant (ex-Indian Army major) who was showing us round one such compound what moral justification there was for this. He was very shocked – he wanted to know what I meant. So I pointed out that Government supplied no services to these people, not even to the extent of providing the shanties. He obviously thought I was a UNIP man because he got a bit annoyed. "It's Government land, isn't it?" he said. I replied "Quite so, quite so", trying to calm the poor fellow down.

At the weekend Alan Mclean invited me to his house at Munali. His wife, also from Glasgow, had a baby three weeks ago. They are an exceedingly nice couple and I spent a most enjoyable couple of days with them. They fixed me up with a partner (another Scot from Paisley) and we went out to a restaurant where there was a band and dance floor.

Seven years later I became one of the architects of housing policies for the urban areas of Zambia. By then, 1968, migration to the urban areas was in the hundreds of thousands not the tens of thousands as was the case in 1961. It was financially impossible for the Government to afford to build houses for all of the urban immigrants. Instead, areas were prepared around the major towns with roads and piped water supplies. Plots were allocated to families who were encouraged to build their own houses. They were helped with loans and with technical support. With the funds available, ten times as many families could be helped to build decent housing as would have been the case if Government had undertaken the total house construction itself. These were known as site and service schemes and were taken up by the World Bank as a model for low cost urban housing.

Chalimbana
13 June 61

It is now only two days to the end of the Course though it is difficult to realize that we have been here for nigh on three weeks for everything merges together as one looks back over that period.

Last Friday we visited the High Court and there saw two trials in progress. One was a civil action and the other a murder trial with seven men in the dock. They are Luluas from Kasai in the Congo who had a fight with some men of a rival tribe, Balubas, in one of the unauthorized compounds outside Lusaka in which some Balubas were killed.

At the time of our arrival, the trial was in its eleventh day and the case for the prosecution was still being put. In fact, the trial is expected to take three weeks. The proceedings are made slower because everything that is said has to be translated for the accused. There is no jury system in Northern Rhodesia because of the difficulty of finding qualified jurors and because of the possibility of a biased verdict if questions of colour or tribe arise. It is strange how dispassionate the law is in the face of a matter of life and death.

Later in the day we visited the Urban Native Court. In this court, all civil actions and minor crimes involving Africans are tried. The bench consists of three assessors, picked from the region whence come those involved in the case. Thus if a Lozi is involved in an action with a Bemba, there will be a Lozi assessor and a Bemba one ▶

▶ and one neutral and together they can pronounce authoritatively on questions of differing tribal custom, damages and so on.

Senanga
27 June 61

The results of the Language Exams came with today's Government Gazette and you will be amazed to hear that I have passed both Oral and Written parts of my Higher Lozi. I regard myself as very lucky to have passed but I am certainly not complaining. My friend David Salmon at Namushakende, unfortunately failed both parts but since he is out of normal district work, it is very difficult for him to keep up his Lozi.

I wish I could say that I was now getting ahead with my swotting for the Law Exam but I can't. At Chalimbana too much talk put paid to it and here I seldom seem to have a spare minute. It is going to be worse next month when for part of it I shall be the only person on the Boma. The DC will be away on a three weeks Copperbelt tour of Lozi communities (he will be accompanied by two indunas) while John Wyatt and Tony Hellen, my two juniors (!) are both due to go off on tour during the month.

Last weekend I went up to Mongu with the Edyes and John Wyatt to see the Barotse National Agricultural Show.

While in Mongu I was told by the DC that the Resident Commissioner had asked for me to be seconded for three months to work out standardized methods of calculating estimates of the District Native Treasuries throughout the Protectorate. So from the beginning of August till about the end of October I shall be based in Mongu and possibly making visits to the various District Native Authority Headquarters during that period to see how each handles its estimates, how new buildings are costed and what rates of pay are in force.

When I wrote that I had been lucky to pass the Higher Lozi exams I really meant it. In the week before, I read a biography of King Shaka of the Zulu people. In the Written paper the passage for translation from Lozi into English had been taken from that book. As soon as I scanned it I found that I could render the English version with ease. It was like winning the lottery.

Twenty-five today and feeling every minute of it.

Mr Heath, the Resident Commissioner, came to lunch last Wednesday and the Farrans and John Wyatt were also there. I gave him a sort of Russian fish pie which was voted the culinary success of the year. The RC that we have now is a very different type from his predecessor. He is very approachable and a fantastic talker. On Wednesday evening, I had dinner at the Edyes' house and the Resident Commissioner spoke almost non-stop all evening. He likes to hear his own voice but he certainly manages to be interesting.

Two financiers are coming here for three days. They are coming up by plane, I think, though it is possible they are also arranging for a landrover to come as well so that they can inspect the forests they are interested in from the ground as well as the air. There are five in their party and as the rest house has only four beds, I shall have to put up one of them.

Life is fairly busy at the moment as I am doing the Nalolo Trial Balance again and on Tuesday the DC goes away for a three-week tour of the Copper Belt centres with two Lozi Indunas in order to visit the Lozis who migrated to the towns. This kind of visit is made every year by a DC and Native Authority representatives from each main tribal group in Northern Rhodesia to acquaint the townsmen of changes in their home districts, to answer questions and generally show that although they have gone to the towns their traditional leaders are still concerned with their welfare.

For the next few weeks I am going to be busy because for part of the time I shall be the only one on the station (the other two being on tour) and because the Governor-General of the Federation is due in mid-August and preparations for his visit will have to be set in train in the next week or two. Also, at the beginning of August the annual audit inspection of the Boma and Native Authority books by a team of auditors from Lusaka falls due and this requires doing another trial balance just beforehand. ▶

▶ Goodness knows how I'm going to find time to do my study for the law exam. It is not only that there is no time during the day to do any swotting but in the evenings, there is so much entertaining done that it is extremely difficult to get a solid piece of work done. Of the last six evenings, I have been out on five of them; two because of the Resident Commissioner's visit, one when I had to entertain the visiting Protectorate Cooperatives and Marketing Officer, one ordinary party and tonight supper at the Farrans.

How stupid Macleod has been to depart from his original proposals. As they were, it was all Kaunda could do to persuade his party to agree to consider them. To modify them because of Welensky is to fail completely to face realities and to give backing to the moderate tactics shown by Kaunda over the past year. It is quite obvious that the side which gives the hardest tweak to the British Government's ears wins the day but time will show that Kaunda and his party can give them a much stronger tweak than Welensky. Why Macleod has gone some way to meeting UFP objections to his original White Paper proposals I cannot really understand. The power of this party is bound to diminish very rapidly.

The missionary from the Seventh Day Adventist mission at Sitoti, on the opposite bank of the Zambezi, fifteen miles south of Senanga, was stranded here having missed the last pontoon crossing so I gave him a bed for the night. He is a nice fellow but quite misguided!

Ian Macleod was an enlightened Colonial Secretary who had set up the Monckton Commission to ascertain the popular mood towards the Central African Federation. The Commission reported that there was overwhelming opposition to the white-dominated Federation and that the two British Protectorates of Nyasaland and Northern Rhodesia should be allowed to secede from it. This was the death knell of the Federation, and infuriated Sir Roy Welensky, the Federation's Prime Minister, and his white electorate.

At the same time, Macleod started inter-party talks to establish a new constitution for Northern Rhodesia which in its first draft promised an extension of the franchise. It would have given many more Africans the vote and a possible majority in the NR Legislature for the nationalists. It was opposed by Welensky who was supported by the right wing of the British Conservative Party. Macleod and his Prime Minister caved in to these pressures and came up with revised proposals that tilted the likely electoral balance in favour of the white supported United Federal Party in Northern Rhodesia. I was correct in predicting big trouble ahead.

Letter to Christian Fraser

Senanga
12 July 1961

My dear Christian

It is mid-winter here and in the early mornings and late evenings one shivers in temperatures of 65 to 70°F.[86] It seems to be much colder this winter than last but perhaps it is only my blood that is becoming thinner. This is the best time of the year and it would be wonderful if it were like this the whole year round. Unfortunately, the seasons here have a predictability totally unknown in Britain. One knows that around the beginning of August temperatures will start rising gradually until by mid-September the thermometer is steady in the nineties.

It is amazing how quickly the sun goes down at this time of year. Towards sunset the sun becomes a great red ball moving slowly onto the edge of the Earth. Then someone seems to grasp it and pull it quickly out of sight.

The Zambezi River is at its loveliest at sunset when the colour of the water changes from russet to red to pink. It is especially beautiful returning home in a boat at this time of day because the extending ripples and waves that follow the boat's wake make the colours come alive. I never tire of watching men paddling their canoes up or down or across the river, so graceful and silent is their passage.

The flood that covers the Barotse Plain every year is now falling fast and during the past two weeks the villagers have been moving themselves and their chattels from their "temporary" villages on ▶

---

[86] *16-18°C.*

the forest edge to the villages on the Plain that they had to abandon some five months earlier in the face of the rising flood waters. Many have to cross the river to get back to their villages because at Senanga the eastern forest edge of the plain comes down close to the river and it is easier for people on the west side of the river to make their flood-season villages on the eastern forest edge than to trek some ten or fifteen miles across the plain to the western forest edge.

In returning to the Plain, they take their cattle with them and at this time of year one can see large herds being swum across. In fact, they are not swum across but rather down river. The cattle are slow in the water and are whisked downstream by the fast current. As they go, herdsmen in canoes gradually nudge them into midstream and into a current which draws the cattle into the opposite bank. It requires a great deal of skill and nerve on the part of the boatmen but even in the strongest currents the Lozi control their canoes effortlessly.

Cattle swimming across the Zambezi while being nudged along by the herdsmen in canoes

Last night, amongst others who came to dinner was the richest man in Central Africa, a businessman with important interests in just about every industry outside copper mining. He flew up to Senanga with two other plutocrats to inspect some forests in this District with a view to their commercial exploitation. They impressed me with their toughness and shrewdness but that's about all. Theirs is not a very humane way of life and I would not change places with them for any amount of millions.

Senanga
26 July 61

I have just returned from a three-day trip to Nalolo. I left Senanga on Sunday afternoon with the DC in Kit Farran's speedboat and it took us about five hours to reach Nalolo and of that, one hour was spent in replacing a broken sheer pin which keeps the propeller in place. If we had used the Boma boat, it would have taken a minimum of twelve hours to do the journey.

At Nalolo, we stayed in the guest house at the Mission and Jameson was able to use the kitchen of the missionary's house, because the missionary and the nursing sister are not at present in residence.

I spent my time working with the Treasury Clerk and his assistant, clearing up various points prior to the visit of the Auditors next week. I also had morning tea each day, along with the DC, with the Mulena Mukwae and her husband in her palace and lunched with them on the Monday. On the Tuesday, instead of inviting us over to lunch, she sent us two large fish and seventeen eggs, so that we should not go hungry while in her capital.

Yesterday morning, after morning tea, I took photos of the Mulena Mukwae and her husband, standing in front of the palace, in the inner court. As I was getting the camera prepared, the Mulena Mukwae suddenly remembered she was not wearing stockings and would have gone away and put on a pair if the DC and I had not assured her it was a matter of no importance! Also, I said I would only like a picture of the upper half of her person, so she was satisfied.

> In the afternoon, I called in to see her and to take my formal leave – one has to observe the proper form, you know. The Lozi are extremely punctilious about these sorts of courtesies, little less so I am sure than at the Court of St James. We exchanged flowery compliments and mutual regret was expressed at my imminent departure for Mongu.

My departure for Mongu was in connection with the previously mentioned three-month assignment to systematise the Native Authority accounts throughout the Protectorate as proposed by the Resident Commissioner (perhaps he had been impressed with my work on the Nalolo Treasury Accounts).

> I must say that I have enjoyed my visits to Nalolo because it is a colourful and interesting place and one is always received there with the greatest of courtesy and friendliness.

> The DC spent long hours talking with the Mulena Mukwae and the Kuta mostly about the details of the Governor General's visit to Nalolo on the 16th August. On matters such as this, the Nalolo Kuta does very well, because preparing for distinguished visitors is something to which they are traditionally accustomed. However, I hope that they remove before the visit, a large banner which occupies a prominent position in the Kuta, on which are the words, in large white capitals "God Save the King" (George VI?). This formed part of the decorations which festooned prominent buildings in Nalolo while we were there, which had been put up to mark the second anniversary of the enthronement of the present Mulena Mukwae. She is the sixteenth to sit at Nalolo and only three of her predecessors, all near the beginning of the line, have been men.

> On Monday afternoon, some Makishi dancers had arrived in Nalolo to dance in front of the palace, to honour the Mulena Mukwae. After I had finished my work I went over and watched them. There were two men dancing, and three drummers accompanying them. They were dancing under a huge tree that grows in the centre of Nalolo between the Kuta and the palace and a large crowd had

gathered. The men were dancing with convulsive jerking movements of their limbs and often they imitated animals or enacted various comedies. I stood under the tree taking photos and enjoying myself watching the dancers and drummers and the reactions of the bystanders at close hand.

I had hardly been standing there for more than fifteen minutes when a kapasu came up and said the Sambi was inviting me to

make use of his chair from which to view the dancing. The Sambi (chief councillor of the MM) was sitting on a bench in front of the offices along with other councillors and the chair he had provided for me was standing on a mat in front of the palace in isolated splendour though a couple of councillors were squatting on the mat beside the chair. So I sat in state till the DC came out from the palace courtyard at the end of his deliberations with the Mulena Mukwae.

Likishi Dancer (photo: LW Jarrett)

Senanga
1 August 61

I have now been in Senanga for close on two whole years having arrived on the 4th August 1959. Little did I think when I stepped off the plane that I would outlast all the members of the deputation who welcomed me at the airfield – David Acheson, Iain Stuart, Jonathon Cole and Peter Wilson. I can remember the scene as clearly as if it had only taken place yesterday.

At the same time, it seems an awfully long time ago. So much has happened since, that it is difficult to imagine them on the station once again, doing the jobs that I am doing now. I feel as though I have always been doing the Native Authority work and not David Acheson and Iain Stuart before me.

The weather has taken a decided turn for the hotter during the last four days. Summer is a comin' in. I had to turn up the flame underneath the fridge quite considerably to prevent it from defrosting. This paraffin fridge is a battered old object – not like the sleek model that graces your kitchen. It does not even own a handle so that to open it you have to poke your little finger into the hole where the handle was and unsneck the catch.

Letter to Christian Fraser

Senanga
1 August 1961

My dear Christian

Right now I am feeling rather unsettled because in less than a week's time I am setting off for a three months' secondment to the Resident Commissioner's office in Mongu to reduce the annual estimates and accounts of the Barotse Native Government into some sort of ordered system.

Also I have applied for a transfer to the Ministry of African Agriculture which is presently looking for another economist. I learned of this during the three week course near Lusaka when I was spending a weekend at the house of Alan McLean and his wife, having met Alan on the course. He is an English teacher at Munali Secondary School just outside Lusaka. At the house of the head English master who is a Scot from Aberdeen, I met the one and only economist on the above-mentioned Ministry's staff. He was very enthusiastic about his job and thought I would have a good chance of getting the other unfilled economist's job if I applied. So when I had a free day after the Course I called in at the Ministry and saw various officials who were fairly encouraging. They advised me to see the Director of Agriculture who was pretty lukewarm, pointing out my lack of research experience, etc. He told me, moreover, that I would be foolish to stay on in the Provincial Administration because he thought that there was precious little future for Europeans without specialist qualifications in this country and that my specialist qualification in economics diminished in value with every year that separated me from my graduation.

If my own bosses had some bright ideas about the continued effective use of European officers in the PA after Independence I would be happier about staying on. Our Minister[87] for example, in the course of delivering a talk to us on the Chalimbana Course assured us that there was a thirty year future ahead for the European administrator who might have to face changes but not ▶

[87] *The same person, Mr George Billing, whom I entertained to lunch in Senanga a couple of months after arriving there.*

any greater than experienced by him in his thirty years of service. He also spoke a lot of guff about facing up to the fact that we could not expect to be Sanders-of-the-River type administrators. He seems quite unable to admit that the revolution that will be created in the administration by the granting of independence under a nationalist government will be far, far greater than he experienced when a Labour Minister stepped into the Colonial Office in 1946.

I won't be particularly worried if I don't get this job I have applied for. In some ways, I am quite happy to sit still and let things take their appointed course.

Yours

Callum

Office of the Resident Commissioner
Mongu.
7 August 1961

This is the evening of August Bank Holiday Monday but it has been no holiday really because today I have "flitted" from Senanga to Mongu. There is no worse job than packing all one's belongings. I found it depressing removing the pictures from the walls, the books from the shelves, the karosses from the floors and leave but the featureless shell of a house, no longer a home. Not only depressing, but exhausting, as I had to get the work done in one day, being kept too busy at the office to set about the work more gradually.

I am now installed in the Rest House in Mongu. I have a bedroom to myself which has a wash basin and a writing table as well, but I shall have to eat in the rest house dining room and have my meals cooked in the rest house kitchen.

During this three-month period, I am likely to be out on tour to the different District and District Kuta headquarters so it does not matter so much that I am living in rather cramped quarters at present. One great advantage this place does have – electricity. What a boon and how nice after paraffin lamps!

> The situation in much of Northern Rhodesia looks tense at present, especially in the Copperbelt and Northern and Luapula Provinces where there have been fatal clashes between police and African demonstrators and blowing up of bridges, etc.

> It is likely that these happenings have been instigated by UNIP members though Kaunda has denounced the violence. He has little control over the lower ranks of his party. This violence is reprehensible but I am sure that the Government has brought it upon its own head by its compromises to the original Macleod proposals for constitutional change.

In the thick of the troubles in Northern Province

Kasama
Northern Province, NR
16 August 1961

I arrived this evening in Kasama, the administrative centre of Northern Province where, as you may have read in newspapers, there has been a lot of trouble in the last few days. I have been sent up with David Salmon and two other DOs to help the local administration until the trouble is over and the situation back to normal.

Life has been really hectic since last I wrote. Sunday morning, the DC Mongu informed me of this assignment and that I was to fly from Mongu on Tuesday afternoon, half an hour after the law exams were due to finish. Naturally, this announcement did not help my concentration very much. In the middle of the night my bedroom became a maternity ward while my dog gave birth to puppies. It was not conducive to sleep.

On Monday, there were two exams of two hours each, and considering my debilitated condition and lack of preparation, I did as well as could be expected. On Tuesday, another six hours of exams, then back to the Rest House to pack a few clothes and arrange for the safe-keeping of my belongings and then a dash to the airport to board a plane specially sent from Lusaka to pick up me and David.

▶

> Reached Lusaka at 8 p.m. to be met by an officer from the Secretariat who handed us each a letter which informed us that we were now District Officers having been confirmed in our appointments.

> We rose before 5 a.m. this morning and drove with Murray Armor, David's former DC in Kalabo, in his car the five hundred and fifty miles from Lusaka to Kasama. There were no incidents on route, the roads having been cleared by the police earlier in the day.

c/o DC Kasama
21 August 1961

This is the first night of my first tour in Northern Province and it is much like that of any tour in Barotseland. I went first to the Native Authority headquarters to pick up the kapasus and councillors who are coming with me on this tour. These headquarters are forty miles from Kasama along well surfaced laterite roads. Then I went to visit the chief another five miles away, and was able to make my visits and complete my business there, all in the space of three hours. In Senanga, it would have taken a whole day.

The Native Authority set-up is different here to Barotseland's. There is a Paramount Chief, called Chitimukulu, and under him there are six chiefs who appear to function pretty well independently of him. The chiefdoms are on the whole smaller than in Barotseland. Senanga, for example, is all under the control of the Mulena Mukwae who is herself in essential matters under the control of the Paramount Chief. But in Kasama District, which is the centre of Bembaland, there are half a dozen chiefs and their areas of jurisdiction are so small that they do not have sub-chiefs under them.

I don't know how accurate the reports (if any) are that are reaching you on the Northern Rhodesia situation. In 1958, there were political troubles in Northern Province and in March 1959, the party then called the Zambia African National Congress (ZANC), led by Kenneth Kaunda, was banned and its leaders detained under a state of emergency.

Until four months ago, UNIP which was in effect ZANC under another name, was unable to function openly in Northern Province because the chiefs were encouraged not to give their approval to the registration of UNIP branches in their areas. However, in April, Government reversed its policy believing that UNIP was pledged to a policy of peaceful change by constitutional means. The chiefs and the common people did not understand Government's reasoning and felt that it was merely capitulating to pressure from Kaunda and others and that they, the chiefs, would be in for a sticky time in future if they did not do as the local UNIP leaders told them.

The NR Government was caught off balance because of the later changes decided upon by the British Government in the new Northern Rhodesia constitution. These benefited Welensky's UFP to the detriment of UNIP and led to the total rejection of the proposed constitution by the latter. Moreover, Kaunda has spoken of a "master plan" with which he intends bringing the state to a standstill without specifying how such an object is to be implemented, and although he has condemned violence he has said that he cannot be held responsible for the actions of his subordinates whose patience is not inexhaustible.

And so it has proved. The local UNIP leaders are according to all reports a rather ruffianly lot. Several have criminal records and the rest are mostly men who have returned discontented from the Copperbelt. For the last two months, they have been going round the villages enlisting support and threatening to burn houses, destroy gardens and even kill those who refuse to join them.

As everyone believed that sooner or later these men were to be the Government of the country, there has been no one to resist them. So they have persuaded hundreds to burn their identity cards, to block roads by felling trees and to destroy bridges. Gangs armed with spears, staves and bicycle chains started trying to ambush cars and burn down stores and schools.

UNIP, therefore, was banned about ten days ago in this Province. To date, in Chinsali District, twenty-two out of the forty-two schools have been burned down; in Kasama District, six churches and a Native Treasury and some cattle kraals have been burned. In

Abercorn District there has been arson and road blocking and in Luwingu District a large Roman Catholic mission station has been destroyed by fire as have several churches, schools, stores and bridges. Other Districts in this and in Luapula Province, which lies between it and the Congo have been affected to a similar degree.

The NR Police and the Kings African and Northern Rhodesian Rifles have been called in to help put down the disturbances. The theory is (and I think it is largely correct) that the active malcontents and arsonists are only a very small proportion of the community but by terrorist tactics they are getting the remainder or a sizable portion of it in certain areas to follow their lead.

So far, 16 people have been killed in clashes with the police and military. In some cases, these deaths have occurred when the forces of law and order have been fired on. More often, they have been killed on the army's initiative. That is, when an unlawful assembly is encountered which does not break up when told to, a warning shot is fired in the air and if that fails to disperse the crowd, one of the obvious ringleaders is picked out and shot. That usually does the trick.

But it seems to me an excessively extreme method. One reason is that the soldiers have no training in the putting down of civil disturbances with baton charges, etc. and are being used only because the police forces are insufficient to cope. Also, where the opposition is armed with spears, a baton charge may be an extremely hazardous operation for the baton-wielders. That having been said, from the security reports coming in, it would appear that the military have not behaved on some occasions with the restraint and common sense that one should expect of them.

In the area I am touring, three churches and the Treasury offices of the Native Authority have been burned, the offices and two of the churches just last night. The arsonists seem not to have come from this District but from the neighbouring one and it seems likely that they have returned from whence they came.

Burned out Chief's headquarters

I have four District Messengers with me, with three rifles between them, lest someone comes in the middle of the night to burn down the camp. They will take it in turns to keep watch.

I shall be on tour for nine days, cycling round the villages putting out counter-propaganda to UNIP's and trying to re-establish the people's confidence in the Native Authority and Central Government.

Back from a most enjoyable tour and now off on another, though a very different one in less than an hour's time. This is very much a scribble but I shall write at length when I get back in a few days' time.

About the tour which I finished two days ago. In each village we spent about an hour talking to the people. Most of the talking was done by me and I was pretty tired of speaking by the end of the tour as you can well imagine.

On the whole I spoke sweet words to the people because I felt that if we are to keep the mass of them on our side we have to distinguish between the leaders and the led. Government's case is on the whole a good deal stronger than UNIP's. For instance, in one District in this province alone, twenty-two schools have been burned by UNIP members and in other districts, schools, churches, native authority offices and the kraals and houses of anti-UNIP Africans have also gone up in flames - the work of UNIP "freedom fighters".

So I talked about the length of time needed to build a strong nation, the meaning of freedom, the importance of peace and law and order as well as Government's intention to hunt down ruthlessly those responsible for the arson and terrorism. To illustrate how long it takes to build a modern society, I explained how my grandfather had been a fisherman with very little money. How my father had been the only one of eight children that his parents had been able to send to university with the help of a wealthy uncle. How this enabled my father to become a teacher and then a head teacher and how he was able to send both his sons to university. So I explained that these developments take more than one generation; that education is the key to progress so the burning of schools harms ordinary people and their children greatly and that if they were patient their children and grandchildren would enjoy much better education in future and better jobs too.

These acts of arson and violence started the week after a Province-wide tour by Kenneth Kaunda. To what extent he is responsible for the dastardly deeds of his underlings I would not know but his attitude towards them has been equivocal to say the least. ▶

▶ On this tour we arrested sixteen UNIP leaders and freedom fighters. A poor bunch they were too, for the most part with little or no education and relying mostly on force to get their way with the locals.

I came back to Kasama two days ago and since then, until lunch time today, I have been working in the Provincial Operations Room. This meant working from 7.30 a.m. to 6.30 p.m. with an hour for lunch. During this time, I was coordinating operations in the Province and acting as secretary at meetings of the Provincial Operations Committee which makes the necessary important policy and tactical decisions. Quite interesting but as the whole situation is becoming quiet now with the UNIP leaders scattered and hiding in the bush, I was not very busy. Moreover, I felt it was a waste of my abilities which lie more in field work so I agitated for a shift. The DC Kasama did likewise, so I am back in the DC's office. Now I have got to go and pack for a short tour in which I am representing the civil power in an operation by some army units to catch leaders hiding on some islands on a river to the east of Kasama.

At the end of the tour, the Administrative Officer of the Native Authority who had been my translator told me that the local people were saying "Who is this white man? Is he a missionary?"

The people's response to what I said may have been because I did not berate them for the acts of arson which had taken place in their district. Or perhaps it was because I spoke of my own family background which made them realise that I was not so different from them.

I last wrote last Wednesday evening before going out on a short operation with the army to round up some UNIP-inspired wrongdoers. I did not enjoy this operation very much. It went as follows.

First of all, about 5.30 p.m. I set out from Kasama and travelled for about fifty miles along side roads until we reached a village on the edge of the Chambeshi River. Parts of these roads had been blocked with trees earlier in the month and one or two small bridges destroyed. As we drove along it was easy to see just where the roadblocks had been made, for although the road had since been cleared, felled tree trunks and branches still lined the road. Our task was to find the people responsible for this and for beating up a party of kapasus and district messengers who had gone to arrest a man in that area, and to find some UNIP men who were said to be hiding on islands on the Chambeshi.

I reached a rendezvous with the Major in charge of the army company who were on this exercise at about 8 p.m. and at 8.30 I set off up the Chambeshi to meet another patrol under an African Sergeant Major (a Lozi) with whom I was to work. There were also two other patrols engaged on sweeping out the islands and then moving in parallel towards a road along which a DO was carrying out a tour of the villages bordering it.

The paths leading onto this road were all guarded by troops and it was hoped to drive people into these traps. I reached my patrol between 9.30 and 10 p.m. and got to sleep soon after.

I was up just before 2 a.m. and set off with the soldiers looking for canoes to take us to the island which we were required to search. Searching the island was our most important task. I had been told it was important to get on to it and surround it before dawn. But over three hours were spent in looking for canoes. We found plenty, but only two paddles. Moreover, the canoes were thin affairs, all right for a lightly clad fisherman travelling alone but no use for carrying more than a single heavily armoured soldier. ▶

The situation was complicated by the fact that more than half the soldiers did not know how to paddle a canoe. Also, the kapasu who was acting as our guide led me to believe that the island was a long way off and that to get to it one had to negotiate a particular part of the Chambeshi which was thickly populated with hippos.

However, towards first light, he had the bright idea of taking us to the village from where it was best to make a crossing to the island. By this time, it was becoming light and on our arrival at this village the people were beginning to get up. The island, instead of being miles away as I had been led to believe, was separated from the mainland by about one hundred yards of water and with the help of men from the village we crossed this in about ten minutes.

The island itself is flat and treeless, full of bogs, and not at all hospitable even to the most hardened of criminals, but the kapasu maintained there were men there and the villagers backed him up to a certain extent.

So off we went to the island and soon got soaked to the knees ploughing through the long dew-laden grass. Only two men were found and they were only innocent fishermen on their way to their nets. Two more were sighted and took to a canoe on the far side of the island and escaped across the river.

Just as we had finished searching the island and returned to the mainland, a boat came chugging up river with the Major and his men and some prisoners on board, the prisoners being men who had run away from their villages and were camped on the river's edge. Once on shore they were identified by the District Messenger and kapasu who were with me as being among the crowd who had attacked them. The men denied this and so the Major took a step forward and slapped two of them across the face for their impertinence!

Then he left and I proceeded on my way through the villages alongside the river. We arrested another twenty-nine men who had allegedly been involved in road blocking and assault on District Messengers and kapasus. The soldiers, when we started off were yelling and from time to time buffeting their prisoners and in the villages, hectoring the people. I told their Sergeant Major after I had seen this happening in the first village we had come to that all this had to stop as they were supposedly coming as friends of loyal citizens and not as representatives of the hated Federation. That stopped all the nonsense.

We finally got to camp at 6 p.m., utterly exhausted, having covered over thirty miles since rising at 2 a.m.

Next day, we set off at 4 a.m. to walk about ten to twelve miles to a village where there was a UNIP branch chairman supposed to be hiding. We reached the village after a rapid march through woods in the beautiful light of the moon, only to find that the man we were looking for had already been arrested.

We camped in a wood above a rushing stream at 10 a.m. and did nothing more that day.

At 4 a.m. the following day, Saturday, we set off once again and reached the main road some three hours later. Eventually, transport came out for me and I set off for Kasama with my soldiers and prisoners.

Half way to Kasama, we came to the Court of the Paramount Chief Chitimukulu's Chief Minister, the Mwanangu. He was conducting preliminary investigations into the cases of the men arrested on this operation to see which were guilty of minor and which of major offences, the latter to be sent to Kasama for trial. So I handed over my thirty-eight prisoners to him and he handed me twelve prisoners for transporting to Kasama.

The men I off-loaded were immediately set upon by the kapasus and District Messengers in attendance at the Mwanangu's Court. They were pushed and pummelled and shoved into line and then marched off in squads. The squad of the worst offenders was marched off and made to lift up a forty-four gallon drum of water above their heads at arms' length for about ten to fifteen minutes, being whacked about the buttocks with sticks if they weakened.

Then, together with the other squads, they were made to drill, sometimes with their hands above their heads, saying aloud in Bemba "Welcome, sir, welcome, sir", the traditional Bemba greeting.

I was horrified but could hardly put a stop to it without making a fool of the Mwanangu so I had to wait until I returned to Kasama to tell the DC about it. The DC said that strict instructions had been issued by him that there was to be no beatings-up or unduly harsh methods used at the native courts to extract confessions of guilt and in fact he had placed a DO at the Mwanangu's Court while the men arrested on this operation were on trial but he had to go away to attend to some other business that very morning.

It may be of course that we are too lily-livered about this and that the Native Authorities know better than we do just how much force should be used against people who have revolted against their authority and that of Central Government. I think their idea is that UNIP intimidation can only be countered by an even greater show of intimidation by the Native Authority and the Central Government.

This, I believe, is very largely mistaken. UNIP owes its power to more than intimidation. It has been able to build up resentment against the chiefs and against Government among certain villagers. UNIP's influence, by the way, varies very much from village to village, depending usually on the character of the headman. There are good reasons for some of this resentment. In other matters, the resentment is based on misconceptions and ignorance. It cannot be removed until their misconceptions have been corrected, the ignorance dispelled and the grievances satisfied.

None of these objects can be achieved if touring by DOs becomes impossible without soldiers to hand; the old basis of trust has got to be re-established. If excessive force is used against even minor malefactors – men who have been led astray by UNIP agitators and the excitement of a UNIP meeting – this trust will never be re-established.

Kasama
5 September 1961

On Sunday evening I set off on another operation. At 8.30 p.m. I left Kasama, driving first to the Musumba (headquarters) of the Chief whose area I had toured a week before. There, I picked up three kapasus and the Administrative Councillor. The Councillor was at a school concert when I arrived and his wife was entertaining one of the Court Assessors and his wife, and the eldest son of the Chief, to beer.

The Councillor arrived and I went into his house to discuss the operation with him. The Chief's son was very tipsy and insisted on telling me his life story, how honoured he was to meet me, what a wonderful Christian speech he had heard me give in one of the villages on my tour, etc., etc. Everyone was highly amused as he insisted on standing to attention while making this address and every now and then flashing a salute.

The beer was in a round calabash which sat in the middle of the floor and there was an iron pipe through which people wishing to partake sucked the beer out of the calabash. It was the first time that I had seen beer being consumed in this way.

The plan of the operation was to make a dawn swoop on a village in the next District, just over the border from Kasama District, where some UNIP "Freedom Fighters" wanted for arson of the Treasury offices at Chief Munkoya's Musumba, were supposed to be living. Involved in this swoop were the Native Authority personnel I have mentioned, five District Messengers and sixty soldiers with two officers because it was also reported that these wanted persons might be in a wood near the village.

By 12.30 a.m. we had reached the river which marks the District boundary. We had to cross this river, which was about one hundred yards wide at this point by means of planks, some six feet wide, as the old bridge had been burned down and a new one was in process of construction. We edged our way across the planks, some of the soldiers being so scared that they crawled across on their hands and knees. I don't have a high opinion of either their discipline or their courage.

▶

▶ On the far side of the river we found a rather incompetent guide to show us the way to the village which we reached at 5.20 a.m. after a four-hour march which often took us through bogs. I felt miserable, suffering as I was from stomach pains. It was now becoming light though the sun was not yet up and we surrounded the village and then started knocking people up. Through the incompetence of the soldiers, two men managed to escape through the back door of one of the huts but several people who had fled from Chief Munkonge's area, including two or three "Freedom Fighters" were captured. They were taken to Munkonge's Musumba for a telling-off and resettlement in their villages and possibly a fine as well. The Freedom Fighters will no doubt be brought in today for trial in Kasama. White Chibesa, the man we were really looking for, had escaped the day before having heard of arrests that had been made on the other side of the river some days earlier. However, I managed to find out the name of the village to which he had gone and as soon as I got back to Kasama I sent off a radio message to the DC of the District involved. This morning I learned that, as a result of this information, Chibesa had been captured. So the operation has been worthwhile and the DC here is greatly pleased.

Before leaving the village, the soldiers helped themselves to chickens, axes and spears. I told the officer in charge that I thought it quite wrong and I forbade my District Messengers to follow suit. Their Officer in Charge said he allowed it because the village was a bad one and deserved to be taught a lesson and that his men deserved a perk!

Some truth in this, I suppose, but I was appalled. For this sort of reason, I don't like working with the military, especially when I know that, but for my presence, their behaviour would be far worse.

On the way back to our transport I nearly went to sleep on my feet, being utterly exhausted from the long walk and lack of sleep.

I slept all afternoon and am once more refreshed. As far as I know, there is nothing planned for tonight, but tomorrow night I think I shall be going out on an expedition which will take about three days to complete. ▶

> The situation is quietening down considerably with an occasional act of arson here and there. I expect that within two or three weeks we will have tracked down most of the people who are now in hiding after committing arson and intimidation. After that, I shall probably be sent back to Barotseland.

There were other night expeditions to arrest arsonists and other offenders in which I took part as representative of the civil authority each similar to the two I have described.

DC's Office

Kasama

19 September 1961

I have been sitting in the office since last I wrote and there are no more trips planned for me at present as things seemed to be quietening down. Today, for example, not a single incident was reported from anywhere within the Province. Of course, we should be setting out on proper touring, but as the Governor General, Lord Dalhousie,[88] is due on the 3rd of next month for an eighteen day tour of the Province, all spare hands are being used to prepare for his visit. A damn great waste of time is the comment of practically everyone from the Provincial Commissioner downwards.

Dalhousie has got the reputation of being an absolute blockhead who demands to be kept amused and the only way of doing this is by laying on huntin' and shootin' trips around the Federation. If he had any ability at all he would be up to his eyes in work at the present time keeping himself up to date with Government papers and exercising a restraining influence on Welensky.

Instead of that, he comes and harries busy officials who have enough on their plates without organising visits of VIPs to places of interest, fishing spots, baby clinics and elaborate garden, cocktail and dinner parties. Not to mention the expense of such a visit (approx. £10,000) at a time when the Federation's finances are in a parlous condition.

[88] A Scottish peer and landowner.

> I don't expect to be in Kasama much longer because things have been so quiet. When out on a visit to some rapids on Sunday with the Provincial Commissioner and his family, the PC told me that the Secretary of the Ministry of Native Affairs who had visited Kasama the previous day had said that it was time that the officers shifted up to Northern Province during the disturbances should be sent back to their stations. However, the PC said he still needed us and that if they were to go back it would have to be at the Secretary's request, not his.

Safe and sound in Senanga again

PO Box 1,
Senanga
4 October 1961

I am now back in Senanga, staying with the Edyes while I unpack. We now have a box number and I suppose this means progress. Some changes are visible just in the short time that I have been away: some new clerks' houses, the road near Senanga straightened and improved etc.

There is going to be a lot of work ahead of us for the next few months as we are behind schedule with our touring programme, there are cattle sales due to commence at the end of this month and various Native Authority works to be completed. It really is very good to be back and to know exactly what is going on.

I can't remember why I was not asked to continue with the task of reforming the accounting system of the Barotse Native Government. Perhaps an accountant from the Provincial Accountant's Office was given the task, a much better idea from my point of view. And I presume that Ian Edye, the DC, was pressing for my return.

Senanga
9 October 61

Dear Mum and Dad

Nothing much to report except that "It's too darned hot". Luckily we now have a swimming pool into which we can jump and cool off but when the heat is at its worst, 2 to 3 p.m., we are still slogging away in the office.

Senanga does not sleep completely as I think I indicated by the physical changes since my departure that I mentioned in my last letter. The biggest change will result from the work of a Government Forest Survey Unit which in the next two years will survey all the forests in this district with a view to their commercial exploitation very shortly afterwards.

So within three to five years at the outside it is likely there will be a railway pushed up into this District to extract the timber (Rhodesian teak mostly, to be used for railway sleepers etc.), and large saw mills employing hundreds, perhaps thousands of labourers. This will make this quite a lively place to administer in the very near future.

The man in charge of the Survey Unit is from Stonehaven,[89] called Adam Wood. I met him for the first time this afternoon when he came in from his camp to post some mail. He came and had tea with me before going back again. He struck me as being a very agreeable person.

I think I mentioned in my last letter that the Farrans had been transferred to Mazabuka where the HQ of the Vet Dept. is situated and their place has been taken by a West countryman from Zoomerset called Tim Nicholls and his wife Kathleen who looks as though she is about sixteen though she is no doubt twenty. Both speak with very broad West Country accents.

This anticipated development of the timber industry in Senanga District never took place; there turned out to be insufficient supplies of teak to make them financially viable to exploit.

[89] *A fishing town 14 miles south of Aberdeen where my paternal ancestors came from.*

Yesterday the District Officer attached to the Special Branch arrived to find out at first-hand what the security situation was like and also to give us the lowdown on the security situation in the Territory as a whole. It was an extremely interesting session in that he revealed that the degree of penetration of the nationalist parties in Northern Rhodesia by the Special Branch is very high indeed.

Last night, I was wakened in order to take an expectant mother to the hospital. This was at about 1.30 a.m.; the woman had been carried up the Zambezi by canoe since midday. The only landrover on the Boma was at my house and as the Duty Messenger had not wakened a driver I took the landrover down to the landing stage near the Boma offices and drove the sick woman (she is badly crippled) to the hospital.

On the way there near the WNLA depot the landrover stopped and as the petrol gauge was very low, I thought I had run out of petrol. I managed to wake up the WNLA mechanic who siphoned a gallon of petrol out of his car for me. He told me it might be that the valve in the carburettor was sticking and sure enough although I started off all right after putting in the petrol, the engine soon started stuttering.

However, I reached the hospital and the patient was carried off to bed on a stretcher. Dr. Casalis was wakened (for the third time that night, poor thing) to come and see how the woman was.

Then I set off home, but after going fifty yards the landrover packed up. Luckily, a few hefty whacks with a spanner on the carburettor put it to rights and I finally got home more than two hours after setting off.

This morning, the DC and I slogged away at the Native Authority books and eventually worked out correctly the Quarterly Trial Balance. Tomorrow, we set off for Nalolo where we will be for three days at the Annual Estimates meeting. If we did not keep at them all the time, work such as this would never get done.

▶

▶ There is a great deal of latent discontent against the traditional Barotse Native Government set up, both amongst the educated minority and the villagers who realize that it is because of the Boma's presence that anything is done for them by the BNG.

One thing is certain, if the Northern Rhodesia Government manages to force the BNG to allow UNIP to register members freely in Barotseland, UNIP will spread like wildfire. But because at present UNIP is not allowed to register here, it cannot hold meetings without the special permission of the Mulena Mukwae or whoever the District Chief is, nor can they raise funds, take subscriptions, etc. So UNIP has to remain underground; even so, its influence is gradually spreading around Senanga and along the road to Mongu.

Mulonga Kuta
23 October 1961

I last wrote just before setting off for Nalolo with the DC for the annual Estimates meeting. We had barely gone ten miles from Senanga when the engine started playing up and eventually gave up the ghost altogether. Since the carburettor had previously caused similar trouble, we gave it a few bangs with a spanner and proceeded on our way. But we hardly progressed a mile before the engine pegged out again. It restarted and again faded away.

We concluded that one of the jets in the carburettor must be blocked. We dismantled the carburettor and blew through all the jets to make sure there were no blockages, put everything back and set off. This time we hardly got a hundred yards before the engine stopped.

Just then, a landrover came down the road from Mongu and who should it be but the chief mechanic from the Government Mechanical Workshops in Mongu on a tour of inspection of vehicles and plant at Senanga, Sesheke and Mankoya. He soon diagnosed the fault – a loose connection to the coil - and quickly rectified it. It was quite a piece of luck that he appeared on the scene because I doubt if we would have discovered what was wrong. ▶

▶ We had wasted an hour or two in the blazing sun and it was nearly 4 p.m. before we had reached the Zambezi at the ferry crossing opposite Nalolo. The Sambi had arranged for a paddle barge to wait for us there and they paddled us to the Mission which was devoid of Europeans, the Nursing Sister having gone on six weeks' local leave to Southern Rhodesia and the Missionary and his wife still being over at Mooyo. We stayed in the Guest Room[90] and Jameson cooked for us in the kitchen attached to the Nursing Sister's house.

Next morning, we walked the half mile to Nalolo and I was welcomed back with a show of gladness by the Indunas and the Mulena Mukwae and Ishee Kwandu. Eventually we got down to business, taking first Revenue Estimates. We buzzed through these fairly rapidly, while I chalked up on a blackboard the figures for this and last year's tax collections to show how badly their tax collectors were doing.

The Indunas' interest picked up when the Estimates of Expenditure came up for discussion; naturally, because they had all asked for salary increases. For the Mulena Mukwae, they requested an increase of £244 and the Sambi gave two or three very weak reasons why this increase was so necessary.

Then the Kuta asked for an increase of about sixty pounds for the Ishee Kwandu (who gets less than a quarter of his wife's salary) and an increase of thirty pounds for the Sambi, though here the Sambi stepped down metaphorically from the platform and let another Induna speak on his behalf. And so on; but no proposals for increasing the salaries of carriers or labourers who earn two shillings per day in their employ.

These Nalolo Indunas are a pretty crummy lot. For the most part they are uneducated and all are all over 50 years old, with little interest in the affairs of government other than their own salaries. One feels that even the low calibre UNIP leaders that I saw in Northern Province could only be one degree more self-centred than these Indunas and might even get certain things done more quickly and efficiently. The Indunas owe their appointment to their family ▶

---

[90] *It contained a couple of beds and a separate bathroom. On the wall of the bedroom was a large poster entitled "FRANCE" and a picture of three jets with vapour trails, Bleu, Blanc et Rouge, zooming over the Arc de Triomphe in Paris.*

background, sometimes being related to the Barotse royal family. Ability to do any of the specialist jobs that they are called on to do is not a requirement. On the other hand, many of them may have an excellent knowledge of traditional law and may be well fitted to pass judgement on the cases that come before them.

So it went on for two days. On Wednesday evening, the last of our sessions having ended at 6 p.m., we set off back to Senanga, getting home at 10 p.m. Next day, I got down to the work of drafting the estimates for submission to the Litunga (Paramount Chief) and the Resident Commissioner and by Friday had finished the bulk of the work. I handed everything over to the DC, tidied up my desk and went home to pack for a tour of several silalos to explain about the importance of supporting the upcoming cattle sales organised by the Cold Storage Commission.

I left Senanga at 3 p.m. and by 6 p.m. had reached Kaunga Kuta where my first camp was. The Kuta building[91] is a fine new construction of burnt brick, cement plastered and roofed in corrugated iron. It is the best in the District, though I say so myself, and it was I who did all the donkey work for it, ordering the materials from Livingstone, getting them delivered to Kaunga, finding a responsible bricklayer, and sorting out the various difficulties that cropped up while the building was going on. The Induna in charge of this Kuta is a very fine person, well over 6 feet tall and with a commanding and humorous personality.

Next morning, the landrover took our goods to the next camp. We addressed a large gathering of villagers on the forthcoming cattle sales, the need to pay taxes, and UNIP. The Veterinary Induna from Nalolo,[92] a weaselly little man, explained about the sales, at tedious length, the Silalo Induna explained about the tax collections and I said "beware UNIP". Not at all an easy discourse. Some very shrewd questions were asked of me at the end of it, mostly of the kind "If UNIP did such and such in Northern Province, why are the UNIP leaders in Lusaka allowed to go free?"

[91]See my letter of 7 December 1959.

[92]Whenever I was accompanied by a departmental Induna from Nalolo it would have been because I had suggested to the Mulena Mukwae beforehand that his presence would be helpful and enhance the value of my tour.

> This morning, we took leave of the Kaunga Induna and set off into Mulonga Silalo, arriving at our camp beside the Kuta at midday. The camp is beautifully situated in the deep, cool shade of muzauli trees. We addressed a meeting at 2 p.m. and then after 4 p.m. set off to visit a large village about thirteen miles away to explain about the sales, etc., getting back to camp just after 6 p.m.

All of these meetings were conducted in Lozi. Long gone were the days when I relied on an interpreter.

Mutomena Camp
Sitoti-Bushanjo Silalo
Senanga
28 October 1961

Instead of the slow plodding of my two previous tours I am speeding around in a landrover. Villages which took us three hours to reach previously are now arrived at in less than an hour. As we approached the camp here, I recognised the path, the wood which we were skirting on our left and a shallow pan on our right and thought, well there is just a broad plain to cross and we will be in

One of my camps

camp. But as we rushed across the baked ground, the broad plain disappeared, swallowed up by our speed, and lo and behold we were already at the gate of the camp.

Today we covered approximately the same area that has required a heartbreak of a trudge in each of the last two tours. In fact, on my first tour I split the journey between two days, on the first of which I walked twenty five miles and was at my last gasp when at 5.30 p.m. I staggered into camp. The next day I had sufficiently recovered to walk eighteen miles.

Last year, with a bicycle to render a little assistance, I combined these two journeys to make one of about thirty two miles. I left at daybreak and returned at sunset.

Today, I did not set out until 10 a.m. because I had first to inspect the nearby school and take part in addressing a gathering of people about cattle sales and other matters. Notwithstanding this late start, we finished our journey by 2 p.m. In fact, instead of going back to that camp, which is at the Kuta, we turned aside, and travelled to the next one.

I can see two important changes in the silalo since first I came here. Everywhere people have been building themselves bigger and better houses, with tall walls, high roofs, and windows, with wooden shutters set into the walls.

The other change is in the water supplies. The people obtain their water in the dry season from wells which they dig in the ground. The walls of these water holes, being of sand soon start to fall in, and this process is hastened by cattle which come to these water holes in search of water and at the same time help to pollute them.

Back in 1959 I promised I would see what could be done to provide proper wells and by dint of agitating here and there not only got the DC to put up a request for special funds for the wells, but also the Provincial Health Inspector, who last year acquired a well-digging team and equipment, to regard this area as priority no. 1 in Barotseland for his well-digging project. So now all the large villages have a well with concrete walls, windlass, chain and bucket and a permanent supply of good water.[93]

[93]See my letter of 24 October 1959 where I describe the foul wells of this area.

▶ As I think I mentioned in my last letter, I have taken my tape-recorder on tour with me. I have held three recording sessions so far in which I have recorded songs of the people living in this silalo.

The people have on each occasion been utterly astounded by this machine which hears them, catches their voices and then lets them go again. It is one of the original Seven Wonders of the World. They are also delighted to hear their voices being played back to them. At the beginning they tend to be shy but once they hear themselves singing, they want to go on singing so that they can have the pleasure of hearing themselves broadcasting.

It will be nine days before I get back to Senanga but the last four of these will be at the cattle sales to be held on the west bank of the Zambezi, twenty-five miles south of Senanga. There are likely to be very many cattle at this sale as the people to whom we have spoken seem to have been very impressed with the prices that will be paid.

Apart from the sale at Senanga last year (also held by the Cold Storage Commission, a semi-public meat-canning concern), the people have in the past received very poor prices for their cattle, the main buyers being a firm called Susman's that has many retail stores in Barotseland and also deals in meat and hides.

On Wednesday, as we were driving along a forest road we saw ahead of us some creatures on the road and as we drew closer, realized that they were giraffe. We were able to come to within twenty yards of them, two adults and two babies (twelve feet tall!). They were a beautiful sight and I was especially moved because they were the first that I had seen here.

What a difference there is between seeing them in the zoo and in their natural habitat. It is only when you have seen them moving slowly through the trees and then starting to gallop, their frames floating over the ground, that you can appreciate their marvellous colouring which so well conceals them and the speed and the grace at which they can move when alarmed.

That day, I camped beside the Zambezi near Sioma, at a lovely spot. It is refreshing to see this river again and it is easy to understand how attached the Lozi are to it, for from it they get the food they most relish, fish, and also the floods which each year refresh the flood plain. Moreover the river is a constant source of fresh water even in the longest droughts.

A view of the Sioma Falls looking upstream

On Wednesday, I travelled along the main road which runs alongside the Zambezi. A meeting was held at a particularly beautiful place on the banks of the Zambezi, where there is a Boma camp. I did not stay the night as I had a long day ahead of me and wanted to go further north to the Government Rest House at Nangweshi.

After talking to the people at this spot, I was left alone with one of the indunas and some of the older men, while the tax clerk was finishing his tax gathering and the landrover was still carrying our equipment to Nangweshi. They told me about two European brothers who used to have a carpenters' business at a place across the river from Sioma. Listening to these old men chatting away about the old times, about the barges that they had made under the supervision of these two Europeans, and sitting at ease under the shade of a tree, I felt completely at peace. How nice to build myself a house here and settle far from the madding crowd, H bombs and all.

I told the men this – build myself a house, sit under this tree all day long and watch my cattle cross the river by the ford yonder just as these cattle are doing now, on their way from their island grazing to their kraal. The men were tickled pink by the idea. How glad they would be to have me as their neighbour! On the day I arrived, my new neighbours would come to greet me in their canoes; why, so many men, women and children would be aboard that some canoes would be in danger of sinking!

Next day, I had to address a meeting of people who had come together at a new school near Nangweshi. The villagers are building this school providing materials, mainly wooden poles and sun-dried bricks, and labour. Equipment and teachers' salaries are paid for by the Government. In this case, the villages around here have been very slow to get the building completed and I had to take them to task. Afterwards questioning the headmen about the building materials that their people had brought in, I found one headman whose village had done better than most and he was possibly the most enthusiastic about having the school.

▶ Yet on the following day at the meeting to publicise the cattle sales I found that he is the doctor who was to provide the medicine to scare away the crocodiles and so ensure a safe passage for the cattle when they will be swum across the river at the end of the sale on the start of their trek to Livingstone.

On Friday, the cattle sales began at Nangweshi. It was terribly hot that day, in comparison to the proceeding five days which were marvellously cloudy and cool. Since then, it has been hot and humid into the bargain. This afternoon has seen clouds overhead and the heat has abated somewhat.

The cattle sales were fairly uneventful. Three hundred and thirty cattle were sold, ninety-five percent being from the Sitoti-Bushanjo area which I toured fairly intensively. The other two areas, Kaunga and Mulonga may send most of theirs to the next sale at Liliachi.

Senanga
13 November 61

Last Tuesday there came a very pleasant surprise in the mail. It was a copy of a letter from the Permanent Secretary of the Ministry of Native Affairs to the Provincial Commissioner, Northern Province, to say that he had been instructed by the Governor to inform him that he warmly commended Mr MAB Christie on his excellent Kasama Tour Report. That he completely agreed with Mr Christie's views on the need for frequent administrative tours at this time and especially endorsed the final sentence of Mr Christie's Report. This came with a covering letter from the Resident Commissioner conveying his congratulations on this commendation.

Last Tuesday took me up to Nalolo where I stayed three days, drank many cups of tea with the Mulena Mukwae and worked moderately hard in the shambolic Treasury office to produce a Trial Balance for the month of November and saw about various other matters.

Excitement in Barotseland centres at present round the trial and imprisonment of the Lozi-born Treasurer of UNIP by the Saa-Sikalo Kuta at Lealui when he, Nalumino Mundia, refused to obey the Kuta's order to leave Barotseland within twenty-four hours under the Undesirable Persons Order. The other main talking point centres on the efforts of the Litunga (Paramount Chief) and Kuta to have Barotseland declared the fourth state of the Federation.

Mundia who came ostensibly to visit his mother spent his time in Mongu organising the UNIP branch and leading a demonstration against the Mongu hospital to complain about the doctor-in-charge. The Barotse Native Government (BNG) told him to get out and when he refused, summoned him to appear before the Lealui Kuta.

He came before the court with about forty of his supporters and delivered a peroration that had very little to do with the offence charged. Against a hubbub of noise from his supporters the Kuta questioned him and then found him guilty, sentencing him to one year in prison with hard labour.

When judgement was pronounced there was uproar and Mundia was quickly surrounded by his supporters who successfully defied the kapasus to arrest their leader. They had stones as weapons which they had transported from Mongu in the UNIP landrover, a sackful or two of which were found aboard it later.

Mundia and his men ordered the Indunas to leave the Kuta but the latter sat tight. A District Officer tried to persuade Mundia to come quietly but failed and he had to go and phone for the Police Mobile Unit. Before it came, the crowd had grown from one hundred and fifty to five hundred and all were waiting to see if UNIP was going to stage a successful revolution against the Paramount Chief and Kuta.

▷

> If the Indunas had left their traditional seats the revolt would have been accomplished because the UNIP men would then have destooled the Indunas and then gone to the Palace nearby and dethroned the Litunga and put the leading contender for the throne, who had come from Lusaka with Mundia, in his place.

Then the Mobile Unit came and Mundia beat it to his landrover and drove it across the Plain as far as he could and then legged it for cover. Next day, he gave himself up at Mongu Boma.

BNG and NRG are at present at loggerheads over the question of constitutional progress. In short, BNG does not want it and yesterday the Litunga and a Barotse delegation met Mr Maudling[94] at Livingstone to press their point of view that Barotseland, while sharing in NR revenues, should avoid the onward march of nationalism that proceeds in the rest of NR.

At present, UNIP is not allowed to register in Barotseland because of the BNG's resistance to it but in the long run BNG is going to be steamrollered out of the way. Sad, especially as the mass of the people either don't know what is happening or just want to back the winning horse.

Sad, too, were it not for the fact that BNG are a pretty hopeless lot. At Nalolo, three-quarters of the Indunas are moribund, decrepit and dying. And although one can deplore the excesses of nationalism, as the Mulena Mukwae does, one must also do something positive to alleviate the real problems that not only exist but are growing and to which the Mulena Mukwae and her Kuta are making no attempt to formulate solutions except "bash 'em!".

---

[94] *Recently appointed Colonial Secretary in place of Iain Macleod.*

On tour of Lumbe Silalo by Landrover

Mate Camp
Lumbe Silalo
Senanga
10 December 61

I managed to get away on Tuesday on the Lumbe tour and drove south to Sioma. At Sioma, I crossed the Zambezi with the landrover on a rickety paddle pontoon which we had shifted a few months ago from another river crossing where it was very seldom being used. Reaching the other side, I met one of the silalo indunas, the court clerk and the kapasus at our first camp about three miles from where we crossed the river.

Since beginning the tour I have been working like a slave. In a landrover, and with little time to spare – I have got to be back in Senanga on the 16th December – one is tempted to take on a little more than one can chew each day. The result has been that I have never managed to be finished before 6 p.m. any day, and sometimes have been working until dusk, sometime after 7 p.m.

In fact, in the course of these 11 days on tour, I shall be covering an area that took me about four weeks last year. However, I am not doing the area as intensively as last year. Instead of walking to every village, I am counting people at camps or at central points and just visiting villages if they happen to lie on our route from camp to camp.

On this tour, I have been trying to trace the origins of the villages established in this silalo. Around Sioma, most of the villages have been established in the last century by various Paramount Chiefs to act as guards on the Sioma Falls against enemies coming into Barotseland from the south. One such was established here well over one hundred years ago after one Paramount Chief had returned from a successful expedition against a tribe living in what is now Southern Province. These people were left behind to keep watch for possible retaliation from the other tribe. The people of this village originally came from Kalabo District.

Other villages were moved here to haul the Paramount Chief's canoes and barges round the Sioma Falls when he went downriver to Sesheke or Livingstone. Most of them were established during

Lewanika's rule, about 1900, as Lewanika made several journeys to Livingstone. He also had a canal dug to shorten the haul round the Falls by about two miles or so. This canal was about ten feet deep and fifteen to twenty feet wide but it was never completed. Another canal was dug in Paramount Chief Yeta's time to make a short cut. This canal is about a mile long and eventually meets Lewanika's. The canal work was supervised in about 1923 by the son of the Induna who had superintended work on Lewanika's canal. Lewanika's canal is partly constructed through rock but for the most part follows a natural valley so there was not much difficult digging to be done. It ends where the ground rises and thick forest begins. About two hundred yards from its end I came across another which has been blasted through solid rock from the Zambezi, about four to five miles below the Falls. This canal is about ten – fifteen feet deep and twelve feet wide and is probably about four miles long. The holes drilled for the sticks of dynamite are clearly visible.

The man responsible for this last canal, by the name of Sampson, was a trader in Senanga in the 1920s and he blasted his canal about that time. Why he stopped when only two hundred yards from Lewanika's canal, I don't know. I hope to find out when I get back to Senanga. With this canal he obviously hoped to avoid the expensive porterage of goods around the Falls.

Proceeding up the Lumbe valley, I found that most of the villages moved from the Central Barotse Plain about sixty to one hundred years ago, either to get away from the dynastic troubles between various Barotse royal families or because of the good hunting to be had, animals having been driven out of the Barotse Plain by the press of human population.

Two or three villages were also established about one hundred and forty years ago, after a victorious struggle with the tribe occupying Sesheke District, which lies on Senanga District's southern border, to levy tribute on these people and watch the various fords over the Lumbe river.

There are also elements of tribes who came from Portuguese West Africa (Angola) about 1920. At that time there was widespread fighting between Angolan Africans and the Portuguese mainly over the subject of taxation.

1962: THE WHEEL OF FORTUNE FAVOURS THE NATIONALISTS

If 1961 was the year when violence was either being threatened by the European political leaders or actually being created by the African ones, 1962 was the year when the leaders of both camps decided that a peaceful democratic process should be given a chance. This process began with the acceptance of the once again revised election arithmetic, too complicated to go into here. Both sides felt they had a chance of forming a winning coalition with whichever middle-of-the-road party was likely to win the majority of the National seats where the victorious candidates required a minimum of support from voters on both the Higher (mainly European) and Lower (African) rolls. The publication of these new electoral provisions took place in March. Once they had been accepted the registration of voters could begin apart from Barotseland where the Litunga and his Council were still opposed to allowing it to go ahead.

In the meantime, Welensky tried to throw a spanner in the works by suggesting to the Litunga that a new Federation consisting of Southern Rhodesia, the Copperbelt, Katanga and Barotseland could be formed, leaving the remainder of Northern Rhodesia to become separately independent.

This bizarre scheme was put to the Commonwealth Secretary, Duncan Sandys, while he was on a visit to Salisbury in February. Sandys agreed to this plan. It was also agreed to by Godwin Mbikusita, a member of the Barotse royal establishment who had moved from being the first president of the ANC in Northern Rhodesia to becoming a UFP member of the Federal Parliament. Accompanied by Mbikusita, Sandys flew to Mongu where he succeeded in securing the Litunga's signature to a document requesting the British Government to allow Barotseland to secede from Northern Rhodesia and remain in the Federation.

Sandys did not endear himself to the Provincial Administration in Mongu. The Resident Commissioner, following the Governor's orders, had been trying to persuade the Litunga that his best course was to participate in the forthcoming Northern Rhodesian elections in the expectation that a party representing the wishes of the Litunga for autonomy for Barotseland within Zambia would win the Barotse seats.

Sandys' arrival threatened all this diplomacy. As described by my colleague, David Salmon, Sandys impressed all the PA officers from the top downwards as being

"One of the most miserable, awkward and selfish people possible".[95]

Sandys' intervention achieved nothing because Reginald Maudling, Iain Macleod's successor as Colonial Secretary, refused to be diverted from his constitutional plans. Once these became public the Administration had again to persuade the Litunga to accept them and allow voter registration to take place in Barotseland. It took a visit to the Litunga by the Minister of Native Affairs and the Attorney General to persuade him to allow the registration of voters in Barotseland and for all political parties to be allowed to operate there. Thus registration of voters in Barotseland began in late May a month later than elsewhere in Northern Rhodesia. I was given the task of coordinating the voter registration throughout Barotseland with only a month available to complete it.

The election took place in late 1962 with some of the National seats having to be decided after a second round of voting because in the first no candidate had managed to obtain the minimum percentage of votes of both upper and lower rolls. Eventually a coalition government of UNIP and ANC was formed with UNIP having fourteen seats to ANC's 5. This established the first African government in Northern Rhodesia which ruled for over a year until further elections in January 1964 established a majority for UNIP.

Zambia became independent on 24th October 1964.

[95]From an unpublished thesis "The Creation of Zambia" by David Salmon.

Senanga
9 January 1962

Life here is rather uneventful. Today's mail brought confirmation that my leave has been approved so I will be able to fly from Lusaka as planned on the 3rd July.

The Resident Commissioner and Ian and Judith Edye and some other Senanga residents came to dinner last Saturday.

I excelled myself and no doubt ensured promotion into the bargain by producing pieces of steak wrapped in bacon, first quickly fried for a minute or two and then allowed to cook slowly in a sauce of old Chianti wine which had become undrinkable but which imbued the meat and the sauce with a marvellous flavour.

Senanga
15 January 62

I have no time to write letters these days so busy am I! For a week now I have been working till 10 p.m. on the Nalolo account books trying to make them balance and today... I succeeded, thank goodness!

Since then I have been drafting the nasty remarks about the Nalolo Treasury for the covering letter that will go with the Trial Balance for the end of the year to the Mulena Mukwae, getting the launch ready for a visit I am making there tomorrow, inspecting the new football pitch that we are laying and trying to act the part of Solomon in a complicated dispute between an African storekeeper and his capitao.

It began to rain fairly steadily a few days ago so breaking a long and unwelcome spell of dry weather, and it may have come in time to save some of the late planted maize and sorghum. The river is rising fairly fast and for this time of year is slightly above average – which bodes ill for those with gardens on the Plain who hope to harvest before the flood comes up.

▶

▶ Mr James, the WNLA representative in Senanga is coming to Nalolo tomorrow to visit the Mulena Mukwae. If not the first visit ever by a WNLA representative, it is certainly the first for a good number of years.

The James's, by the way, are a very nice couple indeed, of middle age, but very sporty for their years. They are still nifty on the tennis court. Yesterday, they took John Wilson, myself and the Edye family downriver on a big WNLA launch for a picnic.

It felt quite like home for it rained most of the way and we had to pull canvases down over the open sides to keep the rain out. So dark and cloudy was it, we might have been in a fall-out shelter. However, never a dull moment, except in the very literal sense, as there was plenty to eat and drink.

The Mulena Mukwae's ceremonial carriage which I never saw in use, and doubt if it was ever more than a museum piece

I flew to Livingstone the day before yesterday for dental treatment because my teeth have been giving me jipp for two or three weeks. Yesterday, I had three fillings done but one of the teeth that has been filled is still sore and yesterday evening it was very painful indeed. I took some codeine and also soaked a wad of cotton wool in neat whisky and applied it to the gum. This latter method is an excellent way of killing toothache.

It is now 6.20 a.m. and my plane on which I'm returning to Senanga leaves at 9 a.m. However, the dentist told me to come in and see him if my teeth were still sore today so that he could look at them again and it may be that if there is something badly wrong I shall miss the plane and have to make other arrangements for my return. However, I am hopeful that this does not occur as I am supposed to be going off on a ten-day tour next Monday.

The appearance of the town of Livingstone is no credit to the good doctor's name. There is one long main street which houses all the shops and the buildings there are of unmitigated ugliness. They look as though they have come straight out of a Western for they all have these false stucco fronts with a veranda in front and corrugated iron for a roof. One waits expectantly but in vain for some hombre to unsaddle and tie his bucking bronco to a hitching post.

However, if the town is ugly the people are friendly. The dentist, for example, invited me to his home for lunch. He is a keen naturalist and in his garden there is a pond on which swim several species of ducks some of them quite rare, and some other types of water birds including a pair of cranes. He sometimes comes up to Barotseland looking for birds.

In the late afternoon, when I had returned to the Government hostel here, the Warden took me out in his car to visit the Falls which are a marvellous sight.

I am back in the wee but 'n' ben once again but not for long because tomorrow I leave to go on a ten-day tour to superintend an election for a representative to speak for one of the five areas in this District which sends representatives to sit on the Katengo Council. It meets twice a year at Lealui and represents the popular assembly of Barotseland, the council of commoners, which sounds good but which has so far been quite ineffectual.

There are five constituencies in this District, each comprising two or three silalos. Each silalo puts up as many candidates as it pleases for anyone may stand so long as he does not have a criminal conviction – the people here have yet to hear of "Prison Graduates". Generally speaking, the people have got the reputation of choosing the best man (by our standards) to represent them – i.e. someone who is reasonably well educated and experienced though that is not saying a lot in many cases.

On the other hand, the people of a silalo seldom vote for a candidate from another silalo which means that if one candidate comes from one silalo and three from another, other things being equal, the first mentioned will win because the votes of his silalo will all go to him but the votes of the other silalo will be split between three.

Tomorrow I hope to go to Lukona Mission to pay a visit to Trudy (who was sister-in-charge of the Nangoma Mission Dispensary for some months in 1960) and the Missionary–in–charge, Remy Anker, who used to be at Senanga. Lukona is in Kalabo District but is not far from the Senanga border where I'll be starting my tour.

The Law results came out in this week's Gazette and I am sorry to have to tell you that I've failed, surprise, surprise! I have no excuses at all.

I now come to the subject of Duncan Sandys' visit to Roy, the Honest (two aces up his sleeve) Welensky. The sight of British Cabinet Ministers trotting out here with their bland smiles and briefcases is getting very nauseating especially when they start grovelling at the feet of the Welensky.

> I had my first day off work in bed last Thursday, the first for many, many moons – because of severe toothache which gave me a slight temperature and a distinctly unwell feeling. However, codeine helped cure the pain and penicillin injections cured the infected gum which was causing the trouble and I am now practically better.

> I hope you are well. Good to hear that the Dons and Scotland won on Saturday; best news there has been for a long time.

Letter to Christian Fraser

Senanga
21 February 1962

My dear Christian

I received your letter when I returned from a very interesting and enjoyable tour. I was organising the election of a member to represent the people of three adjoining sub-districts (silalos) in this District. As you might expect, the people who turned up at the dozen or so election meetings that were held, though largely illiterate and uneducated, were nevertheless quite capable of asking intelligent and shrewd questions of the candidates. As a result, an ex-mission schoolteacher who had to leave his work after fifteen years' service because he took a second wife, was the winner.[96] He was in my view the best candidate both on his qualifications and his ability to represent forcefully in the Council the interests of the people of his constituency. Myself, I believe that it is not so much an intellectual grasp of policies that is required of an electorate (as Welensky and Co. seem to demand when they go on about voter qualifications) as sufficient intelligence to distinguish between a good and a not so good candidate.

The winning candidate in this election will sit on the Katengo Council, the equivalent of the House of Commons of seven hundred years ago – i.e., when kings and barons held all the power.

---

[96] See reference to the Katengo Councillor on page 79.

Last week I went to Nalolo and stayed there for three days, or rather three nights but only two full days. On the first of these I lunched with the Mulena Mukwae and during the two days shared with her about two gallons of tea. I barely survived but just had enough strength left over to stagger into Mongu for the weekend.

Mongu is alive with "alarums and excursions" at present and I am very glad that I am in the comparative seclusion of Senanga. It does not seem to me that the latest constitutional changes give much to the African Nationalists but they seem to have riled Roy. The Federal Government, as I prophesied in my letter to you some weeks ago, is trying to prise Barotseland out of NR and set it up as an independent state which would opt to stay in the Federation.

I think the British Government is firmly against this if it can ever be said to be firm about anything. Certainly, NRG is dead against it. Certainly, too, there are going to be difficult days ahead for Barotseland if Her Majesty's Government allows it to become a pawn in Welensky's struggle for power.

Exciting times these for Central Africa. It is a pity that the central figures in this situation are so hapless. For example, the debate in the Rhodesian Federal House of Assembly just before Welensky declared its dissolution contained the highest percentage of reported drivel that I have ever had the misfortune to hear. Most speakers had got a bee in their bonnet whose buzz was so disconcerting to each speaker's sanity that they all put forward the idea of splitting up Northern Rhodesia into three or four parts, the unwanted unprofitable regions to be gifted to Nyasaland and Tanganyika, Barotseland to be given independence and the Copperbelt and line-of-rail to be joined to Southern Rhodesia. Truly amazing!

▶ Now Welensky is going to seek a mandate from the people!! The UFP leader in Nyasaland said that this election would help to bring home to the people of Nyasaland that they were still within the Federation.

I wonder if Welensky will resort to force to maintain the Federation. It hardly seems feasible and his officers, most of whom are British, will be committing high treason (and mutiny?) if they obey his lunatic orders.

Last Friday four teachers from the local Upper Primary school came round for dinner. The headmaster is a very intelligent and well-informed person, the first African that I have met here with whom I could argue on equal terms. I would have said that he was the only nationalist amongst the teachers who visited me because he felt it was essential that Barotseland should not split from Northern Rhodesia and that Lozi interests should be subordinated to those of Northern Rhodesia as a whole.

The other three teachers were Lozis first, Northern Rhodesians second, and wanted Barotseland to separate from Northern Rhodesia so that come independence they would not be subordinate to other tribes who were jealous of them and who would try to remove their rights to their land. At the same time, they still wanted to retain their share of Northern Rhodesia's copper revenues.

Although they were divided about the future of Barotseland they were all against the present structure of the Barotse government which does not allow men of their position any say at all. They complained that everyone who criticizes the present system is branded as a UNIP supporter when in fact much of the criticism comes from men who, while sharing the same goals for Barotseland as the indunas and chiefs who control the present set-up, deplore the manner in which the present Barotse government is run and its obliviousness to informed public opinion.

The flood has reached its maximum and is now retreating though it may come again later on, an event that does not happen very often. The flood peak, if it is the peak, is the lowest for the past six or seven years and has been reached slightly earlier than usual which means that with luck the plain will also dry earlier than usual and allow people to plant in good time before the next flood.

The economy of the Barotse Plain is quite complex, and delicately poised – a slight difference in the timing of the flood can make the difference between famine and plenty, not that there is ever serious famine on the plain because when the grain supplies are scarce fish and milk are plentiful. The only time really when people may be in desperate straits living on the Plain is when the flood has come up early, the fish thereby scattered and the new crops not yet harvested.

A man suspected of theft was arrested and brought into the Boma about three days ago. It turns out that he is not guilty of this offence. On the other hand, he has not paid tax for six years and he is a self-confessed witchdoctor complete with his "tool kit" of python skin amulet, various poisonous roots, white beads, wing of a bird, etc., etc., all contained in a rusty tin box.

He claims to cure peoples' ills rather than point out or divine witches. This makes him relatively harmless I should say but nonetheless he is committing a crime by so doing. Sentencing men like this for such acts seems slightly ludicrous if we believe that the law is no more than the embodiment of the rules that society feels must be obeyed if peace and good order are to prevail. In fact, ninety-five percent at least of Africans in Barotseland believe that witchdoctors have some sort of special gifts and that they are not just tricksters.

In many illnesses our District Messengers (the arm of the law in most rural districts) will go first of all for treatment to a witchdoctor and only if that fails will they undertake "European" treatment.

The Witchcraft Ordinance makes interesting reading - I wonder if there is still something similar, or if there ever was such a thing, amongst the English or Scottish statutes.

Yesterday, Sunday, I was roused from my bed at 11 a.m. by a drunken senior clerk and a Messenger with the announcement that a man had been stabbed with a fish spear and that the assailant was resisting arrest. So I went out to the village about seven miles from Senanga with four Messengers armed with staves in case he was still in a violent mood. By the time we arrived, however, he had calmed down and had submitted to questioning by the local induna. He was a big lout of a man, well over six feet tall and I certainly would not like to have met with the business end of a fish spear wielded by him.

After depositing him in the local goal I went up to the hospital where I learned that the spear had entered at the top of the injured man's arm, had gone right through it, into the shoulder and finally emerged behind the shoulder blade. Luckily the chest had not been pierced so the injured man is in no danger of dying though he had to have an operation for the removal of the spear, a nasty thin barbed weapon on the end of a long, narrow, willowy shaft.

Senanga
28 March 62

In two weeks' time I am sitting my Lower Cibemba exam. I was rather foolish entering for it, I suppose, as I am now having to work like a slave to get to anywhere near the standard and there is no one with whom I can really talk the language though one or two Messengers have a smattering. The DC is going to invigilate at my Oral so I can't really ask him for advice on ticklish points of the language. Besides, he is working for his Higher Lozi and does not remember all that much Cibemba these days.

Yesterday I went to Mooyo to check the books of the court clerks in the north of the District and got back this afternoon feeling rather under the weather because of an abscess under one of my back teeth. I shall go to Livingstone probably next week to have it extracted. I have really had very good health since coming out here but in the last two or three months my teeth have been giving me quite a bit of bother.

I had dinner last night with the Baumgartners at Mooyo. He is the Missionary there alternating between Mooyo and Nalolo according to the flood. This annual flit is quite a headache for his wife. They are a very nice couple. It may be that they will manage to visit Scotland in September which would be splendid as I am sure you would enjoy meeting them and it would also be an opportunity to repay them for some of the hospitality they have given me on my numerous visits to Nalolo.

The pleasures of local dentistry (photo: Rev JL Baumgartner)

The Kuomboka of the Mulena Mukwae is on the day after tomorrow when she moves in procession in her royal barge from Nalolo to Mooyo. I shall not be going as I have a bad chill and don't relish a day out on the river in the full sun. I hope to give my camera to someone else going and get photographs that way.

Senanga
9 April 1962

Last Thursday after my tooth extraction in Livingstone I had dinner with the Dinwiddies (the DC and his wife) in Livingstone and afterwards, having lent me a blanket, water-sack and given me food for the journey, Mr Dinwiddie drove me to the Zambezi Sawmills railway where I boarded a carriage from the Victorian era and made myself at home with a compartment all to myself.

I managed to sleep fairly well even though the train left at 3 a.m. and stopped at half hour intervals for the locomotive to fill up with water.

I rose about 7 a.m. and enjoyed myself gazing out at the countryside as we chugged along at speeds of up to twenty miles per hour! At our watering places, Africans came with dried fish, meal, cassava roots, maize cobs and hens to sell to the African passengers. Most of the train consisted of flat carriages for carrying equipment for the Sawmills, etc., but there were also two ▶

▶ passenger coaches, one for the poorer passengers (ie. Africans) and one for Europeans who could afford a compartment (ie. myself and a policeman in the next compartment).

At Mulobezi, the end of the line, I met John Wilson and we drove to Sesheke where I spent a very enjoyable evening with a cadet from Edinburgh and his wife. Next day we drove back to Senanga.

The day after tomorrow we all go to Mongu for the language exams. If I had another week, I might pass!

Letter to Christian Fraser

Senanga
30 April 1962

My dear Christian

Apart from a couple of joy rides to Livingstone for dental treatment and one to Mongu to sit a Bemba Oral Language exam[97] I have been stuck in Senanga ever since a two week Katengo Election tour at the beginning of February which I told you about. I would have been out on tour again 'ere now but for the fact that I am expecting to be called to Mongu any day to handle the Registration of Voters in Barotseland for the next Northern Rhodesia elections.

However, the Barotse National Council has not yet come to a decision about this election and NRG is no doubt trying to decide what to do regarding the registration of voters in Barotseland if the National Council either refuses to allow Barotseland to participate in the election or stalls so long that registration will only be possible for a week or two before the rolls are closed. In the meantime, I have packed up nearly all my earthly goods and possessions, and how few these are, and am sharing a house with the Cadet, John Wilson. He, luckily, is a good type who shares my political views and disagrees with me on every other subject from religion to beauty.[98]

▶

[97] I passed it and earned a £50 bonus for passing a language exam additional to the minimum requirements of the service.

[98] John was keen on blondes while I preferred brunettes.

Despite the machinations going on behind the scenes at Mongu and Lealui (the Government and Native Authority centres respectively in Barotseland), life in Senanga maintains its even tenor although that includes people being stabbed at big beer drinks brewed from the millet that is being harvested at this time of year.

The millet is generally grown in drier sandy soils on the edge of woodland that has often been recently cleared by one of the Mawiko (people from the West – Angola) tribes, principally the Mambunda in Senanga District. This is their preferred grain rather than maize which is the staple cereal grown by the Lozi in or on the edge of the Barotse Plain.

The only event of any note this last week was the Federal General Election which so far as Senanga was concerned was a complete farce. On polling day, three, repeat three, voters cast their vote and those represented seventy-five percent of the Federal electorate here. Only Federal citizens by birth or adoption (and that cuts out most UK civil servants) qualify to vote and moreover, you must possess high income and education qualifications as well. This disenfranchises most Africans. To collect these few ballot papers at each of the outlying Barotse stations a plane flew up from Lusaka. It

This is a typical Mambunda hut – quite small, with millet drying on a mat. Three spears are propped against the thatched roof. The Mambunda are woodsmen and skilled hunters. The blue trunk may have been brought from the mines in South Africa by the husband. He would have filled it with gifts for his wife and a few extra clothes for himself that he bought with his miner's wages. The door of the hut is merely a reed screen. A Lozi-built hut would usually be substantially larger and would have a proper wooden door

must have cost the Federal Government at least twenty pounds per ballot to collect the votes cast in Barotseland.

As for the result of the election which gives of course a sweeping victory to Sir Roy Welensky's United Federal Party and about ninety-five percent of the seats in the Federal Assembly (how one-sided the debates are going to be) – just what does this result mean? It means, of course, no more than that Sir Roy still has the backing of most whites in Northern Rhodesia but hardly their enthusiastic support for only fifty percent bothered to vote.

After the election Welensky claimed that this UFP victory was a pointer to what would happen in the NR Territorial Election. Monstrous self-delusion; his party will be lucky if they win one-third of the seats. If that does happen it will be interesting to see if Welensky tries to put into operation one of the many blood and thunder threats that have been so prominent in his speeches of late.

The two African nationalist parties, UNIP and ANC are stepping up their election campaigns. One of their methods is to break up the meetings called by their rival. In the last two weeks, more than 10 people have lost their lives in such disturbances and meetings are now banned on the Copperbelt without special permission. With such goings-on it is difficult not to sympathise with the Barotse National Councillors who want most of all to keep Barotseland out of the arena of party politics and continue on holding on to often very cushy jobs for which they are not particularly qualified.

I become Coordinator of Voter Registration in Barotseland

Senanga

14 May 62

Last week, following a visit to Limulunga, the Barotse capital during the flood season, by the Minister for Native Affairs and the Attorney-General, the National Council and the Paramount Chief changed their minds about the forthcoming election and agreed to allow the registration of voters and canvassing by all political parties to take place in Barotseland.

I have been given the job of coordinating the registration of voters in Barotseland and shall be visiting all districts probably with a film unit to spread publicity and help District Commissioners with their registration campaigns.

I was speaking to one of the local Indunas today about this and he was very gloomy about the whole thing, being convinced that Senanga will soon become a centre of slogan-shouting, disrespectful young African nationalists. I feel rather sorry for the old guard. It is they rather than we who suffer from the changes that are taking place and will continue to do so at an ever-increasing pace.

PO Box 26,

Mongu

22 May 1962

I am now firmly installed in the big city – well not exactly firmly because the day after tomorrow I set off on a tour of the whole of Barotseland by landrover in conjunction with a film unit from the Information Dept. to publicize the forthcoming elections and to register voters.

Since coming here last Thursday, I have held three film shows in Mongu, one at Namushakende and one at a school about thirty miles from Mongu. These meetings have been quite interesting in so far as I have had to answer some extremely tricky questions from the local UNIP men especially about various points connected with the voters' rolls and the elections.

▶

At each meeting I have tried to answer these questions in Lozi fairly concisely and afterwards have interesting discussions at a more detailed and serious level with these people but last night after I had made a fairly fluent speech in Lozi about voters' registration after a special film on the subject, I made rather a mess of answering some of the questions put to me partly because my Lozi failed me when I tried to express some rather abstruse points and partly because the questions required more than a brief, slick answer.

Only people with certain qualifications may qualify to vote and there are two rolls: Upper and Lower. To justify all this is very, very difficult especially as I can't wholly agree with Government policy though naturally I have to stick up for it as best I can.

Yesterday I went and had an interview with the Litunga (Paramount Chief) and later with the Saa-Sikalo and Mongu District Kutas and explained about registration and I think persuaded them to give me their backing and to get as many of the headmen and indunas, who can on the whole be expected to vote for conservative candidates in the Election, to register. Tomorrow I'll give a film show in Limulunga, the Litunga's capital, before going off to Mankoya.

A Witch Doctor at work

Box 26,
Mongu
4 June 62

I am now on the last day of my voters' registration tour of Senanga District. Last night I slept once again at Shekela, and probably for the last time too. The drums started beating in a nearby village and just before 9 p.m. I decided to go and see what was happening. My District Messenger decided to come with me and we walked for about a mile before coming to the village from whence the drumming emanated.

There we found the villagers together inside one of the lapas (the fence which surrounds most huts, forming a courtyard). They had come to help a witchdoctor cure three people and when I appeared those who could, tried to run off, but when I said I had only come to watch, the session continued.

In the middle of the courtyard there was a fire and sitting on a stool beside it was the witchdoctor, a woman. By the fire was a small black cooking pot which contained her medicine. In the middle of the circle formed by the villagers around the fire were the patients, or at least two of them, the third not appearing till later. One was a man and the other a woman and both were stripped to the waist and their faces, arms and legs were smeared with, I think, white cassava meal.

As the drums were beaten the witchdoctor led the women in song, the rhythm being rattled out by the witchdoctor as she shook a tin can full of mazauli seeds on the end of a short stick and by the rest of the women as they clapped their hands. The patients who were sitting down with their legs stretched out in front of them and their hands upon their knees, seemed to go into a trance. Their eyes closed, their heads drooped and then they started moving their legs convulsively in time to the drum beats. ▶

First one leg would start twitching, then the other, then with both legs moving up and down the patients became mobile and twitched their way on their bottoms out of the circle of spectators. By this time the drummers had reached a crescendo and the women were clapping fiercely and hallooing.

Then suddenly the drums would stop and the witchdoctor's assistants attended to the patients by tying pieces of bark rope round their legs and anointing them on their limbs with some medicine. Then the patients were brought into the circle again and from the small black pot bubbling on the fire the witchdoctor removed a small bundle of bark rope which she tested for temperature on her leg and then applied to the legs of the patients, sometimes just patting the joints, at other times wiping them clean of the cassava meal.

Before she did so, she spat lightly on the bark rope, then into the fire and then onto the ground and threw something invisible into the pot.

Abracadabra! – nothing much happened! For when they stopped for a breather the patients got up and stretched their limbs and both were hobbling. They were suffering from a disease called "singongi sa Mawiko" which my Messenger thinks is the same as rheumatism! Maybe this is a form of physical therapy but it struck me that the patients were more likely to contract a cold by being inadequately dressed on a perishing cold night than being cured of their rheumatics.

The third patient made only a brief appearance. He, too, received attention from the witchdoctor's assistants in the dark outside the circle of villagers round the fire, and then he was assisted into the middle of the circle where he immediately started moving around uncontrollably when the drums started beating. First he started sliding along the ground towards the fire and when he was forcibly prevented from reaching the fire, he started causing chaos amongst the circle by moving hither and thither on his bottom his legs waving up and down to the rhythm of the drums, so he was secured and led away to his hut.

The thing that surprised me was the almost total lack of tension at the session. It was more of a party than anything else, a chance to clap and sing and beat the drums while doing good at the same time by helping the witchdoctor with her work.

On Tuesday I went to Mooyo where I met John Wilson and showed him how to check the Cash Books and Ledger of the Nalolo Sub-Treasury, drank tea with the Mulena Mukwae, went back into Mongu for my compulsory pre-vacation leave medical examination and came back to Mooyo and arranged a film show inside the Mulena Mukwae's courtyard for herself and her indunas.

The Mulena was greatly taken with the films. If we'd had enough films, we could have continued till midnight and after without boring her. After the film show, John and I had tea with her and a chat about the films during which the Mulena joggled all over with mirth at all the funny and marvellous things she had just seen on the screen.

Next day we worked at the Cash Books until I had to go and address the local headmen about registration. The Mulena had chosen her most intelligent induna to accompany me and he also explained about registration, the elections, etc. Unfortunately, the silalo induna whose headmen we were addressing, also made a speech which only served to confuse and that, together with the natural reluctance to be hurried into something led to very few people registering.

Elsewhere, especially in places distant from Mongu and Mooyo, where people have been aware of BNG's reluctance to participate in the forthcoming elections, those who are eligible have registered though they are a terribly small percentage of the whole. Even amongst headmen who can be voters if they are literate, about eighty percent fail to qualify because they cannot read the simple questions written in Lozi on the registration form – e.g. "What is the name of your village?"

▶ At Senanga, I stayed with the Edyes who had insisted that I come and stay with them during my night in Senanga. I must say I have been very lucky in being stationed with them for so much of my tour.

I arrived there on Wednesday night and on Thursday, at midday, or so, I took the pontoon to Kalongola and drove to Kaunga, calling in first at Sitoti Seventh Day Adventist Mission to register some teachers. Next day we went to Sinungu where two meetings including a film show were held. There, becoming anxious to at least have one of the headmen as a voter, I showed one of them how to write his name by writing the characters on the dusty ground and then got him to copy them onto the voter registration form. That way I couldn't be accused of forging his signature. Then to Shekela with stops en route to register people. At Shekela, we registered the only two literate people living there – the two indunas.

Tomorrow I go to Lukona to hold a meeting and register people and spend a week in Kalabo District. Tomorrow, too, I shall probably try and go to Kalabo to get more petrol and post this, so you should get it in reasonable time.

Now only thirty days till I see you! Almost unbelievable.

Soon after he arrived, Ian Edye gave me the best piece of advice I had in my three years in Senanga. "Always remember", he said, "that we are public servants. That means we're here to serve the public, not the other way round". Perhaps he felt it necessary to say these words because he detected signs of arrogance in my attitude to some of the Africans who came to the office each day with requests for help in one way or another. He never said so, but in any case I tried in my work to put these words into practice. His deeds were as good as his words.

Letter to Christian Fraser

PO Box 26
Mongu
4 June 1962

My dear Christian

Thanks for your letter which reached me just before my bosses had transferred me from Senanga to Mongu within two months of the end of my tour. Since then, I have been continuously engaged on disseminating propaganda about the need to register for the forthcoming elections in Northern Rhodesia which take place in October and the actual job of voter registration throughout the length and breadth of Barotseland.

So far, I have visited three of the five Districts in Barotseland with a film landrover unit from the Information Department, holding meetings, showing films about the elections and other subjects and registering those who are eligible to vote.

It has been an interesting journey so far. In Mongu, in response to questions mainly put by members of the local UNIP committee, I had to explain as best I could in the vernacular the history and principles of the qualified franchise. These and other questions of a related nature gave me at first hand and especially in spirited discussion after the meetings, some insight into the thinking of the young African intelligentsia.

In passing, it should be mentioned that I explained and defended the limitations of the present franchise only in my capacity as a civil servant. In fact, it is virtually impossible to do any such thing without wounding the legitimate self-esteem of one's listeners who cannot qualify to vote. In my opinion, it boils down to the fact that a poor man is not necessarily an irresponsible one and an uneducated man is not necessarily a stupid one. Unfortunately, the present franchise equates poverty with irresponsibility and ignorance of the three Rs with stupidity. One is left feeling rather sick about the whole thing after trying for the umpteenth time to explain the reasons for the present franchise. Now I tell the questioner to see me ▶

afterwards and then I inform him it is just a dodge to get round Welensky and the white settlers by continuing to pay lip service to their notions of responsible government.

Equality of man aside, there is a fantastic disparity in informedness between townsfolk and those living in most parts of Barotseland. One of the questions on the Registration Form is "Have you lived in the Federation of Rhodesia and Nyasaland for the past two years?" Most people answer "NO" because they are under the impression that although Federation has been talked about often enough, Northern Rhodesia, and Barotseland in particular, never got round to entering this entity. So part of one's job is either to tell the chap just to write "Yes" and forget about it or explain to him about the divided responsibilities of the Federal and Territorial Governments.

Kalabo
11 June 62

The Voter Registration Journey continues and I am now on my last full day in Kalabo. Tomorrow I shall leave in mid-morning and sleep tomorrow night at Nangweshi in Senanga District, the half-way point between here and Sesheke.

Here in Kalabo I have continued with my registration of voters work but at an easier pace than elsewhere. On the 5th June, my first day in Kalabo, I arrived at Lukona and met again the Ankers and Trudy. There, and at the local Kuta, I found that no one had been warned of our arrival. I wondered if there had been a last minute change in my programme so I drove another forty miles to Kalabo Boma and about five miles short of the Boma, I met a landrover carrying the Induna chosen to accompany me on the tour. He continued to Lukona and I went on to the Boma.

The DC is a chap from Portsoy[99] called Alex Smith and he thought he had told Rev Anker when I would be arriving and had asked him to tell the local indunas. If he did so, he was a bit slack; he should have also sent a Messenger to tour the local villages to

[99] A fishing village north of Aberdeen.

inform them of my coming or sent a formal written request to the indunas. At some of the other places I visited I found inadequate notice had been given of my arrival so that in part my visit here has been rather a waste of time.

At Lukona, where I stayed a night, I had a most enjoyable evening and we went on talking together till 1.30 a.m. after they watched "my" film show. Two nights later I stayed at a Capuchin Fathers' mission and was very hospitably received. One of the Fathers there is an expert linguist, has started his own fish ponds, and is altogether a most interesting person to speak to. In fact, our conversation did not end until well past midnight.

A Man dances with his Shadow

At one of the schools where we gave an evening film show and talk to the assembled villagers, the place was lit up by the powerful lights of the Information Department lorry. Loud dance music sounded from its loudspeakers to attract the people from the surrounding villages. Into the spotlight strode one of the teachers. The lights were focused on the whitewashed wall of the main school building and when he came into the arena his long shadow was cast on the school wall. He started to dance not alone, but with his shadow. He and his shadow were inspired; oh, how well they twisted and gyrated, totally in love with one another. The crowd was mesmerised. He danced for ten or fifteen minutes, and then feeling perhaps he had done enough to entertain us all, he stopped. A great din of applause and ululation from the women greeted his performance.

It was after that meeting that the Induna accompanying me told me that some of the people wanted to know who I was. Was I a missionary? "Why would they ask that?" I enquired. "Because you speak Lozi much better than a District Officer usually does, more like a missionary really." Wow, that was a complement. The fact was that I had mastered the vocabulary of voter registration and all the likely questions I would be asked about the new constitution and other related political issues during the first few meetings I

▶ had held in Mongu. I had achieved quite a fluent delivery in my address to the subsequent meetings and in the question and answer sessions that followed.

This was put to the test at a daytime meeting I held in this District when some of the leading UNIP officials from Lusaka, including some who were Lozis, were present. They listened to what I had to say without comment and then left to proceed with their own campaign.

During my few days here the Governor came on a one-day visit. I was not at either of the two public functions laid on as I was not included on the Guest List, no one having been aware that I would be here at the time. I wasn't downhearted, quite the contrary as these "do's" are the end.

However, I did meet him when returning to the Boma in the launch. I was admiring the lagoon and as we got close to the bank I looked up. There was the Governor, his wife, his ADC, the Resident Commissioner and the DC all standing on the bank looking like a reception committee. I was wearing a dirty pair of shorts and an equally dirty shirt but the RC gallantly introduced me to the Governor with whom I chatted for a few minutes about registering voters, etc.

PO Box 26
Mongu
21 June 62

I returned to Mongu yesterday afternoon after having spent a few enjoyable days in Sesheke District. As most of the registration of voters had already been done there, my task was merely to visit some of the more important centres in the District and give a talk at the evening film show. For the rest of the time I mostly lazed around in the company of whoever was my host for the day.

At the Native Authority Headquarters, I stayed with a Livestock Officer who has a house overlooking a beautiful lagoon of the Zambezi. He is a Scot from Islay. So as you can imagine we had a very enjoyable "we think Scotland is great" session.

Last Saturday, I went down to the football field with David Salmon to watch a game of football and ended up as the referee not only of that game but also of the one that followed.

On Sunday I managed to get up and go to church at 9.30 a.m. by a great feat of willpower and in the afternoon had an exhausting game of football. Every time I or David Salmon (we were the only white players taking part) kicked the ball the crowd shouted "Kwacha!", the UNIP slogan, meaning "Dawn". It was all good humoured which we took in good part. Football is amazingly popular and even in an out of the way place like Mongu there are about six or seven teams playing every week and some quite good players amongst them.

Stay well and let's keep our fingers crossed till we meet a week tomorrow.

THE RETURN HOME

I landed at Heathrow on a freezing cold (to me) early July day to be met by my parents and a salesman who presented me with the keys of the Volvo B18 saloon which I had ordered. They were as impressed as I was by the car's gleaming appearance and its smooth performance on the road to the north. There were no motorways then apart from a section around Preston so there was no hardship in obeying the instruction to drive at a moderate speed for the first few hundred miles until the engine had been bedded in. My parents had booked a cottage for two weeks at Nethybridge on Speyside, my mother's home area. There I played golf and walked and talked with my parents who wanted to know much more about my three years in Africa than I had been able to convey in my letters.

I arrived back in Aberdeen at more or less the same time as Christian, who had been on a motoring holiday in Scandinavia with our friend from university days, Rhona McGhie. Christian shared a flat with her widowed mother and it was there that I called on my first evening in Aberdeen. We drove to a point where the River Don enters the North Sea, parked the car, and set off on a stroll, hand in hand, along the wide deserted beach. Soon we were lost amidst the high sand dunes in a world of our own.

Six weeks later, after we had spent a weekend at the Edinburgh Festival, and while waiting for the car ferry at South Queensferry (there was no Forth Road Bridge in 1962) I asked Christian "Will you marry me?" and she replied "Yes". Two months later we were married, on her birthday, and after another two months set sail for Africa, where we drove from Capetown to Northern Rhodesia across the Karoo Desert, the Transvaal and Southern Rhodesia on our way to Samfya District on the shores of Lake Bangweulu. What an idyllic spot it was to start our married life; our house was on a ridge from where we had a wonderful view across the Lake and it was there that we brought home our first child eight months after our first arrival there. Life was bliss!

WHAT BECAME OF BAROTSELAND?

As has been described already (letter dated 14th May), the Litunga and the National Council agreed in May 1962 to allow the registration of voters for the forthcoming Northern Rhodesia elections. They also agreed that all political parties would be allowed to campaign freely in Barotseland. They did so because they had been told by the British Government that they would not be supported if they sought secession from Northern Rhodesia and they also believed that neither UNIP nor ANC had significant support in Barotseland. They backed the formation of a traditionalist party called Sicaba (i.e. National) which would promote support for Barotseland's secession from an independent Zambia.

I, a non-Lozi and merely a junior District Officer, could have told them that the educated younger generation of Lozi would support UNIP because they had become so dissatisfied with the Barotse Native Government which was controlled by the older, very conservative generation. I, however, lived outside the Lealui-Limulunga bubble and was coming in contact with the generation of school teachers and other white collar workers who wanted change. Moreover, UNIP took care to nominate Arthur Wina, the son of a former Ngambela,[100] and two other prominent Lozi, as their candidates. UNIP's supporters were keen to register whereas, as I found out when touring the rural areas of Barotseland to enrol voters, many of the village headmen were either too cautious to do so or were too illiterate to fill in the voting form.

It was no surprise to me when the UNIP candidates in the Election that was held in October 1962 were elected with huge majorities over the Sicaba candidates.

In August 1963 elections were held for the Katengo Council (the Council of Commoners) and UNIP candidates won all 25 seats leaving the Litunga and his traditional elite even more isolated. However, the new councillors turned out to be as keen as the old guard to retain Barotseland's autonomy within Zambia. After the National Election in January 1964 when UNIP won all seven seats in Barotseland, the Barotse delegation comprising elected and traditional representatives was agreed that Barotseland's special

---

[100] *The Litunga's Prime Minister.*

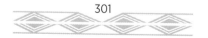

status which it had enjoyed under the British should be recognised within the Zambian constitution. Kaunda refused to agree to this and instead a separate Barotseland Agreement was signed by Kaunda and the Litunga, and endorsed by the British Government, which agreed to preserve the autonomy of Barotseland and the traditional rights of the Litunga.

After Independence the Agreement was torn up within five years. First, all the traditional courts were put under the Ministry of Justice where previously they had been independent, and in late 1965 a Local Government Act abolished the Barotse National Council and set up a District Council for each of the Districts within Barotseland. Their headquarters were to be alongside the Boma, not at the traditional capital of each District, ie, in the case of Senanga District, at Senanga not Nalolo. No longer would the Mulena Mukwae and her Kuta have any power. She would become just like any other chief in Zambia, as would the Litunga and the other District chiefs in Barotseland.

By 1968, the Barotse public had become so disenchanted by these reforms and the gradual whittling away of the Litunga's rights[101] about which they had not been consulted that in the national elections of that year UNIP lost most of its seats to Barotse nationalist candidates. Those who lost included three Cabinet members, Arthur Wina, Sipalo and Konoso. To this setback Kaunda responded in 1969 by announcing that Barotseland would be renamed Western Province and that the 1964 Barotseland Agreement would be cancelled by an Act of Parliament. Thereby the Litunga lost all the powers assured in Agreements signed with the British from 1890 onwards. All the traditional rights that he and the other chiefs and traditional councillors had enjoyed were extinguished. All their fears of what their fate would be under an independent African Government were seen to be justified.

Barotse nationalism has to this day (2015) not disappeared. There are still outbreaks of low-level violent protest at what the people of Barotseland see as slights to their historical identity by the Zambian Government.

The 1969 decision to rename Barotseland as Western Province was a case in point: a misguided attempt to defuse Lozi nationalism. As a Scot, I could have told President Kaunda and his Government that this would have a contrary effect. Try telling the Scots that from now on Scotland is to be renamed the Northern Province of Great Britain. Just imagine the outcry! It would be seen as provocative and disrespectful to the Scottish nation as no doubt the renaming of their land appeared to the Lozi nation.

---

[101]*See section, The Paramount Chief and his Government, pages 19-21.*

POSTSCRIPT: 50 YEARS LATER, A VISIT TO SENANGA

In 2012, a couple of months before my return visit to Senanga, I had written to the Provincial Commissioner in Mongu to tell him of my wish to visit Senanga and call on the District Commissioner. I never received a reply but the DC was expecting me. When I entered his office we put our arms around each other in a warm bear hug. I think he was astonished and delighted that I had travelled such a long way to revisit Senanga, and I was equally delighted to be back and to be given a warm welcome.

The DC gave his assistant the task of showing us around the town. We visited the hospital, the two secondary schools, the PMS mission station and the Harrington compound. We were fortunate in meeting William Harrington the grandson of Arthur Harrington about whom I have written so much in my letters from Senanga. The picture of his grandfather painted by William was very different to the one which the old man had presented to me and the other Europeans who used to visit and drink with him. To William his grandfather was a kindly old man who used to walk hand in hand with him around the family compound. He was a person he revered.

On the edge of the Harrington compound there is a small graveyard where Arthur is buried, his tombstone standing next to his African wife, the mother of Willie who took over his father's trading and boat building business and who in turn was father to William who was showing me around. Willie had become the Member of Parliament for Senanga as a representative of Kaunda's party, UNIP. William has succeeded his father as Senanga's MP and recently had been Minister for Tourism. He resides in Lusaka and makes regular visits to Senanga. He told me his aim was to turn his house in Senanga into a hotel. William told me he has siblings, nephews and nieces spread throughout the urban areas of Zambia. The Harrington name continues and its holders live lives unimagined by the old man who founded this dynasty. He would have been amazed and, I think, delighted.

In Senanga now there are shops, a petrol station and the bus terminal with a gleaming new bus ready to set off for Lusaka.

What impressed me most was the community high school where the local people are responsible for financing the construction of classrooms and the Government funds the teachers' salaries.[102] On the gable walls of the main classroom and administrative block the Head teacher had inscribed inspirational quotations for his pupils and their parents.

"The foundation of every state is the education of its youths" – *Diogenes.*

"When books are opened we discover we have wings" – *Helen Hayes.*

I asked the Head teacher, Mr Malumo, who had founded the school a decade earlier what his philosophy was. He replied, "To light the enthusiasm for learning in the minds of my students". My father who was a head teacher for many years in Scotland would have used much the same words.

September 2012 – meeting the present Senanga District Commissioner (on left) and his assistant

[102] *Exactly the same system for financing primary schools in colonial days which I described in my letter dated 6th November 1961.*

September 2012: In front of the Old Boma where I worked. It is now the Senanga Police Station

September 2012: standing with Mr William Harrington on the front veranda of his house. The bench in front is dedicated to the memory of his grandfather, Arthur Harrington

September 2012: Matauka (Community) High School with its Founder and Headmaster, Mr Henry Malumo

Sunset on the Zambezi at Senanga

Farewell

INDEX

List of Photographs

All photos by the author except where otherwise mentioned within the text. The copyright in this book applies to all photographs except those attributed to Rev J-L Baumgartner, R. Paterson and L. Jarrett.

CLINICAL
SOCIOLOGY